# FLORIDA ON THE BOIL

Xlibris

# FLORIDA ON THE BOIL

Recommended Novels And Short-Story
Collections Set In The Sunshine State

## KENNETH F. KISTER

Artwork by
David O'Keefe

To order additional copies of this book, contact:
Xlibris Corporation
1-888-795-4274
www.Xlibris.com
Orders@Xlibris.com
23927

# Contents

For Clarice,
Wife, Lover, Best Friend

Perhaps the best prescription for a Florida worth living in and writing about is to see to it that the peoples who inhabit it know about it, love it, and care for it. To that end, the more of Florida we have on the bookshelves of our homes, schools, and libraries, the better the chances for keeping the Legend of Florida a living one.

Stetson Kennedy
"Viva La Florida!" in
*The Book Lover's Guide to Florida*

# Preface

This little book is a guide for people, young and old, who love to read. More specifically, it is a guide for people who love to read fiction, a form of imaginative writing that, at its best, both entertains and educates. And most specifically, it is a guide for people interested in reading good fiction that takes place in Florida, a unique subtropical peninsula that is as much a state of mind as it is a state of America.

The guide—entitled *Florida on the Boil: Recommended Novels and Short-Story Collections Set in the Sunshine State*—reviews 305 titles, all commendable works of fiction based on such evaluative criteria as literary quality, social significance, and popular appeal. In addition, approximately 300 other pertinent titles are mentioned or briefly described within the reviews. The guide also serves to identify authors, past and present, who have made a meaningful contribution to the creative literature of Florida.

The guide's underlying premise is that reading good fiction is a good way to learn about a place and its inhabitants—in this case, Florida and Floridians. Of course, fiction is not intended as a source of encyclopedic or factual information; on the other hand, novels and short stories do often provide illuminating insights and profound truths not found in works of nonfiction. This is not an original idea or new proposition. Years ago the British writer E. M. Forster remarked in his influential *Aspects of the Novel* (1927), "We know each other approximately by external signs, and these serve well enough as a basis for society and even for intimacy. But people in a novel can be understood completely by the reader, if the novelist wishes; their inner as well as their outer life can be exposed. And this is why they often seem more definite than characters in history or even our own friends." More recently the American writer Peter Matthiessen echoed Forster, pointing out in an interview that fiction allows authors and their readers to plumb "deeper truths" about people and the world in which they live. Likewise, E. L. Doctorow, another prominent contemporary American author, has described fiction as a "mega-discipline," suggesting that imaginative writing has the capability of drawing on and incorporating information from various fields of study (history, sociology, psychology, geography, biology, etc.) in the effort to uncover and communicate those deeper truths.

"To understand the Russian Revolution," says Doctorow, "read Tolstoy." And we might add, to understand the motivations and consequences of William Tecumseh Sherman's devastating march through Georgia and the Carolinas near the end of the American Civil War, read Doctorow, specifically his recent novel *The March*. Or to understand Florida's resilient pioneers called Crackers, read Marjorie Kinnan Rawlings. Or to understand the African-American experience in Florida, read Zora Neale Hurston. Some years ago A.J. Anderson, a professor at the Simmons College Graduate School of Library and Information Science in Boston, neatly summed up the premise this way: "The purest story-form often conveys a greater and more accurate truth about human nature in its various manifestations than any abstract or generalized literature, dogma or dialectic or deduction of science. . . . [F]iction and drama have at all times daringly probed the inner recesses of the self, explored the often unconscious sources of action, and grappled with the intricate and conflicting traits and impulses of human behavior."

Here are some other particulars you should know about *Florida on the Boil*:

- The guide's emphasis is on recently published titles, though a number of worthy older works and classics are included.

12

- The guide covers a broad range of fiction, from mysteries, fantasies, and adventure stories to historical novels, family sagas, and literary masterworks.
- The guide is limited to English-language publications.
- Most of the books reviewed in the guide are for adults, though some are intended expressly for young readers and labeled as such. Bear in mind, however, that age suitability labels are arbitrary and therefore best taken with a large grain of salt. Young people have varying levels of maturity, and some are intellectually and psychologically capable of comprehending and benefiting from literature considered adult in nature. Certainly bright young people should not be limited to reading material classified as "young adult" or "juvenile." The flip side is equally true: Adults should not be reluctant or tentative about reading books said to be for children or young people. For instance, there's no doubt that **Freddy Goes to Florida** (see entry 23) by Walter Brooks is primarily for young readers, but many adults will also enjoy the novel—if they can get passed the notion that it's a "kid's book."
- Books reviewed in *Florida on the Boil* are arranged alphabetically by author. To locate specific titles, subjects, Florida locales, and coauthors and editors, consult the index at the back of the guide. Titles of books reviewed in the guide are printed in **bold** type wherever and whenever they appear. Cross-references, which cite entry numbers (*not* page numbers), are provided throughout the text; see, for example, **Freddy Goes to Florida** in the preceding paragraph.
- With few exceptions, books reviewed in the guide can be borrowed from—or through—your local public library. If the library does not own the

book you want, it usually can be obtained via interlibrary loan, a system that has greatly improved in recent years thanks to the automation of library catalogs and the creation of computerized library networks.

- Some of the books reviewed in the guide are "in print" (that is, currently available in retail bookstores or from book wholesalers or the publisher or distributor); others are "out of print" (or no longer available through customary channels). Check Bowker's *Books in Print* or Amazon.com, reference sources found in practically all libraries, to determine the availability of any book; if it is in print, both *Books in Print* and Amazon will indicate which edition or editions are available (hardback, trade and/or mass market paperback, audio, large print, etc.). In most instances, books that are out of print can be acquired through online booksellers that deal in secondhand and remainder copies. Amazon.com, Barnes & Noble.com, and Alibris.com are among the largest and best known of these dealers.

- Caricatures of Florida writers that appear on the guide's cover and in the text are the work of David O'Keefe, an award-winning illustrator for the *Tampa Tribune*, one of Florida's largest daily newspapers. Thank you, David.

It is my hope that students, teachers, librarians, and the general reading public will find *Florida on the Boil* a useful source of information about novels and short stories that take place in the Sunshine State. The book naturally will be of greatest interest to Floridians, but it is for anyone who has ever resided in, visited, or fantasized about the state. And who hasn't? As Carl Hiaasen, one of Florida's sharpest contemporary writers, has observed, "Everybody has some Florida connection or some Florida experience. Florida has a universal connection with people."

Finally, comments about *Florida on the Boil*—positive, negative, argumentative, off-the-wall, whatever—are welcome. I'm especially interested in hearing about titles not included in the guide you believe should be. My email address is: kfkister@msn.com.

Happy reading!

Kenneth F. Kister
Tampa, Florida
May 2006

# Abbreviations

*BLGF* ........ *The Book Lover's Guide to Florida* (Pineapple Pr., 1992)

*BL* ............. *Booklist* (American Library Association., 1930- )

Co ............. Company

ed.............. edition

*FHQ* ......... *Florida Historical Quarterly* (Florida Historical Society, 1908- )

*FL* ............. *Florida Living* (Florida Media, 1981-May 2001; continued by *Florida Monthly*)

*FM* ........... *Florida Monthly* (Florida Media, June 2001- ; originally *Florida Living*)

*LJ* ............. *Library Journal* (Reed Business Information., 1876- )

*NYTBR* ..... *The New York Times Book Review* (New York Times, 1851- )

PD ........... police department

PI .............. private investigator

Pr .............. Press

*PW* ........... *Publishers Weekly* (Reed Business Information, 1872- )

sf ............... science fiction

Univ ......... University

YA ............ young adult

# Introduction:
# Florida Fiction Q & A

*What is "Florida fiction"?* In this guide Florida fiction is defined as novels and short stories set completely or partially in the American state of Florida (1845 to the present) or the Florida territory (from prehistory to 1845). Historical note: During pre-Columbian times the Florida peninsula was the domain of various native tribes, most prominently the Calusa, Tequesta, Timucua, and Apalachee. In 1513 Juan Ponce de León, a Spanish explorer, "discovered" Florida during Easter week, claiming the territory for Spain and naming it *Pascua florida* ("feast of flowers") in honor of the season. Spain explored, colonized, and ruled Florida for approximately three centuries, from 1513 to 1763 and 1783 to 1821 (the territory was briefly ceded to the British during the 20-year period 1764-83). In 1821 the fledgling United States of America acquired Florida from Spain via treaty, largely the result of military pressure exerted by U.S. General Andrew Jackson, who became the first American territorial governor of Florida. Finally, on March 3, 1845, Florida joined the nation as its 27th state.

*What was the first significant Florida novel or story and when was it published?* According to the best evidence, the first major work of fiction set in Florida was *Atala, ou Les amours de deux sauvages dans le désert*, a short novel written in French and published in Paris in 1801. The author, François-René de Chateaubriand, a French diplomat and noted romantic writer, had visited Spanish Florida some years earlier while traveling in North America. Well-received in France, *Atala*, a tragic love story about an aboriginal couple in the New World, was quickly translated into English and in 1802 an English-language edition appeared in both Great Britain and the U.S. For more about Chateaubriand's historically important novel, see Janette C. Gardner's *An Annotated Bibliography of Florida Fiction, 1801-1980* (Little Bayou Pr., 1983), p. 23; and *The Florida Reader: Visions of Paradise*, edited by Maurice O'Sullivan Jr. and Jack C. Lane (Pineapple Pr., 1991), pp. 92-94, which includes a substantial excerpt from *Atala*.

**Did publication of Atala prompt a great wave of Florida fiction in the 19th century?** No, quite the contrary, relatively few works of fiction with a Florida setting were published in the 19th century. Gardner's aforementioned *Annotated Bibliography*, a reasonably thorough record of Florida fiction issued during the period 1801-1980, identifies only 133 titles for the whole of the 19th century, and most of these (89 titles) were published late in the century, between 1880 and 1900. Some impressive Florida fiction did appear during this time, including Ellen Call Long's **Florida Breezes** (see entry 166), Maurice Thompson's **A Tallahassee Girl** (see entry 270), and Constance Fenimore Woolson's **East Angels** (see entry 298)—all local-color novels, a genre popular in post-Civil War America. In addition, one of the best known of all Florida short stories, Stephen Crane's "The Open Boat," was first published in 1897; frequently anthologized, "The Open Boat" is the lead story in Kevin McCarthy's collection, **Florida Stories** (see entry 184). Still, the fact remains that comparatively little 19th-century fiction had a Florida setting and those novels and stories that did were, with a few notable exceptions, not memorable.

**Why was so little Florida fiction published in the 19th century?** History and geography provide the answer: Florida in the 19th century was mostly a very hot, humid, bug-infested, swampy, heavily wooded, sparsely populated subtropical wilderness. What towns there were offered scant amenities, and woefully poor transportation, yellow fever outbreaks, and "Indian" wars added to the inhospitable environment. In the early 1800s when Spain ceded Florida to the United States, the territory had only an estimated 12,000 inhabitants, most living in the far northern part of the peninsula clustered around either coast. Antebellum Florida also had a number of agricultural plantations concentrated in the Panhandle around Tallahassee and along the northeastern section of the Atlantic coast. Southern Florida on the other hand was largely devoid of civilization until near the end of the century. For instance, in 1845 when Florida became a state it had a total population of 69,000, but Miami at the time was little more than a South Florida outpost with just 314 settlers, and places such as Miami Beach and Coral Gables did not yet exist. Not only was 19th-century Florida a low-population state, its people tended to be a motley mix of illiterate or minimally educated farmers, small-time cattle ranchers, local merchants, hunters, adventurers, and loners; and some were outlaws, including runaway slaves and a few hundred Seminole Indians, the latter secluded in the Everglades to avoid removal to territories west of the Mississippi River per the federal Indian Relocation Act of 1830 (another legacy of Andrew Jackson). A frontier mentality pervaded Florida throughout the century, and education, culture, reading, writing, and books were, to put it charitably, not a priority.

After the Civil War and especially the end of Reconstruction (1877), the state did begin to attract more newcomers and visitors, thanks to improvements in transportation and basic living conditions. By the 1870s steamboats had opened up portions of Florida's interior, most notably the inviting St. Johns River area, and railroads and first-class hotels constructed by millionaire moguls such as Henry Morrison Flagler and Henry Bradley Plant were enticing fashionable travelers eager to experience Florida's sunny winters, pristine beaches, and other intrinsic assets. Around the same time, Hamilton Disston, a wealthy northern industrialist, purchased four million acres of Florida swampland for 25 cents an acre; after dredging and draining, much of the land was eventually converted into towns and ranches and canals in the central and southwestern areas of the state. Florida's population had increased to 325,000 in 1880 and by the end of the century it topped the 500,000 mark. The notion of the state as the setting for a novel or short story ceased to be an oddity by the end of the 19th century, but it was not until the next century that Florida—alluring, mysterious, forbidding Florida—would emerge as one of the hottest U.S. locales for imaginative writing.

*What caused Florida fiction to boom in the 20th century?* Essentially the Sunshine State went from a 19th-century backwater to a 20th-century colossus at warp speed. Modern technology and industrialization helped tame huge portions of the Florida wilderness, ultimately rendering the peninsula a desirable place for ordinary people to live, including northern retirees, who began flocking to the state in large numbers after World War II. Capitalizing on its great tracts of virgin land and numerous natural attractions, Florida in the 20th century developed at an explosive rate, growing and thriving due to the advent of the automobile . . . and paved roads and superhighways . . . and air conditioning . . . and insecticides . . . and air travel . . . and Disney World . . . and a multitude of lesser theme parks . . . and scores of golf and tennis resorts . . . and baseball's spring training . . . and students' spring break . . . and the establishment of hundreds of new cities and towns . . . and thousands of subdivisions and retirement communities . . . and dozens of military installations . . . and a national center for the exploration of space. Because of these and similar developments, Florida metamorphosed from an almost completely rural state in 1900 to an increasingly urban one by the latter half of the 20th century, and by the end of the century it had emerged as a giant among the American states. In the 2000 Census Florida ranked as the country's fourth most populous state, behind California, Texas, and New York; and demographers predict that not too far into the 21st century its population, currently approaching 18 million, will surpass New York's.

As 20th-century Florida surged in popularity and prominence, literacy rates improved, embryonic educational institutions expanded and many new ones were created, and interest in culture and the arts, including literature, increased commensurately. At the same time a host of talented American fiction writers—Ring Lardner, Ernest Hemingway, Marjorie Kinnan Rawlings, James Branch Cabell, Theodore Pratt, Lois Lenski, Wyatt Blassingame, John D. MacDonald, Don Tracy, Charles Willeford, and Patrick D. Smith, among others—discovered Florida. These writers, all born and raised elsewhere, quickly realized that the Sunshine State was not only a good place to live, either permanently or part of the year, but fertile ground for their work. They assimilated the Florida experience and found it offered a wealth of unique ideas and material for all kinds of stories, long and short. Some drew on Florida's rich history for inspiration while others were stimulated by the state's diverse social and ethnic composition or its blistering weather or exotic flora and fauna or distinctive environment or many beguiling places such as historic St. Augustine, ritzy Palm Beach, glittering Miami, the vast Everglades. Marjorie Rawlings is a perfect case in point: Not until Rawlings came to live in Central Florida at age 32 after buying an old farmhouse and citrus grove in rural Cross Creek did she find a place that set her literary imagination ablaze (see entries 232-235).

Today there are more fiction writers working the unique Florida landscape than ever before, and an increasing number of them are Florida natives (Carl Hiaasen, Connie May Fowler, and Beverly Coyle, to name but a few). The best of these do exactly what the best of Florida's earlier fiction writers did: Inspired by the power of place, they create stories that are exciting, provoking, agitating, pulsating, disturbing—stories that are "on the boil."

***If there were a Florida Fiction Hall of Fame (which there is not), who should be in it?*** Obviously, there's no definitive or correct answer to this question. With that caveat, here is a suggested list of initial inductees, all first-rate writers who have contributed significantly to Florida's literary heritage: *HARRY CREWS *MARJORY STONEMAN DOUGLAS *CONNIE MAY FOWLER *JAMES W. HALL *ERNEST HEMINGWAY *CARL HIAASEN *ZORA NEALE HURSTON *ELMORE

LEONARD *JOHN D. MACDONALD *THEODORE PRATT *MARJORIE KINNAN RAWLINGS *PATRICK D. SMITH *RANDY WAYNE WHITE *ROBERT WILDER *CONSTANCE FENIMORE WOOLSEN.

Other strong candidates for such recognition are Wyatt Blassingame, Edna Buchanan, James Branch Cabell, Beverly Coyle, Carolina Garcia-Aguilera, Edwin Granberry, James Grippando, Rubylea Hall, Stuart Kaminsky, John Katzenbach, Baynard Kendrick, Ring Lardner, Michael Largo, Lois Lenski, John Leslie, Paul Levine, John Lutz, Ed McBain (Evan Hunter), Thomas McGuane, Edith Pope, Laurence Shames, Frank Slaughter, Les Standiford, Don Tracy, Sterling Watson, Charles Willeford, Joy Williams, Philip Wylie, and Jose Yglesias.

*Who are the most promising Florida fiction writers on the scene today?* Fortunately there are numerous currently active writers that belong on this list. They include James O. Born, Tom Corcoran, S. V. Date, Tim Dorsey, Adrian Fogelin, Steve Glassman, Michael Gruber, Vicki Hendricks, Jilliane Hoffman, Jonathon King, Christine Kling, Jeff Lindsay, Susan Carol McCarthy, Janice Owens, Barbara Parker, Nancy Pickard, James Swain, Ana Veciana-Suarez, and Darryl Wimberley.

# RECOMMENDED NOVELS AND SHORT-STORY COLLECTIONS

1. Adler, Warren. **Never Too Late for Love.** Moose, WY: Homestead Publishing, 1995. 288p.

Inspired by the large Florida retirement community where his parents spent their final years, veteran fiction writer Warren Adler provides a bittersweet depiction of love and sex among the state's Jewish seniors in this collection of 15 stories. The titles alone convey a sense of the tales' seductive charm: Consider, for instance, "A Widow is a Very Dangerous Commodity," "Tell Me That I'm Young," "He's Going to Marry a Shiksa," "Why Can't You Be Like the Solomon Brothers?," "At Least You Have Your Bingo," and of course "Never Too Late for Love." You need not be any particular religion or ethnicity to relish Adler's stories, six of which first appeared in his earlier collection, *The Sunset Gang* (1977). Note: *Mourning Glory*, an Adler novel published in 2001 and set in Florida's posh Palm Beach, also deals with women of a certain age in search of a suitable mate.

From "An Unexpected Visit" in **Never Too Late for Love:**

Whenever Harold Weintraub drove through the imposing brick gates of Sunset Village, past the fancy colonial gatehouse, which could summon up images of verboten wasp country clubs, he would smile and shake his head. Under all these trappings, he told himself—the big showy clubhouse, the neatly clipped Florida grass, the little blue ponds and dredged canals, the gaily painted shuttle buses, the tricycles with their pennants crinkling in the breeze—lay, at least in his own mind, the unalterable fact that this was merely a dumping ground for aged Jewish parents of a certain working-class social strata. They were the Jews who never really make it big, a counter stereotype, a far cry from the usual "goyishe" perceptions of the rich kike who knew how to make all that money.

2.    Anderson, Kevin J. & Doug Beason. **Ignition**. New York: Forge/Tom Doherty, 1997. 320p.

At Cape Canaveral a gang of terrorists led by a megalomaniac named Mr. Phillips hijacks the space shuttle Atlantis just a few minutes before lift-off, seizing hostages and demanding that a fortune in gems and a getaway helicopter be delivered within four hours. Only former mission commander Colonel Adam "Iceberg" Friese, grounded by a broken foot, can save the day. "The coauthors, both physicists with firsthand NASA experience, make the space program fertile thriller territory. Although extremely formulaic, this tale sets pulses racing while raising readers' awareness of the many risks faced by our space explorers" (*PW*, Feb. 10, 1997, p. 67). Recommended for both adult and young adult readers.

From **Ignition**:

Mr. Phillips picked up the radio transmitter himself and broadcast on the open band. "Attention NASA. My name is Mr. Phillips . . . the man holding your shuttle hostage?" he said, as if they wouldn't remember who he was. "I'd like to request that you clear the skies for our departure. That includes your chase helicopters and tracking aircraft. Our helicopter has arrived, and we must be on our way. I have Launch Director Nicole Hunter and Senator Charles Boorman as my companions to ensure my safety. Oh, and don't forget that I have my finger on the detonator button that could make quite a mess of Atlantis."

3.    Anderson, Virginia. **Storm Front**. New York: Doubleday, 1992. 446p.

Viscerally, **Storm Front** engages the reader in a heart-pounding search for the Sinkhole murderer, a Ted Bundy-type serial killer who terminates young women in Florida's Big Cypress Swamp deep in the Everglades between Miami and Naples. On another, more contemplative level, the novel raises social and political questions concerning the relentless human encroachment on the state's environmentally sensitive wilderness land. As one character puts it, "We've got people pressing in from both sides like a cancer, people who don't understand why if they've got the bucks they can't live wherever they want, even if they have to drain the town's well dry or plow under the last 600-year-old stand of virgin cypress to do it." Author Virginia Anderson's protagonist, Joe Hope, a special agent with the Florida Department of Law Enforcement, is an especially empathetic character.

4.    Anthony, Piers. **Firefly**. New York: Morrow, 1990. 384p.

A loathsome monster that stalks and kills humans is loose in a remote Central Florida wildlife preserve, enticing its victims in much the same way fireflies attract a mate—that is, by exuding powerful procreative lures, or pheromones. The creature in **Firefly** grotesquely sucks the protoplasm out of each kill, leaving behind only shriveled skin and dry bones. The story line contains a certain amount of raw sex as well as consideration of more complex sexual issues, such as the difference between love and simple copulation. Most reviewers disliked the novel when it appeared: "While some readers may find his [author Piers Anthony's] ideas intriguing, many will be put off by a narrative that verges on the pornographic" (*PW*, Aug. 10, 1990, pp. 431-32); and "The whole thing comes off like *The Creature from the Black Lagoon* redone as a porno paperback" (*BL*, July 1990, p. 2041). Aficionados of horror fiction, however, might disagree, finding redeeming literary and social value in this grisly tale.

5.    Anthony, Piers. **Tatham Mound**. New York: Morrow, 1991. 552p.

Piers Anthony, a well-known contemporary writer of scores of science fiction and fantasy novels such as **Firefly** (see entry 4), exhibits his versatility in **Tatham Mound**, an imaginative reconstruction of how the arrival of European explorers in 16th-century North America led to the wholesale death and in some cases extermination of indigenous peoples. Based in part on real-life archaeological discoveries at a Tocobaga Indian burial mound in Central Florida near where Anthony lives, the story is narrated by Tale Teller, a linguistically accomplished member of the tribe and, one surmises, a mythic version of the author himself. A tribal elder instructs Tale Teller to travel far and wide, identifying potential dangers the Tocobagas might someday face and suggesting ways to avoid them, but the plan ultimately fails as the people succumb to diseases introduced by the invaders. For readers, however, Tale Teller's "35-year journey and the tales of many tribes he gathers provide a moving portrait of the living worlds destroyed when Europe 'discovered' America" (*BL*, July 1991, pp. 2010-11).

6. Atkinson, Jay. **Caveman Politics**. Halcottsville, NY: Breakaway Books, 1997. 301p.

In his spare time, callow Joe Dolan, a young newspaper reporter in Cocoa Beach, Florida, is an amateur rugby player who enjoys drinking beer with the guys and bedding as many young ladies as he can. In a word, he's a troglodyte, a modern caveman. But Joe begins to grow up during the course of investigating an explosive rape case involving a black rugby teammate and a woman who is white—and the girlfriend of a redneck biker. Add to this mix a sleazy district attorney who's all too willing to exploit a corrupt judicial system for political gain, and the result is a memorable first novel. "Atkinson has written a jauntily unpretentious, solidly plotted book that displays good insights into character. Joe is a hero you can care about" (*LJ*, Mar. 15, 1997, p. 87).

7. Ayres, E. C. **Hour of the Manatee**. New York: St. Martin's, 1994. 304p.

Winner of the 1992 Private Eye Writers of America/St. Martin's Press competition for the Best First Private Eye Novel Contest, **Hour of the Manatee** introduces unlicensed sleuth Tony Lowell, a laid-back, divorced, pony-tailed, Zen-reading Vietnam vet and former wire service photographer now living the good life restoring boats in Palm Coast Harbor, a fictional town on Florida's Gulf Coast. In his debut Lowell takes on a case involving the long-unsolved death of a wealthy playboy, which eventually implicates some big-name Florida politicos. The nail-biting climax occurs at the famed Belleview Biltmore Hotel in Belleair, just south of Clearwater.

8.  Ayres, E. C. **Night of the Panther**. New York: St. Martin's/ Thomas Dunne, 1997. 272p.

E. C. "Gene" Ayres' series PI, Tony Lowell, first appeared in **Hour of the Manatee** (see entry 7), then *Eye of the Gator* (1995), and most recently **Night of the Panther,** in which he's recruited by career cop and friend Lena Bedrosian to help investigate the killing of her cousin, a game warden in the Big Cypress Swamp area of the Everglades. "The steamy, alligator-ridden Florida swamp is the perfect setting for Ayres' menacing, suspense-filled mystery. The characters—mostly corrupt, tobacco-chewing good ol' boys driving pickup trucks with rifle racks—are almost too perfectly stereotypical, but Ayres knows how to make them leap off the page" (*BL*, May 1, 1997, p. 1481).

9.  Baker, Larry. **The Flamingo Rising**. New York: Knopf, 1997. 309p.

The Flamingo, a fictional drive-in movie theater located on Florida's Atlantic Coast on the beach between Jacksonville and St. Augustine, is so large that a family—Hubert Lee, his wife, and two adopted Korean children—is able to live in the tower supporting the theater's gargantuan screen. Unfortunately the big, noisy drive-in overlooks undertaker Turner West's quiet establishment, and a nasty feud develops between Hubert and Turner, though in a Romeo-and-Juliet twist Abraham Isaac Lee (Hubert's son and the novel's narrator) and Grace West (Turner's daughter) fall in love. "Larry Baker is writing for grown-ups, but he remembers how it felt not to be one, and renders the experience in unforced, unshowy prose, neither folksy nor formal. The result is a novel that's both modest and surprisingly seductive" (*New Yorker*, Sept. 15, 1997, p. 88).

10.  Banks, Russell. **Continental Drift**. New York: Harper & Row, 1985. 374p.

One bitter cold winter night in December 1979, 30-year-old New Hampshire native, Bob Dubois, couldn't take it anymore, so he abruptly packs up his family and heads for Florida, in search of a better, warmer, less crabbed life. Sometime later 16 desperate Haitians, including young Vanise Dorsinville and her infant child, set out in a small boat headed for Miami, also hoping to improve their lot. Inexorably, unknowingly, fatefully, Bob and Vanise drift toward one another, and when their paths finally cross the consequences are tragic. A modern masterpiece, **Continental Drift** vividly explores the racial and cultural realities of life in contemporary South Florida. "There are raw edges to Banks's novel, and a numbing insistence on the powerlessness of its characters, but there's no denying its almost frightening intensity" (*LJ*, Apr. 15, 1985, p. 85).

From **Continental Drift**:

When he [Bob Dubois] crosses the Miami River in the center of the city, he's downtown and can see Miami Beach across the bay, where people live in hotels and live off hotels, a city where there are no families. Then north along Biscayne Boulevard, past the grandstands from last month's Orange Bowl parade, empty and half demolished and throwing skeletal shadows over the grass of Bay Front Park, until he passes out of downtown Miami and enters dimly lit neighborhoods where there are no more white people—no white people on the sidewalks, no white people in the stores or restaurants, no white people in the cars next to him at stoplights. This is where he wants to be. He knows, from what newspapers and boatmen on the Keys have told him, that he's in Little Haiti now, a forty-block section of the city squeezed on the west by Liberty City, where impoverished American blacks boil in rage, and on the other three sides by neat neighborhoods of bungalows, where middle-class Cubans and whites deliver themselves and their children anxiously over to the ongoing history of the New World.

11.  Barr, Nevada. **Flashback**. New York: Putnam, 2003. 396p.

U.S. park ranger Anna Pigeon, star of Nevada Barr's popular National Parks mystery series, has solved crimes in a number of unusual venues, but none so remote as Florida's Dry Tortugas National Park, a chain of seven small islands at the entrance to the Gulf of Mexico roughly 70 miles from Key West. Needing time to sort out her personal life, Pigeon takes a temporary posting on tiny Garden Key, part of the park and home to Fort Jefferson, the grim, six-sided Civil War-era prison where Dr. Samuel Mudd, the physician implicated in Abraham Lincoln's assassination, spent four years after the end of the war. Pigeon soon experiences mysterious attempts on her life that seem somehow related to the fort's 19th-century history. Flashbacks to that time 140 years ago cleverly intertwine past and present villainy.

From **Flashback**:

The stink of decomposing flesh and the scurrying sound of interrupted diners gushed from the new-made hole, and Anna fell back. She gave the critters a few seconds' head start, then, having kicked the rubble away, stuck her head through, flashlight in hand.

The earthly remains of Theresa Alvarez stopped her from going any farther. As Mack had said, she was shoved in a heap just inside the brick wall. Fighting her gag reflex—to once start vomiting was to have difficulty stopping till not only the smell but the sense memory of the smell were purged—Anna pulled and bashed away enough of the wall [of the dungeon] that she could see the corpse more clearly, not to study it for clues, but to avoid treading on or in any way touching the pathetic thing.

12. Barry, Dave. **Big Trouble**. New York: Putnam, 1999. 255p.

Set in Miami, humor writer Dave Barry's first novel is a comic tour de force. The story focuses on the wayward ways of one Arthur Herk, an alcoholic mid-level executive with Penultimate, a large, successful, (and fictional) South Florida construction company. Barry explains: "Penultimate's formula for success was simple: aggressive management, strict employee discipline, and a relentless commitment to cheating . . . . Penultimate was as good at municipal corruption as it was bad at actually building things. In political circles, it was well known that Penultimate could be absolutely relied upon to do the wrong thing. In South Florida, a reputation like that is priceless."

When Herk's superiors learn he's been embezzling from the firm, they hired two hit men, Henry and Leonard, to rub him out at his Coconut Grove home. In the course of crazy events, Herk survives but a massive python named Daphne gets blown away at the Miami International Airport. Swarming with oddball characters and weird plot twists, **Big Trouble** is "that rarest of all literary creatures, the genuinely funny mystery novel" (*NYTBR*, Oct. 31, 1999, p. 16).

13.  Bartholomew, Nancy. **Drag Strip**. New York: St. Martin's/ Minotaur, 1999. 272p.

Series character Sierra Lavotini—heroine of **Drag Strip** as well as other fast-paced thrillers such as *The Miracle Strip* (1998) and *Film Strip* (2000)—is a tall, sassy, high-class stripper at the Tiffany Gentleman's Club in the Florida Panhandle community of Panama City. Sierra's also a lapsed Roman Catholic, owner of a spunky Chihuahua named Fluffy, and hot for city detective John Nailor. In **Drag Strip** she becomes involved in the search for the killer of a fellow stripper, Ruby Diamond. "What makes this book hum and whir—besides a sturdy plot—is a startlingly agreeable array of local crackpots, including a psychotic but shrewd neighbor, an eccentric millionaire and Sierra's dazzlingly foolhardy mother" (*PW*, Sept. 27, 1999, p. 76).

14.  Beach, Rex. **Wild Pastures**. New York: Farrar & Rinehart, 1935. 313p.

In his day Rex Beach (1877-1949) was a well-known novelist whose tales usually concerned macho men in frontier settings, spiced up with a liberal serving of boilerplate romance. Raised and educated in Florida, Beach left the state in 1900 to search for gold in Alaska, an experience he later (like the better known Jack London) turned into stories, a few of which eventually became feature films. In 1926 he returned to Florida where he farmed, raised cattle, and continued to write. Though mostly forgotten today, Beach had a lively pen, and his novel **Wild Pastures**, which concerns virile young Tom Kennedy, the beautiful Cuban girl he loves, and the state's rambunctious cattle industry from Kissimmee southward to Fort Myers, is still worth the time of any reader looking for a ripping good yarn about pioneer days in 19th-century Florida.

15. Bell, Christine. **The Pérez Family.** New York: Norton, 1990. 264p.

After being incarcerated for 20 years in Castro's Cuba as a political prisoner, Juan Raúl Pérez, 57, frail, and toothless, is released in 1980 and makes his way to Miami via the Mariel boatlift, eventually finding temporary shelter in a tent community at the Orange Bowl. During this odyssey he hooks up with a flamboyant babe named Dottie plus several other colorful Marielitos who become Juan's second "family" in this often funny but ultimately sad book. Once in Miami, Juan searches for his first family, a wife and daughter who fled to South Florida in the early 1960s following his imprisonment. "As **The Pérez Family** bubbles along toward its conclusion, the strangest thing begins to happen. Miami, and human nature, show their tragic side. And it dawns on you that Christine Bell is much more than a lighthearted comic novelist. She's one of those writers like Flannery O'Conner or Isak Dinesen: she doesn't so much write stories as spin tales" (*NYTBR*, Aug. 12, 1990, p. 5). Note: In 1995 a film version with the same title as the novel appeared, starring Alfred Molina, Anjelica Huston, and Marisa Tomei (as the irrepressible Dottie).

From **The Pérez Family:**

"I am not here for political asylum. That's why I left Cuba, to get away from political asylum. And this has nothing to do with government," Dottie said. "I came here to get away from government, for nail polish and rock and roll"—Dottie wondered if this man [a U.S. immigration officer] knew exactly how much a bottle of nail polish cost on the Cuban black market when they did have it—"and for men like John Wayne." Her explanation had worked with the Cuban officials, she saw no reason why it wouldn't work with these officials.

16. Blake, James Carlos. **Red Grass River: A Legend**. New York: Avon, 1998. 382p.

Based on real events, James Carlos Blake's first-rate historical novel tells the story of John Ashley, prominent member of a large and boisterous Florida crime family operating in the Everglades in the early decades of the 20th century. After Ashley kills a Native American, DeSoto Tiger, during a botched bootleg deal, Sheriff Bob Baker—once Ashley's friend but now sworn enemy—arrests him. But in no time Ashley is out, free as the wind in the Glades, having escaped from jail and now back to his old ways, robbing banks, running rum, and generally thumbing his nose at the law. But Baker, a study in tenacity, won't rest until he's recaptured his old pal. "A wonderful tale of outlaw heroics and the growth of south Florida from swamp into vacation mecca—too good to be missed" (*LJ*, Oct. 15, 1998, p. 95).

From **Red Grass River**:

The interrogation did not take long. When Bob Baker asked Ben Tracey where John Ashley might be found, Ben said, "Uck you wid a arden hose." Bob Baker said he had him for bank robbery but would drop all charges against him in exchange for information on John Ashley and his gang. "Aint no rat," Ben Tracey said. Bob Baker stood over him and gently laid a hand on his bandaged chest and repeated his question. Tracey cursed him once more and Bob Baker leaned hard on his chest.

Tracey's quavering screams brought nurses on the run but the two cops outside the closed door would not permit them to enter the room. One of the nurses ran off to find a doctor but she was ten minutes in returning with one in tow and by then Ben Tracey had come to see the wisdom in accepting Bob Baker's deal and had hastily confided all he knew about John Ashley's immediate intentions.

17. Blassingame, Wyatt. **The Golden Geyser**. New York: Doubleday, 1961. 335p.

A prolific writer now rarely read, Wyatt Blassingame (1909-85) set several of his novels in Florida, including **Live from the Devil** (see entry 18), *Halo of Spears* (1962), and his best, **The Golden Geyser**, a cautionary tale about the state's explosive land boom in the 1920s. Bob Nolan's only desire is to be a successful nursery farmer, but his wife, Shirley, and father-in-law, Sam Anders, become players in the heady real estate game, making piles of money—until the geyser suddenly goes dry. In addition to including some smoldering sex scenes between the adulterous Shirley and Lou Kleinman, her scheming lover, Blassingame frequently weaves informative textbook-style history and biographies into the narrative, an unusual technique in a novel but one that works here, aiding reader understanding of social and economic conditions in Florida during the land boom period. "A vivid, accurate re-creation of a twentieth-century phenomenon acted out by lifelike characters" (*BL*, Feb. 15, 1961, p. 353).

From **The Golden Geyser:**

She raised her head and saw Kleinman in the bathroom doorway, sponging the sweat from his body with a wet cloth. "My God, you're an ugly little Jew."

He grinned sourly at her. "That's my fatal fascination. That's why you love me."

"I don't love you."

"Okay," he said almost cheerfully. "You want to go into that again. You don't love me and I don't love you. So what are you doing here? Because sex—just good plain straight ordinary old-fashioned animal sex—can be a hell of a lot of fun, particularly if you don't clutter it up with love and all that kind of crap."

"Yes." She stood up. She was still sleek with sweat; she could feel it sliding between her breasts and down across her stomach. "Give me a washcloth, Lou. I wish I had time for a shower."

18. Blassingame, Wyatt. **Live from the Devil**. New York: Doubleday, 1959. 408p.

Few people think of Florida as cattle country, but it's been a thriving industry in the state and territory as far back as the 1600s. Wyatt Blassingame's **Live from the Devil**, which takes place during the period from 1900 to the dawning of World War II, is set in fictional Tonekka County in Southwest Florida and chronicles the life and times of Matt Prescott, a lusty, brawling, compulsively competitive man who achieves his boyhood dream of becoming a cattle kingpin. Subplots include a tempestuous marriage, sexual infidelity, a troubled father-son relationship, and a venomous feud between powerful business rivals. "So smooth is the plotting, so engaging the writing style that the book will rouse the interest of those who like their literary fare rich and raw" (*NYTBR*, May 10, 1959, p. 28).

19.  Booth, Pat. **Palm Beach**. New York: Crown, 1985. 392p.

Pat Booth's naughty tale about Palm Beach, Florida's foremost habitat of the rich and famous, has been called "pornographic," "steamy," and "vulgar," among other pejoratives. It's also said on good authority to be "the most popular book ever written about the ritzy watering hole" (*BLGF*, 1992, p. 190). The story, which unfolds through the eyes of Lisa Starr, the novel's alluring heroine, conveys a relentless curiosity about the drinking, sexual, and social-climbing habits of the town's pampered elite. Booth, a part-time resident of Palm Beach, dedicates the book to Roxanne Pulitzer, another Palm Beach insider who a decade later produced her own juicy fictional exposé, **The Palm Beach Story** (see entry 228).

From **Palm Beach**:

Bobby wished the color wasn't burning on his cheeks.

"Her name is Lisa Starr. I believe you met her once when lunching with me at the Café L'Europe. A very beautiful, wonderful young lady. I'm very fond of her, mother."

"Who is she?" Caroline Stansfield had had a lifetime's experience of cutting through the shit. He's going to get angry, she thought, picking up on the twin spots of red high up on her son's cheeks, and caring not a bit.

It was pointless to pretend to misunderstand the question, to reiterate that her name was Lisa Starr. His mother hadn't meant that at all. Bobby tried to minimize the damage. "She's from West Palm. Runs a business there." Even as he spoke he knew that, far from minimizing it, he had compounded it.

"Yes?" The word said it all. West Palm for a Palm Beacher had all sorts of hidden meanings. After all, the town across the bridge owed its existence to Palm Beach. It was where the black servants lived. Nowadays they had been joined by a crude assortment of carpetbagging riffraff, retirees from the North, the ubiquitous lawyers and dentists and God knows who else, but to Caroline Stansfield it was a ghost town, inhabited by specters, people without substance, without significance.

20. Born, James O. **Walking Money**. New York: Putnam, 2004. 272p.

Protagonist Bill Tasker, a dedicated state trooper with the Florida Department of Law Enforcement (FDLE), has recently been transferred to the department's Robbery Task Force in Miami. Despite not being fully prepared for the extent and sophistication of South Florida venality, Tasker is given the job of keeping track of a satchel containing $1.5 million that's "about to walk out of a bank. The trick is to keep an eye on the prize once it walks and then as it changes hands over and over again. Honest-cop Tasker is framed, becomes a target, and continues investigating as the body count mounts. A sleek and slick caper" (*BL*, May 1, 2004, p. 1502). A veteran FDLE officer who's currently a special agent supervisor, James Born has served as a technical adviser for two films based on books by renowned crime novelist Elmore Leonard (see entries 156-158). Now he brings that expertise to his own fiction, ensuring a high degree of factual accuracy and verisimilitude regarding weapons, police procedures, the criminal mentality, etc. Note: **Walking Money** merited cover treatment in a recent issue of *Florida Monthly* (June 2004, pp. 29-30), the magazine full of praise for Born's debut: "With perpetual plot twists, deeply developed characters and an eerie feeling that leaves readers wondering what in the book is indeed fiction, James Born has solidly landed among the country's best fiction writers, earning respect page by page." Note also: Born's second and third novels, *Shock Wave* (2005) and *Escape Clause* (2006), are also set in Florida and feature Bill Tasker.

21. Bova, Ben. **Death Dream**. New York: Bantam, 1994. 497p.

Ben Bova sets this futuristic novel inside Cyber World, a fictitious Florida start-up company that produces virtual reality games and simulations, such as walking on the moon and piloting jet fighters. At first Cyber World seems a reasonably normal place, but then strange happenings begin to occur: "We get frantic business dealings, industrial spies, death in a virtual reality aviation simulator and even some sleazy virtual reality sex. The ending is weird. Can illusion become reality? Mr. Bova, author of many works of science fiction, has come up with a scary thriller" (*NYTBR*, Aug. 28, 1994, p. 25).

22. Boyd, Shylah. **American Made**. New York: Farrar, Straus & Giroux, 1975. 373p.

Much of this dazzling but now largely forgotten novel is set in the Florida Keys on fictional Lime Island, a tiny speck of terra firma some 25 miles north of Key West. It's the story of Shylah Dale, an assertive, high-energy young woman growing up in the revolutionary 1960s whose life brims with abundant angst, rebellion, family dysfunctionality, and a strong preoccupation with sex. Author Shylah Boyd's evocative, often intense, always readable rendering of life in the steamy, libidinous Keys is a minor Florida classic that deserves to be resurrected, starting with a reprint edition launched with vigor.

From **American Made**:

Lime Island lay below Bahia Honda [Key]. A separate little off-road from Highway 1 led to a bridge that connected the smaller finger of land to the bigger key—about a quarter mile in distance. It was, of course, what everything else was down here, a resort paradise—but with a slightly higher economic level of activity—the best fishing guides, the best fish, the best fishing, the best swimming, that kind of thing, and the local residences reflected their affluence. Three movie stars had homes here, one President got drunk here, the world's most arrogant and superb golfer lived here, Alice said. It was when we traversed the tiny bridge with its flared curve and Lime lay emerald and sculptured before us—it was then that I began to have that wonderland sense of things—as if I had stepped into a 2:00 a.m. movie starring Dorothy Lamour and a cast of a thousand motels.

23. Brooks, Walter R. **Freddy Goes to Florida**. New York: Knopf, 1949. 208p.

Between 1927 and 1958 Walter Brooks (1896-1958) produced more than two dozen Freddy the Pig novels—charming tales intended primarily for children ages 6-12 though they can be enjoyed by the young at heart of any age. The books, which contain original illustrations by Kurt Wiese, are ingeniously written by Brooks to encourage both character and vocabulary development. **Freddy Goes to Florida**, the first in the series, recounts the adventures of an intrepid band of anthropomorphic barnyard animals living on a farm in upstate New York who decide to migrate to Florida for the winter, a robin kindly providing a map. In addition to Freddy the pig, the smartest and most verbal of the animals, the cast of characters includes Jinx, a cat; Robert and Jack, dogs; Charles and Henrietta, a rooster and his wife; Mr. and Mrs. Webb, a devoted couple of spiders; Mrs. Wiggins, a cow; Hank, a horse; Alice and Emma, ducks; and Eek, Quik, Eeny, and Cousin Augustus, a family of mice. During the course of the trip to the Sunshine State, Freddy and his companions encounter humans of every stripe, get to meet the President of the U.S. and tour Washington D.C. (they're initially baffled by the word "constituent" but quickly master its meaning), outwit a bunch of hungry alligators, recover a fortune in buried gold coins, and much more. Note: In 1987 Knopf reissued all of Brooks' Freddy novels, and in 1998 Overlook Press reprinted them in facsimile editions, beginning with **Freddy Goes to Florida**, which was published originally in 1927 as *To and Again* and retitled in 1949 to reflect Freddy's central role in the series, which did not become evident until book three (*Freddy the Detective*).

From **Freddy Goes to Florida**:

They sniffed the air delightedly.

"Mmmmmm!" said Mrs. Wiggins. "Isn't that good? It's better than clover. I wonder what it is."

"I know," said Jack. "I've smelt it at weddings. See all those little green trees down there? They're orange-trees, and that smell is orange-blossoms."

"Look! Look!" squealed Freddy. "There's a palm-tree."

"It's Florida!" shouted Jinx.

And all the animals shouted together: "Florida!" so that they could be heard for miles, and Alice and Emma hopped about and quacked and flapped their wings, and Charles crowed, and the dogs barked, and Mrs. Wiggins mooed, and Hank, the old, white horse, danced around like a young colt until his legs got all tangled up and he fell down and everybody laughed. Even the spiders raced round and round the web they had spun between Mrs. Wiggins's horns, and the mice capered and pranced.

"So this is Florida!" said Mrs. Wiggins. "Well, well!"

24. Buchanan, Edna. **Cold Case Squad**. New York: Simon & Schuster, 2004. 304p.

In 1986 Edna Buchanan won a Pulitzer Prize for her work as a *Miami Herald* police beat reporter and a short time later she burst onto everyone's bestseller list with *The Corpse Had a Familiar Face* (1987), a nonfiction account of the most intriguing crimes she had covered during her newspaper career. Since that time Buchanan has devoted herself to writing fiction, mainly a series of Miami-based thrillers starring Britt Montero launched with the publication of **Contents Under Pressure** (see entry 25). More recently her novel **Cold Case Squad** introduced a new series about a Miami PD homicide unit dedicated to reopening old, unresolved murders, especially ones that might be solved using state-of-the-art forensic science. The several cases reopened in **Cold Case Squad** are uniformly interesting, the cast of cops and killers satisfyingly motley, and the setting—Miami—naturally exotic. "Buchanan's memorable characters strut their wacky stuff, but, as always, it's the fascinating, hothouse city of Miami that's the real star of the show" (*PW*, Apr. 19, 2004, pp. 37-38). Note: Buchanan's second cold case mystery, *Shadows* (2005), focuses on the 1960s murder of a former mayor of Miami whose home had a basement, a rarity in Florida: Might there be gruesome secrets lurking in that dark, dank area of the house?

25. Buchanan, Edna. **Contents Under Pressure**. New York: Hyperion, 1992. 288p.

**Contents Under Pressure** is the first in a series of popular mysteries devoted to the exploits of gritty Miami crime reporter Britt Montero, a blond, green-eyed Cuban American who is clearly author Edna Buchanan's fictional alter ego. The action begins when a much admired black man, former pro football player D. Wayne Hudson, is killed in an alleged traffic accident while being chased by local police. Was Hudson's death really an accident? Or was it a case of police negligence or, worse, racism? Why is the press, including the pushy Montero, being stonewalled by law enforcement officials? How is the city's African-American community handling the heightened tension? "It's been noted before, usually by Buchanan herself, that Miami manages to corner the market in weird crime, and **Contents Under Pressure** revels in the small details that bring that weirdness alive" (*BL*, July 1992, p. 1898). Subsequent Britt Montero outings include *Miami, It's Murder* (1994), *Suitable for Framing* (1995), *Act of Betrayal* (1996), *Margin of Error* (1997), *Garden of Evil* (1999), **You Only Die Twice** (see entry 26), and *The Ice Maiden* (2002).

26. Buchanan, Edna. **You Only Die Twice**. New York: Morrow, 2001. 304p.

Here Edna Buchanan is at her best as a writer of crime fiction. A woman drowns off Miami Beach . . . but hadn't she been murdered years before? Isn't her husband currently on death row awaiting execution for that very crime? These questions lie at the heart of a puzzling case confronting Britt Montero, Buchanan's resourceful series heroine who makes her seventh appearance in **You Only Die Twice**. "Ah, breathtaking sunsets, warm sandy beaches, swaying palm trees—and a floating corpse off Miami Beach. All of these things make for another tremendously entertaining Britt Montero mystery" (*LJ*, Apr. 1, 2001, p. 131).

New Jersey native **Edna Buchanan** (see entries 24-26) recently told an interviewer, "I envy people born in Miami. When I first saw Miami, it brought tears to my eyes, like I'd finally found my way home. My life went from black and white newsreel to full-color Cinema-Scope. It's a very evocative place. The attraction for a lot of people is, it's down at the end of the map. When people on-the-run run long enough, they all end up in Florida" (*PW*, Apr. 2004, p. 38).

27. Buechner, Frederick. **The Storm**. San Francisco: Harper SanFrancisco, 1998. 208p.

Written by Christian clergyman-cum-novelist Frederick Buechner and based loosely on Shakespeare's play *The Tempest*, **The Storm** is a deftly crafted story of forgiveness, reconciliation, and fatalism. Kenzie Maxwell, a writer and Prospero-type character who lives with his wealthy third wife on fictional Plantation Island off the coast of Florida, is celebrating his 70th birthday, an occasion that brings together a host of people important in Kenzie's life, including his long estranged brother, Dalton (modeled on Shakespeare's Antonio); his disaffected daughter, Bree (Miranda); his current wife's son, sprightly Averill (Ariel); and his uncouth handyman, Clavert Sykes (Caliban), who claims he is the true owner of much of exclusive Plantation Island. During the course of the birthday party, Kenzie works his magic and longstanding conflicts are resolved—but in an ironic reversal of Shakespeare's plot, Buechner's violent storm comes at the end, bringing with it inexplicable tragedy. "Faith is at the core of this novel, as it is in much of Buechner's work, but it is an oddly ambiguous, utterly human kind of faith—characterized not by certainty but by good-humored irony, even world-weariness, and above all, by a profound sense of quiet" (*BL*, Nov. 15, 1998, p. 566). Note: Buechner's much earlier novel, *Lion Country* (1971), is also set in Florida.

28. Buffett, Jimmy. **Tales from Margaritaville: Fictional Facts and Factual Fictions**. New York: Ballantine/Fawcett Columbine, 1989. 250p.

Though born in Pascagoula, Mississippi, and raised in Mobile, Alabama, it's Key West, Florida, and analogous tropical climes that most people associate with popular musician Jimmy Buffett and his hyper-enthusiastic fans, the Parrotheads. Talented and ambitious, Buffett not only writes and sings his own songs ("Margaritaville," "Cheeseburger in Paradise," "Come Monday," etc.), he's the author of a variety of books, including *A Pirate Looks at Fifty* (1998), a memoir; *Where is Joe Merchant?* (1992) and *A Salty Piece of Land*

(2004), adult novels; *The Jolly Mon* (1988) and *Trouble Dolls* (1991), children's fiction written with his daughter, Savannah Jane Buffett; and **Tales from Margaritaville**, a collection of eight short stories and four autobiographical pieces in which Buffett takes readers inside magical Margaritaville, described as a mythical rather than a real place. Florida—especially the Florida Keys—figures heavily in some of the tales. For instance, in "Are You Ready for Freddy?" the reader learns, "Card Sound Road is the back door to the Florida Keys, a straight line going South. It is a two-lane blacktop lined on each side by a stand of Norfolk pines, a road on which speed limits are meant to be broken. It ends as abruptly as it begins, leading back to U.S. 1 near Key Largo, the territory of Travis McGee [of John D. MacDonald fame; see entries 172 & 174] and Humphrey Bogart. I was going all the way to the end in Key West where I would catch the ferryboat to Margaritaville and celebrate my return to Nashville." Note: Jimmy Buffett is one of only a handful of writers ever to have books at the top of *The New York Times* bestseller list in both the fiction and nonfiction categories.

29.   Cabell, James Branch. **There Were Two Pirates: A Comedy of Division**. New York: Farrar, Straus, 1946. 132p.

    James Branch Cabell (1879-1958)—best known for the novel *Jurgen* (1919), a medieval fantasy that achieved notoriety for its sexual content (mild stuff by today's standards)—spent the winter months in St. Augustine between 1935 and 1952 and during that time produced three slight but imaginative works of fiction set in Florida: *The First Gentleman of America* (1942), **There Were Two Pirates** (1946), and *The Devil's Own Dear Son* (1949). Cabell's arch style has long been out of favor with the reading public, but the Florida novels retain a certain campy appeal, especially the fanciful **There Were Two Pirates**, said (in an editorial note by Cabell) to be an edited version of the autobiography of one José Gasparilla, a legendary Spanish pirate who plied his trade off the west coast of Florida in the late 18th and early 19th centuries in an effort to accumulate enough wealth (500,000 pesos) to return to Spain and claim his truelove, Isabel de Castro. Gasparilla, whose home base was Tampa Bay, eventually wins the hand of Isabel, but only after finding her years later—fat, drab, and widowed with five children—aboard a ship he was plundering.

From **There Were Two Pirates**:

I had private and urgent reasons (to which I shall recur in the sequel) for going into Florida without delay; and so, with the assistance of my fellow lieutenant, Roderigo Lopez, and of our chaplain, Father Martin León Verdago, of Seville, a mutiny was arranged upon the festival of the Conversion of St. Paul, whose intercession for our success I duly invoked upon the eve of this momentous occasion.

Thirty-eight out of the ship's crew of sixty joined in with the three of us to dispatch the other officers and the seamen who remained loyal to sentiments such as I, for one, admired as relics of a more highly impassioned era, but for the sake of my own welfare was compelled to discourage. To the last words of our deposed captain, in particular, I listened with reverence; they were biassed [sic] by disapproval; they bordered even upon the denunciatory; and yet, so complete was my affection for the indomitable old gentleman that I blew out his brains in a warm glow of admiration.

30.   Carlisle, Henry. **The Land Where the Sun Dies**. New York: Putnam, 1975. 318p.

Based on historical fact, Henry Carlisle's novel focuses on the fortunes of Florida's Seminole Indians during the period 1818-42 when hostilities between the tribe and the U.S. government led to open warfare. The story, which is both absorbing and enlightening, unfolds though the eyes and experiences of Carlisle's fictional heroine, independent-minded Eliza Hutchins. Eliza's kinship with real-life General (and later President) Andrew Jackson places her at or near the center of momentous events, including the December 1835 Dade Massacre and simultaneous killing of Indian agent Wiley Thompson by the renowned warrior Osceola—actions that sparked the Second Seminole War (1835-42), the bloodiest and most expensive of all the country's many military conflicts with Native Americans.

From **The Land Where the Sun Dies**:

Indians wandered amazed among the bodies. Most had been on raiding parties, some had taken white scalps, but this day was altogether different: Never in memory had there been such a slaughter of those who claimed mastery over them. There was no looting, no spree of mutilation; only the Negroes went about the usual business of victors. As Osceola dismounted, the only celebration was the torches and the cool wind seething in the pines.

He started toward the log bastion, four feet high and studded with lead that shone in the moonlight; near it he found Micanopy [an old Seminole chief] sitting on a log, his head in his hands; Jumper and Alligator came up behind the chief, who looked up and seeing the bloody coat Osceola wore said, "Now they will destroy us."

31. Castañeda, Omar S., Christine Blackwell & Jonathan Harrington, editors. **New Visions: Fiction by Florida Writers**. Orlando, FL: Arbiter Pr., 1989. 224p.

Featuring writers either born in Florida or who have spent considerable time in the state, this paperback anthology consists of 18 short stories, 13 of which have a Florida locale. In their introduction the editors also note that all of the contributors are contemporary authors: "Our anthology, we insisted, would showcase work by living writers only. It would present the work of new writers like Anne Lawrence, Philip F. Deaver, Morris Kennedy, and Lisbeth Kent, as well as that of more established talents such as Joy Williams, Harry Crews, Peter Meinke, Janet Burroway, and Padgett Powell." The stories of two other well-known Florida writers—Enid Shomer and Bob Shacochis—are also included in this valuable collection of short fiction.

32. Chapman, Herb & Muncy Chapman. **Wiregrass Country: A Florida Pioneer Story**. Sarasota, FL: Pineapple Pr., 1998. 361p.

While not great literature, the Chapmans' **Wiregrass Country** does provide an exciting, historically realistic picture of frontier life in the Florida Territory in the mid-1830s prior to statehood. Ace Dover and his family, owners and operators of a large cattle ranch in Central Florida south of Payne's Prairie near Gainesville, battle not only hostile Native Americans but a determined band of rustlers. Lawlessness is rampant, and the Dovers, a doughty bunch, are forced to fend for themselves. Coauthor Herb Chapman, for many years a professor at the University of Florida specializing in the cattle industry, brings his expertise to the story. Note: **Wiregrass Country** is similar to novels in Pineapple Press's popular Cracker Western series, which includes Lee Gramling's **Ghosts of the Green Swamp** (see entry 85) and Jon Wilson's **Bridger's Run** (see entry 295).

33.   Charteris, Leslie. **The Saint in Miami**. New York: Doubleday, 1940. 300p.

Beginning in 1928 Leslie Charteris (1907-93) produced approximately 50 crime novels and short story collections featuring suave Simon Templar, alias the Saint, a flawlessly tailored (Savile Row) Englishman driven by a sense of noblesse oblige to fight wrongdoing whenever and wherever he finds it. In **The Saint in Miami**, Templar's beautiful companion, Patricia Holm, receives a letter from friends in South Florida indicating they're in some sort of trouble and need help. The story opens with the couple luxuriating in the sun on a Miami beach waiting to meet Patricia's friends, but before you can say "tallyho!" Templar is racing off to the Everglades in pursuit of a bloodthirsty gang of pro-Nazi German Americans up to their swastikas in evil schemes. Eventually he meets up with Newton Haskins, a down-home Florida county sheriff who's every bit as rustic as Templar is refined, and together they bring the case to a satisfying conclusion.

From **The Saint in Miami**:

"Son—" The Sheriff's mouth was slightly overloaded. He poured half a tumbler of rye into the water glass and tossed it down. "This warn't exackly a killin'. Mo' like wholesale slaughter, you might call it. Then, it warn't exackly in my county, neither."

"Really?" said the Saint politely. "Then where was it?"

"Way down in the Everglades, in a place not even half the conchs down theah could find. But I heard tell it was shuah one helluva mess. Seems like there was almost a dozen plumb dead bodies left lyin' around. Even that feller Gallipolis we was talkin' to got himself shot down theah."

"Did he? How extraordinary! Do you think he could have tried to play both ends against the middle just once too often?"

"Mebbe." The Sheriff's wise old eyes held the Saint's tantalising blue ones. "You wouldn't know nuth'n about none o' them bodies now, would you, son?"

"Corpses?" Simon protested. "Cadavers? Lying around? . . . What a horrible thought. I always bury my dead bodies in a climate like this. It's so much more hygienic . . . Unless you leave them to drown; and then of course the barracuda take care of them."

"Yep, that's what I thought," Haskins said sagely.

34. Clague, Maryhelen. **Fort Brooke Drummer Boy: A Story of Old Florida**. Kearney, NE: Morris Publishing, 1998. 93p.

Intended mainly for young people (ages 12+) but also recommended for adult readers of historical fiction, this short, intelligently constructed novel is set in Florida in 1835 and recounts the adventures of Army Private Danny Bauer, the drummer boy of the title, who arrives at Fort Brooke (now the city of Tampa) just as the Second Seminole War erupts—a conflict prompted by the massacre of more than 100 U.S. troops, including their commander, Major Francis Dade, by Seminole warriors who ambushed Dade and his men as they marched from Fort Brooke to Fort King (now Ocala). Luckily, young Danny was not with the ill-fated Dade mission, but he quickly gets to test his mettle in a battle with the Seminoles during an expedition sent to bury the dead soldiers. Although Danny Bauer is a fictional character, Maryhelen Clague's story is rooted in fact, and various personages from Florida history such as Osceola and General Winfield Scott make cameo appearances. Note: Clague has written more than a dozen works of fiction, including several romance novels under the pseudonym Ashley Snow. Her latest book is a historical novel set in 19th-century Tampa entitled *This Land of Flowers* (2005).

35. Coffey, Tim. **Miami Twilight**. New York: Pocket Books, 2001. 304p.

Garrett Doherty, a South Florida public relations executive and narrator of this edgy novel set in Miami, earns plaudits from his superiors for landing a very important client: rich and powerful (albeit shady) Cuban expatriate Ernesto Rodriguez who's planning to build a large residential development for millionaires that will encroach on the fragile Everglades. For some, the project raises environmental concerns, whereas for Doherty it's just a matter to be papered over with the right PR, the right malarkey. But then he falls in lust with Magdalena, the hot, sexy wife of one of Rodriguez's compatriots, and as events race along, fueled by the forces of intrigue, greed, violence, and infidelity, Doherty's life spins out of control. In a review in the *St. Petersburg Times* (Sept. 16, 2001, p. 4D), Jean Heller, an accomplished novelist herself (see entry 102), wisely suggests the book's central character "vacillates between needing our sympathy and needing a good beating."

From **Miami Twilight**:

What I recall most vividly, of course, was Magdalena. We were together almost every afternoon although I couldn't see her on the weekends, which stretched out interminably while I accompanied Helen [his wife] to the beach or the movies, or to restaurants I'd once found interesting. On weekdays I enjoyed the anticipation of seeing my lover, and my breath would grow short and quick on my way to our assignations.

Magdalena always arrived first. I'd knock two times on the door, then three. The knocks matched the syllables in my name; we liked having a secret to share. She'd open the door and smile. She'd still be fully clothed because she knew I liked to watch her undress.

We'd kiss and she'd ask how my day had gone so far and I'd tell her, invariably, that it was about to get a lot better. She'd laugh and say I was incorrigible and I'd agree and we'd kiss again and laugh and wrap our arms around each other and after a few minutes she'd step away and unzip her dress and let it fall to the floor and then she'd kick off her shoes and walk toward me wearing only her lingerie. Usually it was black.

36. Cohen, Nancy J. **Died Blonde: A Bad Hair Day Mystery.** New York: Kensington, 2004. 256p.

Beginning with *Permed to Death* in 1999, Nancy Cohen has produced half a dozen Bad Hair Day mysteries starring Marla Shore, a likable, pragmatic Florida hairdresser and beauty salon owner who moonlights as an amateur sleuth. Set in Fort Lauderdale and environs, the lightweight (think bouffant) but popular series also includes *Hair Raiser* (2000), *Murder by Manicure* (2001), *Body Wave* (2002), *Highlights to Heaven* (2003), **Died Blonde** (2004), and *Dead Roots* (2005). In **Died Blonde,** Marla investigates the suspicious death of her archrival, the beautician she worked for before going into business for herself. And in this episode she finally gets engaged to longtime sweetheart, homicide detective Dalton Vail. "Another bright addition to a charming series" (*LJ*, Oct. 1, 2004, p. 64).

37. Cohen, Paula Marantz. **Jane Austen in Boca.** New York: St. Martin's, 2002. 268p.

A professor of English (Drexel University), Paula Cohen sets her delightful modern-day version of Jane Austen's *Pride and Prejudice* in a fictional Jewish condominium retirement complex called Boca Fest in Boca Raton, Florida. The story line focuses on three Boca Fest women and their romantic aspirations as they compete for the resident bachelors and widowers. Especially well-drawn is Flo Kliman, a sharp-tongued retired librarian who's a reincarnation of Austen's Elizabeth Bennet character. "The author's perceptive observations of life among the retirees of Florida are combined with skillful parallels to the plot and characters of the original novel. The narrative flows, and the reader will be chuckling, trying to guess who from Boca is a character from Austen" (*LJ*, Sept. 1, 2002, pp. 210-11).

From **Jane Austen in Boca**:

"And what's your impression of Elizabeth Bennet?" asked Stan, hoping to take advantage of what seemed like a tenuous return to the events of the novel. "Do you like her?"

"Too sarcastic for my taste," noted Dorothy. "I can't say I'd be friends with her."

"I like her," countered May. "She sees things everyone else doesn't, but it doesn't keep her from joining in."

"I agree with Dorothy," said Pixie. "She's stuck-up. Very snooty."

"No," said Lila, who clearly had begun to enjoy the discussion and fancy herself something of a literary critic. "It's the rich one, Darcy, that's stuck-up. He's proud, she's prejudiced. There's the title: *Pride and Prejudice*." She looked expectantly to Stan for approval at this feat of analysis.

38. Comfort, Iris Tracy. **Echoes of Evil**. New York: Doubleday, 1977. 188p.

Though the author is better known for her nonfiction works on scientific subjects, such as *Florida Rocks, Minerals and Fossils* (1994) and *Florida's Geological Treasures* (1998), than as a writer of fiction, **Echoes of Evil** is a little gem of a thriller. Set in North Florida in Jackson County (which borders both Georgia and Alabama), the tightly knit plot concerns a psychic investigator's inquiry into the case of Andrea Hood, a recovering amnesiac whose first glimmerings of recall include hazy memories of the murder of her parents, long an unsolved crime. Soon Andrea's own life is threatened: Is it because she's beginning to remember?? "Though it strains credulity at times, this is a gripping romantic suspense novel with special appeal for those interested in psychic phenomena" (*BL*, May 1, 1977, pp. 1325-26).

39. Corcoran, Tom. **The Mango Opera**. New York: St. Martin's/ Thomas Dunne, 1998. 301p.

Tom Corcoran kicked off his Key West mystery series in 1998 with **The Mango Opera** and since then has added such intriguing titles as *Gumbo Limbo* (1999), *Bone Island Mambo* (2001), *Octopus Alibi* (2003), and *Air Dance Iguana* (2005), all of which are recommended as first-class escapist fare. Alex Rutledge, Corcoran's series protagonist, is a laid-back guy who mostly lives in shorts and sneakers while working as a freelance crime photographer, a job that involves him in all sorts of murder and mayhem. In **The Mango Opera**, for instance, it eventually becomes eerily clear that someone is killing Alex's old girlfriends one by one. "With its sure feel for the Key West that resides beneath the tourist facade and a quirky, hard-edged rhythm pulsing beneath the surface calm, this debut deserves a wide and welcoming audience" (*PW*, May 11, 1998, p. 54). Note: A profile of author Corcoran appears in the November 2005 issue of *Florida Monthly* (p. 16).

40.  Coyle, Beverly. **In Troubled Waters**. New York: Ticknor & Fields, 1993. 324p.

Florida native Beverly Coyle's first novel, **The Kneeling Bus** (see entry 41), received high praise from critics, and her second, **In Troubled Waters**, confirms the judgment that she's one of the state's brightest literary talents on the scene today. As one reviewer put it, **In Troubled Waters** "does exactly what first-rate fiction should do: As it entertains, it helps us better to understand ourselves and others" (*LJ*, Apr. 1, 1993, p. 129). Set in Point Breeze, a fictional Florida town northeast of Orlando, the story unfolds through the ancient eyes of Tom Glover, who's 91, deaf, and crippled, and spends much of his time sitting on his porch reminiscing while also trying, often futilely, to keep track of his son-in-law, Paul, a former teacher and now an Alzheimer's victim. When Tom hires two local boys—one white, one black—to take Paul fishing in the afternoons on a nearby lake, old racist attitudes resurface in the town. Tom, knowing he's near the end, is resigned to the inevitable though he still struggles to make sense of it all, filtering the present through the scrim of the past. "Coyle's orchestration of this multitiered drama is tight yet subtle, while her articulation of the disgraceful legacy of racism, the tragedy of Alzheimer's, and the shadow of impending death is both compassionate and frank" (*BL*, Mar. 15, 1993, p. 1296).

From **In Troubled Waters:**

Who would have thought the sight of one black kid might ease the conscience of a man living as much in the past as he was? A hundred years ago they all used to swim down there together, blacks and whites, too easy in their bones for people to believe nowadays. They had grown up and gone to work picking stump out of every other burned off field in this Florida county. Seminole County. He used to swim down there by the hour with a boy named Lucky Apple who would stand at the edge of the water with a quarter in his mouth trying to make it look like a silver tooth. This was Point Breeze, Florida. In Glover's day she sat a long way east of Orlando—a whole morning rocked to sleep beside Lucky in a wagon. Now politicians and conservationists called everything Central Florida. Everything had exploded into tract housing. Rangers coaxed the two remaining panthers down into the Everglades last year. They were said to survive down there in high-frequency collars. Point Breeze was a bedroom now, a bedroom for another kind of business boom: land too valuable to farm unless one belonged, heart and soul, to Minute Maid.

41.  Coyle, Beverly. **The Kneeling Bus**. New York: Ticknor & Fields, 1990. 224p.

A fifth-generation Floridian, Beverly Coyle was born in North Miami Beach in 1946. After graduating from Florida State University in 1968 she left home, earning a Ph.D. at the University of Nebraska, and then accepted a position teaching English at Vassar College in Poughkeepsie, New York. But in a figurative sense Coyle has never left the place of her birth: All her novels to date—**The Kneeling Bus** (1990), **In Troubled Waters** (see entry 40), and *Taken In* (1998)—are set in her native state. The first of these, **The Kneeling Bus**, consists of eight interconnected vignettes describing a young girl's coming-of-age in small-town Florida during the 1950s. Carrie Willis is the daughter of a Methodist minister (as is Coyle) and, as the book's title subtly suggests, religion plays a significant role in her world while growing up. "Coyle's concluding image, that of Carrie's mother on a kneeling bus—a bus that lowers itself to the sidewalk to help disabled and elderly passengers board—is full of hope and humor. A fine first novel, imbued with the sadness of the past and full of memorable scenes and personalities" (*BL*, Feb. 1, 1990, p. 1069). Note: Coyle's third novel, *Taken In*, concerns a runaway teenage prostitute and the residents of a suburban Florida town who try—with horrific results—to help her.

42.    Cozzens, James Gould. **Guard of Honor**. New York: Harcourt, Brace & World, 1948. 635p.

   To date, only three novels with a Florida locale have won the Pulitzer Prize for fiction: Marjorie Kinnan Rawlings' famous **The Yearling** (see entry 235), John Updike's famous **Rabbit at Rest** (see entry 276), and James Gould Cozzens' not so famous **Guard of Honor**. This is not to insinuate that **Guard of Honor** is unworthy of such a prize or that it is not a fine novel; rather, the point is the book, for several fairly obvious reasons, lacks the broad, timeless appeal of the Rawlings and Updike classics. **Guard of Honor** takes place on the home front during World War II, specifically a three-day period in 1943, with almost all of the action confined to the Ocanara Army Air Base, a large training installation located in the fictional Central Florida town of Ocanara very near the real communities of Orlando and Winter Park (which in 1943, before Walt Disney and Mickey Mouse came to Florida, were not much more than tiny dots on a large-scale map). The base is a beehive of activity, and Cozzens brilliantly juggles an enormous cast of characters and their stories, all designed to give the reader a realistic sense of military life at that time and place. Among the many plot threads: Ugly scenes on the base created by racial segregation (the U.S. military was not integrated until after the war); tension between the base brass and the editor of the local Ocanara newspaper over the issue of Army censorship versus press freedom; a tragic accident that kills of a group of paratroopers; a general whose career goes down the drain because he drinks too much; the intrusion of snakes—water moccasins—in the women's barracks. Today, the novel will appeal most strongly to those with military experience, especially World War II veterans. "As is his custom, Mr. Cozzens looks at his characters with warm understanding, with humor and with tolerance for their failings. Several passages of **Guard of Honor** are exciting as a story and—again this is usual—the author's style is easy and flowing, with the underemphasis that makes for drama. It is necessary to say, however, that **Guard of Honor** is long and that it not infrequently drags" (*NYTBR*, Oct. 3, 1948, p. 5).

From **Guard of Honor**:

Colonel Ross looked at the dark fluid with disgust.

"Nick," he said, "I'd like to ask you a question. Why the devil is there no orange juice in Florida?"

Nicodemus broke into a rich noise of laughter, a spasm of hearty yeh-yehs. "Colonel, they tell me out there in California, that's where they buy it all. Yeh, yeh, yeh—"

"Then you better go out there and get me some tomorrow." Colonel Ross took a swallow of the juice, a puce-colored slop, tasting as you would expect anything that color to taste, and turned his attention to the Ocanara *Morning Sun*. He opened it at once to the editorial page and a column headed: *This & That by Art Bullen*.

Mr. Bullen was the owner of the *Sun*. He was not a native of Florida; but he had come to Ocanara as a young man, and few people born there were so aggressively, in Mr. Bullen's own term, Ocanarans. Perhaps he felt that all was definitely right about a place where a young fellow with nothing but energy and ambition could do so well by himself in less than twenty-five years. Just out of the Army after the last war, he was supposed to have bought the paper, a weekly with a circulation of about one thousand, for fifty dollars.

**Harry Crews** (see entries 43-44) is a tough-guy writer in the tradition of Ernest Hemingway and Norman Mailer. His fiction reflects the pain of a childhood filled with abuse, illness (polio), and injury (a horrible burn suffered during a game of crack-the-whip that accidentally landed him in a cast-iron boiler used to skin hogs). Writing, Crews has observed, "is a process of discovery. You gotta get naked. You can't hide anything. Publishing a book is about as naked as you'll ever get. It's like being in the mall without clothes."

43. Crews, Harry. **Celebration**. New York: Simon & Schuster, 1998. 270p.

The author of some 20 novels, Harry Crews writes what has been called "grit lit": biting, earthy, satirical prose that depicts a darkly comic universe peopled by losers, freaks, deviants, criminals, and the maimed. **Celebration**—vintage Crews—is about old people doing little but waiting around to die in a cheerless Florida mobile home park called Forever and Forever. The park's manager and owner, a man called Stump (he's missing part of an arm), likes things the way they are—deadly quiet—but change comes in the form of a sexy teenage girl with the unusual name of Too Much. Absurdly, Too Much encourages the park's residents to be joyous, to noisily celebrate life, to speak out, and they do. Stump, his control challenged, is flummoxed and goes on a binge. Still, in the end, there's no escaping the ultimate fate: Everyone, including Stump, must come "to grips with the brutal and messy reality of mortality" (*PW*, Nov. 17, 1997, p. 54).

From **Celebration**:

On his way down the narrow hallway from the bedroom to the kitchen, Stump paused at the open door to his bathroom. The huge tub seemed even bigger empty than it did filled with water. It has been four days now—or at least this was the morning of the fourth day—since there had been water in it. Stump could smell the stink in the tangled hair of his armpits and the sour odor of his crotch, urine-tainted and stained by dirty-handed pissing and by three days and four nights without a bath. But by God, he'd promised himself he would leave off with the whiskey, which he had been not so much drinking as pouring down his throat steadily and savagely the last three days—leave off with the whiskey and scour himself down with hot water and soap. Not by sitting in that goddam monster tub alone, though. He could not bear that. For the first time ever, he would use the showerhead he'd had installed above it when he knocked down a wall and put in the huge tub to accommodate Too Much's circus act.

44. Crews, Harry. **Naked in Garden Hills**. New York: Morrow, 1969. 216p.

Among Harry Crews' most notable Florida novels are *Karate is a Thing of the Spirit* (1971), *The Hawk is Dying* (1973), *The Gypsy's Curse* (1974), *All We Need of Hell* (1987), *Body* (1990), *Scar Lover* (1992), *The Mulching of America* (1995), and **Celebration** (see entry 43). Though some critics would disagree, his second novel, **Naked in Garden Hills**, also belongs on this list. Set in a desolate, nearly abandoned phosphate mining town southwest of Orlando ironically named Garden Hills, the tale revolves around two grotesque characters—Dolly, who is said to have an "iron hymen," and Fat Man, the impotent owner of the godforsaken town—who spend much of story in bed in the buff trying to make love. Crews is not a happy-ending writer, and the book's conclusion might annoy—or repulse—some readers. "Macabre and slapstick, howlingly funny and as sad as a zoo, ribald, admonitory, wry and deeply fond. [**Naked in Garden Hills**] lives up to and beyond the shining promise of Mr. Crews's first novel, *The Gospel Singer* [1968]" (*NYTBR*, Apr. 13, 1969, p. 4).

45. Crews, Lary. **Extreme Close-Up**. New York: Lynx Books, 1989. 252p.

Lary Crews—no relation to the better known Harry Crews (see entries 43-44)—has written several original paperback mysteries featuring Veronica Slate, a young, attractive, divorced, cat-loving radio talk-show host in the Tampa-St. Petersburg, Florida, area. The Slate novels have enough frenetic activity—sex, drug busts, car chases, murder, and more—to keep most thriller readers happily turning the pages. Crews also makes good use of local landmarks; for instance, in **Extreme Close-Up** some of the action takes place at the Don CeSar Beach Resort, a historic pink hotel in the town of St. Pete Beach on the Gulf of Mexico. Note: **Extreme Close-Up** was reprinted in 2000 by iUniverse, a print-on-demand publisher.

46. Cummings, Betty Sue. **Say These Names (Remember Them)**. Sarasota, FL: Pineapple Pr., 1984. 296p.

An especially fine historical novel that takes place in Florida during the Second Seminole War (1835-42), Betty Sue Cummings' **Say These Names (Remember Them)** recounts the human toll exacted by that conflict from the perspective of female members of the Miccosukee Indian tribe who, observes Cummings in a prefatory note, were "heroic in their efforts to save their children and preserve their culture." The long ordeal of the Miccosukees, a small Florida Native American tribe closely allied with the Seminoles, is revealed largely through the experiences of a fictional character, See-ho-kee, a young mother who flees with her family from Fort King (present-day Ocala) southward to eventual refuge deep in the Everglades. During her journey See-ho-kee encounters a variety of people, some the product of author Cummings' imagination and some real. Here she describes meeting the very real Coacoochee, an exuberant warrior-chief also known as Wildcat: "She began to think of stories she had heard about Coacoochee, tried to reconcile this contemptuous man to those stories: he loved to stay near the forts, using the white men's food and whiskey until they began thinking of capturing him, whereupon he always slipped away; he dressed himself with more elegance than any other chief, had adorned himself when he went to Fort Payton when he was captured, had carried a white plume for peaceful passage and a beautiful bead-pipe for General Hernandez from Asi Yahola [i.e., Osceola, the famous Seminole leader]; but he had often teased the white soldiers when he ran from them for he ran like a wild cat, and he would stop and jeer and beg them to run faster so that it would be more interesting for him. A strange, wild, comical man, a chief who was hard to know." This meticulously researched novel can be read with profit by both adults and young people.

47.   Dantzler, Rick. **Under the Panther Moon and Other Florida Tales**. Port Salerno, FL: Florida Classics Library, 2001. 349p.

Lucidly written, handsomely produced, and beautifully illustrated (by Winter Haven artist Paul Schulz), Richard E. "Rick" Dantzler's book contains 22 short stories dealing principally with

Florida's natural attractions and threatened environment from the Panhandle to the Keys. A prominent state politician, attorney, and avid outdoorsman, Dantzler makes it clear that the tales, with the exception of one autobiographical piece, are products of the imagination: "While many of the events in this book are based on personal experiences, this is a work of fiction." However, in most instances the stories conclude with an Author's Note that provides personal commentary about the places and issues mentioned in the text. For instance, in the title story, "Under the Panther Moon," Dantzler's note explains the complex problems involved in trying to save the Florida panther, the official state animal and a much endangered species. "This book reaches its audience on two distinct levels: as an oral history of Florida from a man with diverse experience in the state, and also as a collection of stories that will entertain the reader" (*FHQ*, Spring 2003, p. 488).

48. Date, S. V. **Black Sunshine**. New York: Putnam, 2002. 309p.

S. V. Date (the "S" is for Shirish and the last name is pronounced DAH-tay) has an inventive mind and a wicked pen, the requisite ingredients for producing biting satire, which he's been doing on a regular basis in a string of popular novels since the late 1990s. Date's background, style, and concerns are quite similar to those of Carl Hiaasen (see entries 108-111), a recognized master of Florida satirical fiction: Both men are journalists by trade (Date is currently the *Palm Beach Post*'s Tallahassee bureau chief and Hiaasen is a regular columnist for the *Miami Herald*); both unmercifully lampoon Florida's political establishment in their books; both populate their stories with comic caricatures of public figures and low-life criminals (sometimes one and the same); and both convey a simmering outrage over the wanton despoilment of Florida's environment. **Black Sunshine**, Date's fifth novel and one of his best, takes readers inside a wacky gubernatorial election campaign dominated by the Billings—read Bush—brothers and their fat-cat oilmen friends eager to commence offshore drilling up, down, around, and, if necessary, through the Florida coast. It's a slick, greasy gas.

49. Date, S. V. **Smokeout**. New York: Putnam, 2000. 226p.

Though a relative newcomer to writing fiction, S. V. Date has an impressive list of successful novels to his credit, all dealing sardonically with hot-button social and political issues in Florida. They include *Final Orbit* (1997), about the state's space industry; *Speed Week* (1999), about NASCAR racing at Daytona Beach; *Deep Water* (2001), about Disney-style planned communities; **Black Sunshine** (see entry 48); and **Smokeout**, about the tobacco industry and its unscrupulous efforts to influence votes in the state Legislature. Date is especially acerbic in his portrayal of corrupt and libidinous lawmakers in **Smokeout**, which closely apes the real world of Florida legislative politics. As one reviewer observed, "Of course, the characters are no more than vicious cartoons—but cartoons that reflect our blackest fears about the politicians we elect" (*NYTBR*, Jan. 14, 2001, p. 24).

50. Davis, Wesley Ford. **The Time of the Panther**. New York: Harper, 1958. 282p.

It's the 1920s and 14-year-old Tom Jackson, who lives in a tiny sawmill town in Central Florida, experiences a "double-barreled dilly of a summer," during which he learns much about nature's ways by observing the behavior of birds and animals in their habitat, including a scary encounter with a full-grown panther. That eventful summer he also comes to understand the true meaning of responsibility, owing to an incident involving his younger brother. But perhaps most intriguing—and disconcerting—for young Tom is his introduction to the power of sexuality, courtesy of Miss Amie Lou, a hedonistic evangelist passing through town. Skillfully written with both tender and hair-raising moments, Wesley Ford Davis's story has strong appeal for adult and teenage readers alike. "Enriched by absorbing anecdotal material, **The Time of the Panther** comes alive on every page" (*NYTBR*, Jan. 26, 1958, p. 28).

From **The Time of the Panther**:

He had often fancied himself a wildcat, prowling the night woods, silent as a ghost, stalking the spoke-wheeled cluster of sleeping quail, or at twilight or dawn stalking the feeding wood ducks at the edge of stream or lake. Sometimes he was a big red-tailed hawk, circling high, broad-winged, his head moving back and forth to pick up the scurrying movement of the woods rat in the grass and palmettos far below. Or the big pileated woodpecker or the ivorybill, swooping through the tall woods, knocking and slashing the bark off the big trees, filling the woods with a raucous cry.

He opened his eyes and looked at the ducks. They swam to the far side of the lake into the shadows. The female merged with the heavy shadows of bushes overhanging the water's edge. The male was a moving patch of shifting colors. Tom got up and turned away from the lake. He shook his head and spoke aloud. He had to tell himself the truth.

"No," he said, "it isn't to *be* one of these things, bird, wildcat, or duck; it's the knowing of them. No one of them can know himself as he figures in with all the rest."

51.  Deal, Borden. **A Long Way to Go**. New York: Doubleday, 1965. 232p.

When their parents apparently abandon them during a family vacation in a beach town on Florida's West Coast, three young children—Ashley, 10; Brett, 8; and Shane, 6—have no one to turn to. So, using child logic, they begin walking home to Alabama. Traveling northwest along Florida's Gulf Coast, they try, not always successfully, to avoid contact with other people, especially adults. They steal food from open fields to satisfy their raw hunger; soon they suffer sore feet and other minor ills; eventually they acquire a stray dog, Beau. And they argue a lot: Ashley, being the oldest, takes charge but her decisions are constantly challenged by her brothers. After seemingly endless days and nights on the road, the kids finally arrive home—dirty, hungry, and exhausted. But where are their parents?? Then Ashley finds a letter from their mother that explains all. It begins, "*My dear children: If you are reading this letter, you have come home. They told me that you couldn't travel six hundred miles by yourself, but I didn't believe them and that is the reason I have left this letter.*" Mississippi-born

Borden Deal (1922-85), a prolific author who also wrote under the pseudonym Lee Borden, lived the last two decades of his life in Sarasota, Florida, but **A Long Way to Go** is one of the rare instances when he set a story in Florida. Note: Deal's former wife, Babs Deal, who died in 2004, was also an accomplished writer, and two of her novels, *Summer Games* (1972) and *The Crystal Mouse* (1973), take place in Sarasota.

52. DeFelice, Cynthia. **Lostman's River**. New York: Macmillan, 1994. 160p.

An experienced YA writer and former school media specialist, Cynthia DeFelice sets **Lostman's River** in the year 1906 in Florida's Ten Thousand Islands, a dense hodgepodge of small, tricky-to-navigate mangrove islets in the far western Everglades. The novel, intended mainly for young readers (ages 10+), deals with the once widespread practice of killing egrets, flamingos, and other plume birds for their feathers, eagerly sought at the time to adorn women's hats. DeFelice presents a pro-conservation message without being preachy, while the story's central character, 13-year-old Tyler MacCauley, learns a hard lesson about adult duplicity. "The quality of the conflicts in this novel is first-rate—questions of loyalty, honor, trust, value of human life, and environmental concerns focus on the universal struggle between good and evil. What happens to the characters is believable as well as riveting" (*BL*, May 15, 1994, pp. 1679-80). Note: DeFelice's most recent novel, *The Missing Manatee* (2005), is also set in Florida and aimed primarily at young readers.

53. Dexter, Pete. **The Paperboy**. New York: Random House, 1995. 311p.

After being expelled from college in the late 1960s, Jack James, the narrator of this engrossing novel, takes a job driving a delivery truck for the newspaper his father owns and edits in fictional Moat County in North Florida. But when Jack's older brother Ward, an investigative reporter for a major Miami daily, and his corner-cutting partner Yardley Acheman, come to town to reopen a sensational murder case in which creepy Hillary Van Wetter disemboweled the county sheriff, Jack agrees to drive and do odd jobs for them. Pete Dexter—a former newspaperman and author of several other serious novels, including the National Book Award-winning *Paris Trout* (1988)—weaves a multilayered story involving redneck violence, manufactured evidence, a sadistic killer freed on a legal technicality, an egregious breach of journalistic ethics, and a sullied Pulitzer Prize. "The novel's conclusion feels a bit hasty; but for much of its length, **The Paperboy** burns with the phosphorescent atmosphere of betrayal" (*Time*, Jan. 23, 1995, p. 58).

From **The Paperboy**:

Yardley Acheman was despised in the newsroom now by all but a handful of young reporters—some of them with college degrees in journalism—who wrote stories imitating his style. Not having my brother to supply these stories with the weight of incident and facts, however, the pieces they wrote were masturbatory in nature, stuff that even I—a dropout of the University of Florida swimming team—would have been ashamed to have written.

They were the sort of things that Yardley had produced before he and my brother were attached to each other by the editors of the *Miami Times*.

Yardley ignored his critics and encouraged his imitators, praising them extravagantly for the most ordinary and, in most cases, out-of-place prose. Even when this prose was thrown back at them by old-school editors who told them to fill the holes with facts, not flowers.

54. DiCamillo, Kate. **Because of Winn-Dixie**. Cambridge, MA: Candlewick, 2000. 184p.

"It's summer, and 10-year-old India Opal Buloni moves with her preacher father to tiny [fictional] Naomi, Florida. She's lonely at first, but Winn-Dixie, the stray dog of the title, helps her befriend a group of lovable, quirky locals, eventually bringing her closer to her father and the truth about her mother, who left the family when India was 3" (*BL*, May 1, 2000, p. 1665). Aimed mainly at young readers (ages 10+), this award-winning first novel will also captivate adults interested in a well-written, heartwarming story. Note: The eponymous pooch is called Winn-Dixie because he was first encountered at a local Winn-Dixie supermarket, a chain established in Florida in 1925 and long a household name in the state. Note also: A feature film loosely based on the novel and with the same title appeared in 2005, starring Annasophia Robb as Opal and Jeff Daniels as her dad.

55. DiCamillo, Kate. **The Tiger Rising**. Cambridge, MA: Candlewick, 2001. 122p.

Talented YA writer Kate DiCamillo, a Pennsylvania native, spent much of her youth in the South and is a graduate of the University of Florida at Gainesville. **The Tiger Rising**, DiCamillo's second novel, is intended for the same general audience as her widely praised debut, **Because of Winn-Dixie** (see entry 54). This time her main character is a young boy, Rob Horton, who moves with his father after his mother's death from the big city ( Jacksonville) to a small, rural town (fictional Lister) in North Florida. Rob hates his new life: Father and son live cramped in a motel where the senior Horton is a lowly maintenance man employed by the owner, a blustering yokel named Beauchamp; at school Rob must deal with constant taunts by bullies, mainly the brothers Norton and Billy Threemonger; and he's developed an unexplained rash on his legs. Things change however when he becomes friends with Sistine, a feisty new classmate. Together they decide to liberate a wild tiger that Beauchamp keeps caged in an abandoned building behind the motel—the imprisoned cat a metaphor for youthful feelings of futility and powerlessness. **The Tiger Rising** is another solid winner for DiCamillo. Note: In 2004 DiCamillo's literary stature was further enhanced when her third novel, *The Tale of Despereaux: Being the Story of a Mouse, a Princess, Some Soup, and a Spool of Thread*, won the prestigious Newbery Medal for the year's most distinguished contribution to American children's literature.

From **The Tiger Rising**:

"There ain't no point in crying," his father had said afterward. "Crying ain't going to bring her back."

It had been six months since that day, six months since he and his father had moved from Jacksonville to Lister, and Rob had not cried since, not once.

The final thing he did not think about that morning was getting onto the bus. He specifically did not think about Norton and Billy Threemonger waiting for him like chained and starved guard dogs, eager to attack.

Rob had a way of not-thinking about things. He imagined himself as a suitcase that was too full, like the one that he had packed when they left Jacksonville after the funeral. He made all his feelings go inside the suitcase; he stuffed them in tight and then sat on the suitcase and locked it shut. That was the way he not-thought about things. Sometimes it was hard to keep the suitcase shut. But now he had something to put on top of it. The tiger.

56.   Didion, Joan. **The Last Thing He Wanted**. New York: Knopf, 1996. 233p.

Elena McMahon, a jaded, divorced, middle-aged *Washington Post* political reporter assigned to cover the 1984 U.S. presidential election, impulsively leaves her job to come to Miami to visit her ailing father, a secretive man who's somehow involved in the international weapons-trading business. Soon Elena is caught up in both a shadowy scheme that closely resembles the Reagan era Iran-Contra deal and a more intimate, personal effort to sort out her life and relationships, particularly those with men and most particularly with her father. Piecing the action together is an unnamed narrator who acts as a facilitator—really, an auteur—between the characters and the reader. "Brilliantly written and flawlessly structured, Didion's first work of fiction since 1984's *Democracy* employs her trademark barbed-wire prose to tell a highly elliptical tale of political intrigue" (*PW*, June 24, 1996, p. 43).

From **The Last Thing He Wanted**:
What we want here is a montage, music over. *Angle on Elena.*
Alone on the dock where her father berthed the *Kitty Rex.* Working
loose a splinter on the planking with the toe of her sandal. Taking
off her scarf and shaking out her hair, damp from the sweet heavy
air of South Florida. *Cut to Barry Sedlow.* Standing in the door
of the frame shack, under the sign that read RENTALS GAS
BAIT BEER AMMO. Leaning against the counter. Watching
Elena through the screen door as he waited for change. *Angle on
the manager.* Sliding a thousand-dollar bill beneath the tray in the
cash register, replacing the tray, counting out the hundreds.

No place you could not pass a hundred.

There in the sweet heavy air of South Florida.

Havana so close you could see the two-tone Impalas on the
Malecón.

Goddamn but we had some fun there.

The music would give you the sweet heavy air, the music would
give you Havana.

*Imagine what the music was as*: Barry Sedlow folded the bills
into his money clip without looking at them, kicked open the screen
door, and walked down the dock, a little something in the walk, a
definite projection of what a woman less wary than Elena might
(*might, could, would, did, wanted to, needed to*) mistake for sex.

*Close on Elena.* Watching Barry Sedlow.

"Looks like you're waiting for somebody," Barry Sedlow said.

"I think you," Elena McMahon said.


57.  Dorsey, Tim. **Florida Roadkill**. New York: Morrow, 1999.
273p.

A rapid-fire succession of wickedly funny thrillers beginning in
1999 with **Florida Roadkill** and followed by *Hammerhead Ranch
Motel* (2000), **Orange Crush** (see entry 58), *Triggerfish Twist*
(2002), *The Stingray Shuffle* (2003), *Cadillac Beach* (2004), *Torpedo
Juice* (2005), and *The Big Bamboo* (2006) has catapulted Tim Dorsey

into the company of such venerable Florida crime satirists as Carl Hiaasen (see entries 108-111), Elmore Leonard (see entries 156-158), Laurence Shames (see entries 249-250), and S.V. Date (see entries 48-49). Like his literary soul mates, Dorsey peoples his breakneck plots with predatory politicians, manic drug dealers, rapacious developers, rascally sleazeballs, and bodacious babes—all found in great abundance in his facetious version of the Sunshine State from Tallahassee and Tampa to Miami and Key West. **Florida Roadkill**, written while the author worked as a journalist for the *Tampa Tribune*, concerns a $5 million insurance scam and lots of characters (in every sense) chasing the money all over Florida, including Dorsey's most memorable creation to date, Serge Storms, a devil-may-care serial criminal. "Vulgar, violent and gaudier than sunsets on the Keys, Dorsey's roadshow is some fun" (*NYTBR*, Sept. 5, 1999, p. 25).

58. Dorsey, Tim. **Orange Crush**. New York: Morrow, 2001. 300p.

There's a gubernatorial election underway in Florida pitting House Speaker Gomer Tatum, a Democrat as dim as his name, against incumbent Governor Marlon Conrad, a Republican "golden boy" seeking a second term. Marlon, once considered a shoo-in for reelection but now in trouble owing to a sudden attack of honesty, tells his chief of staff, "If we're going to win this election, we'll need the right wheels," and in a flash he's careening around the state in a used Winnebago with the words ORANGE CRUSH in "big bright letters in a tangerine script running the length of the RV." The candidates, their staffs, and the issues—affirmative action, gay rights, capital punishment, etc.—are all fodder for Tim Dorsey's rollicking pen. Note: The cartoonish antihero Serge Storms, first sighted in **Florida Roadkill** (see entry 57), makes a cameo appearance in **Orange Crush** and returns as Dorsey's main character in *Torpedo Juice* (2005) and *The Big Bamboo* (2006), the latter set mainly in California.

Born on April 7, 1890 in Minneapolis, Minnesota, **Marjory Stoneman Douglas** (see entries 59-61) was reared in Taunton, Massachusetts and educated at Wellesley College. In 1915 she moved to South Florida to take a job as a reporter and later columnist at the *Miami Herald*, where she honed a gift for writing that eventually produced several novels, numerous short stories and, in 1947 at age 57, a tremendously influential work of nonfiction, *The Everglades: River of Grass*, a book that literally changed forever the way people think about Florida's natural resources and their preservation. Douglas, who lived to be 108 years old, loved the "real" Florida with a passion and for many years was the state's most prominent environmentalist.

59. Douglas, Marjory Stoneman. **Alligator Crossing**. New York: John Day, 1959. 192p.

Marjory Stoneman Douglas (1890-1998), a great Floridian who had a long and illustrious writing career, is best known for her classic nonfiction study, *The Everglades: River of Grass* (1947), but she also produced a substantial body of fiction, much of it aimed at a youthful audience. A good example is **Alligator Crossing**, the suspenseful story of Henry Bunks, an inquisitive youngster from urban Miami who one day stows away on an illegal alligator hunter's boat and ends up in the Everglades, a much different place than the big city. "**Alligator Crossing** offers young readers [ages 10+] everything necessary for a wilderness adventure: a secret hideaway, travel, a colorful cast of characters." (*FM*, Mar. 2003, p. 16). Note: The novel was reprinted in 2003 in paperback by Milkweed Editions in Minneapolis.

60. Douglas, Marjory Stoneman. **Freedom River**. New York: Scribner's, 1953. 264p.

Among her works of fiction, Marjory Stoneman Douglas cited **Freedom River** as her personal favorite. Set in Florida during the 1840s, the novel involves the shared experiences of three 15-year-old boys—a Miccosukee Indian, a black slave, and a white settler—who form a strong friendship despite racial and social differences. "Although its main characters are adolescents, the story was not written only for young adults . . . . The universality of issues that deal with man's birthright to freedom, and the use rather than abuse of the earth's resources, make this a book of timeless appeal" (*Florida Libraries*, Jan.-Feb. 1998, p. 14). Note: Valiant Press in Miami published a new edition of **Freedom River** in 1994; it includes Douglas's original text and adds 28 evocative black-and-white drawings by Jack Amoroso, a South Florida artist and friend of the author.

61. Douglas, Marjory Stoneman. **Nine Florida Stories by Marjory Stoneman Douglas**. Edited by Kevin M. McCarthy. Gainesville: University Press of Florida, 1990. 216p.

These short stories, all of which originally appeared in the *Saturday Evening Post* between 1925 and 1941, deal with social, cultural, and environmental issues in South Florida, an area Marjory Stoneman Douglas knew as well as anyone. "Plumes," a story based on the despicable and illegal practice of slaughtering birds in the Everglades for their feathers to decorate women's hats, is arguably the finest of the nine selections. Overall, the collection succeeds "as a sample of the early fiction of a farsighted and articulate advocate for the environment, and a picture of life in early south Florida" (*FHQ*, Jan. 1991, 372). Note: In 1998 the University Press of Florida issued a second collection of Douglas's *Saturday Evening Post* stories from the same period; entitled *"A River in Flood" and Other Florida Stories by Marjory Stoneman Douglas,* it also contains nine stories and is edited by Kevin M. McCarthy.

62. Due, Tananarive. **The Between**. New York: HarperCollins, 1995. 280p.

Florida native Tananarive Due's first novel blends two types of fiction, mystery and horror. When the reader first meets them in 1993, Hilton James, a social worker, and his wife, Dede, the first elected African-American judge in Dade (now Miami-Dade) County, are a comfortably off black couple with two lovely children, an attentive dog, and most of the other trappings of middle-class existence. Their lives change radically, however, when Dede (pronounced DAY-day) begins receiving obscene and threatening hate mail connected with her work, and Hilton, plagued by frightening dreams as a child, develops nightmares that appear to foretell the future—a very unpleasant future for him and his family. ". . . this novel is believable, powerful, and chilling. The portrayal of a realistic family with typical problems is refreshing, and even enhanced by the contrast with Hilton's bizarre struggle. Solid characterization seasoned with a perfectly judged pinch of spookiness" (*School Library Journal*, Oct. 1995, p. 166).

From **The Between**:

He had to get out of the house, as far from Kaya and Jamil [his children] as possible. Hilton took painstaking steps across the floor, breathing through his mouth as he read the label Kaya had affixed to the wrapping in her girlish script. To: Dad. From: A friend.

He didn't dare shake the box to better judge its contents. They'd wrapped it, bless them. Charles Ray Goode had mailed a bomb to his house, and his children had gift-wrapped it.

The distance from the dining room to the front door seemed endless, but Hilton breathed a little easier once he was outside. Charlie [the dog] was still standing against the fence, barking his furious warnings. Hilton's extended arms ached horribly. He looked right and left, up and down the empty street. What now?

Beyond the coral wall, Hilton saw the aluminum garbage can and remembered. It was all happening just as Nana had shown him in his dream. Had he won, at last? Was it finally over?

63.   Dunsing, Dee. **The Seminole Trail**. New York: Longmans, Green, 1956. 211p.

The Second Seminole War in Florida began in 1835 and did not end until 1842, but the bloody conflict's most decisive and only major conventional military engagement occurred on Christmas day 1837, when U.S. soldiers fought and routed Seminole and Miccosukee warriors in a pitched battle on the northern shore of Lake Okeechobee. The Battle of Okeechobee not only ended organized resistance by the tribes, it drove their remaining members far into the depths of the Everglades where they continued the fight, relying exclusively on guerrilla tactics. Dorothy May "Dee" Dunsing's enduring novel provides a highly readable, historically credible account of events leading up to Okeechobee and the clash itself—all viewed through the observant eyes of Dunsing's protagonist, Rod Wheeler, a sensitive young man who gets shot during the battle but predictably survives, a scar his only medal. Larry Toschik's black-and-white illustrations add to the book's appeal. Note: A companion novel by Dunsing, *War Chant* (1954), deals with the Seminole conflict in the Fort King (now Ocala) area.

64.   Edwards, Page Jr. **American Girl**. New York: Marion Boyars, 1990. 171p.

Nancy Meade has just left her "redneck professor" husband, returning to her family who owns and operates the Fountain of Youth in St. Augustine, a tacky Florida tourist attraction founded by her grandmother (a character based on a real person) and alleged to be the very fountain Spanish explorer Juan Ponce de León sought and failed to find in the 16th century. Nancy, the "American girl," has money, brains, and good looks but they "mask a dark soul," which author Page Edwards explores in this "short, exquisitely wrought novel" (*PW*, Sept. 21, 1990, p. 65).

From **American Girl**:

"A job would keep you busy" said my uncle. "And I could keep my eye on you."

"You don't want me working there, Uncle Jack. I might tell the tourists the truth."

He laughed at me. "You've agreed not to do that—at least not all of it. Besides, if you cause the attendance to drop, you're only hurting yourself."

I could never cause the attendance to drop. I wouldn't want to anyway. I love the fountain as much as Uncle Jack does—for different reasons. The part of the truth I'd agreed not to tell in my master's thesis was how the property came into the family in the first place. Some St. Johns County Circuit Court cases in the 1900's indicate that my grandmother and grandfather, whom she divorced, might have swindled the property away from the previous owner. Accusations were made. The charges were dropped. I'd promised my uncle to leave that part out of my thesis.

As if to mock me, Uncle Jack turned on the huckster in him: "What is the Fountain of Youth? Step right up, folks. Let us cast a veil of magic over your eyes. Come sip from the legendary well and be revitalized. Regenerate your hopes. Restore your potency."

65.   Elkin, Stanley. **Mrs. Ted Bliss**. New York: Hyperion, 1995. 292p.

Elderly but still attractive, Dorothy Bliss is a widow whose husband, Ted, died of cancer before the story begins. She lives on the seventh floor of the Towers, a Miami retirement condominium overlooking Biscayne Bay where her public persona—Mrs. Ted Bliss—is irrevocably fixed as the wife (or appendage) of her dead husband. Typical of retirees who have lost their spouse, her existence is often lonely and humdrum, though there are occasional moments of exhilaration, surprise, and shock, as when at novel's end Hurricane Andrew strikes the Towers. "**Mrs. Ted Bliss** may not be Stanley Elkin's best, but it is a smart, generous, melancholy, funny, even elegiac work by a prodigious practitioner. Passages—all right, shticks—stay with you after you've given up on the plot: There's Mrs. Ted out shopping with her visiting health-nut daughter-in-law, Ellen, who announces that her doctor recommends coffee high colonics. A few pages later, Mrs. Ted awakens to the smell of fresh coffee: 'Great, thought Mrs. Ted Bliss, she's making herself an enema'" (*NYTBR*, Sept. 17, 1995, p. 7).

66.  Evans, Mary Anna. **Artifacts**. Scottsdale, AZ: Poisoned Pen Pr., 2003. 290p.

**Artifacts** is Gainesville, Florida, author Mary Anna Evans' first novel, and it's a jewel, offering readers both an intelligently constructed present-day murder mystery and an informative glimpse into Florida's plantation past. Faye Longchamp, a student of archaeology, has been hanging onto her ramshackle ancestral home, once a great Gulf Coast plantation house, by illegally selling historical objects she unearths in a nearby national wildlife refuge. But when she digs up a human skull of recent vintage, Faye must either inform the police, which might jeopardize her felonious cottage industry, or do some investigating on her own. "Evans introduces a strong female sleuth in this extremely promising debut, and she makes excellent use of her archaeological subject matter, weaving past and present together in a multilayered, compelling plot" (*BL*, May 1, 2003, p. 1542). Note: **Artifacts** received the Florida Historical Society's 2004 Patrick D. Smith Florida Literature Award, given annually to a work of fiction that stimulates the promotion and study of the state's heritage. Note also: The intrepid Faye Longchamp returns in Evans' second novel, *Relics* (2005).

67.   Falco, Edward. **Winter in Florida**. New York: Soho Pr., 1990.
300p.

Bored with his upper middle-class life on Long Island, preppy
Jesse "Sky" Skyne, 23, heads for Florida where he lands a job as a
groom at a racetrack near Orlando. He quickly falls in with a bunch
of rough, vulgar characters more interested in drugs and sex than
horse racing. Eventually their leader, a sadist named Jack Winter, is
shot and stabbed with a screwdriver, which elicits a vicious retaliation.
"There is no one to like much in this story of foul-mouthed misfits,
yet Falco has the power to make us care what happens to them" (*BL*,
June 15, 1990, p. 1958). Note: Edward Falco is a poet and award-
winning short-story writer; **Winter in Florida** is his first novel.

68.   Fielding, Joy. **Whispers and Lies**. New York: Simon &
Schuster/Atria, 2002. 315p.

At first when Terry Painter, an unmarried woman of 40 and
a nurse at a small, private health facility, rents the cottage in back
of her home in the oceanside city of Delray, Florida, to Alison
Simms, a vivacious young lass who's just moved to the state, all goes
swimmingly. But as the tale unfolds it becomes apparent that Alison
is no ordinary tenant, that in fact she has a secret agenda to worm her
way into Terry's life. But for what purpose?? An experienced novelist
who lives part of the year in another Florida seaside community (Palm
Beach), Joy Fielding writes exceptionally well and knows how to keep
a plot boiling. "The brutal denouement will shake readers lulled by
the tale's cozy trappings, but those familiar with Patricia Highsmith's
particular brand of sinister storytelling will recognize the mayhem
Fielding so cunningly unleashes" (*PW*, July 29, 2002, p. 53).

From **Whispers and Lies**:

"Chicago," Alison answered.

"Really? I love Chicago. Where exactly?"

"Suburbs," she said vaguely. "How about you? Are you a native
Floridian?"

I [Terry Painter] shook my head. "We moved here from Baltimore
when I was fifteen. My father was in the waterproofing business.

He thought Florida was the natural place to be, what with all the hurricanes and everything."

Alison's green eyes widened in alarm.

"Don't worry. Hurricane season is over." I laughed, finally locating the corkscrew at the back of the cutlery drawer. "That's the thing about Florida," I mused out loud. "On the surface, everything is so beautiful, so perfect. Paradise. But if you look a little closer, you'll see the deadly alligator lurking just below the water's smooth surface, you'll see the poisonous snake slithering through the emerald green grass, you'll hear the distant hurricane whispering through the leaves."

69. Fogelin, Adrian. **Crossing Jordan**. Atlanta: Peachtree, 2000. 140p.

A serious and accomplished YA writer, Adrian Fogelin moved to Florida some 25 years ago and each of her novels to date, beginning with **Crossing Jordan** and including *Anna Casey's Place in the World* (2001), **My Brother's Hero** (see entry 70), *Sister Spider Knows All* (2003), and *The Big Nothing* (2004), is set in the Sunshine State. In **Crossing Jordan**, Cass, a 12-year-old white girl and the story's narrator, becomes friends with Jemmie, a black girl of the same age, when Jemmie's family moves next door to Cass's in a working-class neighborhood of Tallahassee. When both girls' parents actively discourage the friendship, racial prejudice becomes the central issue in this absorbing, emotion-stirring novel. A key incident occurs when Cass overhears Jemmie's grandmother, Nana Grace, singing a song about "that river of Jordan" and wonders what it means. "Crossing Jordan," she learns, was code among slaves in the antebellum South for the forbidden dream of freedom. The novel's message: Despite decades of progress, many of us, black and white, are still trying to cross that metaphorical river. Intended mainly for young people (ages 12+), **Crossing Jordan** is also highly recommended for adults.

From **Crossing Jordan**:

Jemmie was shifting from one foot to the other. "You won't tell Mom about Cass, will you, Nana?"

Nana Grace squinted one eye at Jemmie. "An' why not?"

Jemmie made lines in the dust with her bare toes. "You know how she feels about the fence [put up by Cass's father after Jemmie's family moved next door], the way she calls Cass's family a bunch of redneck bigots."

When she said that I felt like I'd had the wind knocked out of me.

"Jemmeal!" Nana scolded.

"You know she does!"

Nana Grace stared at Jemmie until Jemmie looked away, and then Nana Grace turned to me. Her brown eyes were pale and flecked with green. "I hope you'll understand. When Jemmie's mama was growing up, Tallahassee was a whole 'nother place. Seemed like black and white folks had a war going. Jemmie's mama was just little then, but she got caught in the crossfire. She ain't learned to forgive yet."

70.  Fogelin, Adrian. **My Brother's Hero**. Atlanta: Peachtree, 2002. 224p.

Adrian Fogelin's third YA novel deals with the instinctive need all children have for parental love. Ben Floyd, 13, and his little brother Cody, 7, are thrilled to spend the Christmas holiday in the Florida Keys helping their parents manage a family-owned marina, but Ben's enthusiasm and ego take a hit when a marine biologist and his bright 11-year-old daughter, Mica, sail in and dock. Mica seems so cool, so grown-up, so superior to Ben; to add to his misery, Ben's parents treat Mica like one of their own. Before long, however, Ben discovers that Mica's father is a heavy drinking, emotionally cold man, and that she envies Ben and Cody their warm, caring, loving parents. ". . . this story has plenty of action, but it's the emotional drama, revealed in funny, realistic dialogue and spot-on descriptions, that distinguish the novel" (*BL*, Feb. 1, 2003, pp. 993-94). Like Fogelin's other novels (see entry 69), **My Brother's Hero** has what YA publishers call "crossover appeal"—that is, the book can be enjoyed equally by young adult *and* adult readers.

A Florida native originally from the St. Augustine area, **Connie May Fowler** (see entries 71-73) writes like an angel but she had a devil of a childhood, including an abusive father who died when she was seven and a controlling, alcoholic mother who succumbed to liver cirrhosis ten years later. Today, Fowler, now in her mid-forties, is the author of five acclaimed novels and writer-in-residence at Rollins College in Winter Park, Florida.

71. Fowler, Connie May. **Before Women Had Wings**. New York: Putnam, 1996. 272p.

Connie May Fowler, a 1983 graduate of the University of Tampa in Florida, later earned an advanced degree in English literature at the University of Kansas. She emerged as a promising writer of serious fiction in 1992 upon publication of her first novel, **Sugar Cage** (see entry 73). Subsequent novels—*River of Hidden Dreams* (1994), **Before Women Had Wings** (1996), **Remembering Blue** (see entry 72), and *The Problem with Murmur Lee* (2005)—have solidified her reputation as a first-rate literary voice. A general consensus exists among critics that the semiautobiographical **Before Women Had Wings** stands out as Fowler's most accomplished work to date. Though narrated by a nine-year-old child, Avocet "Bird" Jackson, the story is thoroughly adult in substance and style. Early on, Bird's hard-drinking father, Billy, commits suicide and her abusive, alcoholic mother, Glory Marie, moves from North Florida to the Gulf Coast city of Tampa, settling herself, Bird, and Bird's older sister, Phoebe, in a run-down trailer park in an undesirable part of town. There Bird, a sensitive and intellectually curious youngster, is befriended by a grandmotherly black woman and fellow seeker, Miss Zora. Beautifully rendered, the novel received enthusiastic notices, including this prepublication rave: "Fowler sweeps the narrative along with plangent, lyrical prose. Mixing the squalid details of Bird's life with the child's magical dreams of hope and healing, she has fulfilled the promise of her highly praised debut, **Sugar Cage**, and established herself as a writer of formidable talent" (*PW*, Mar. 11, 1996, p. 41). Note: In 1997 **Before Women Had Wings** was made into an Oprah Winfrey Presents TV movie, starring Ellen Barkin with young Tina Majorino as Bird. Note also: In 2002 Fowler published a nonfiction version of the story entitled *When Katie Wakes: A Memoir*.

From **Before Women Had Wings**:

Old Sam [Bird's dog] and I followed her in. Her door was not locked. I said, "Why don't you lock your door when you're not home? Mama says there are burglars everywhere in Tampa."

"Well, child," Miss Zora said as she set down a basket full of grasses and flowers and weeds she'd picked in the field, "if anybody needs what I have, they are welcome to it."

That was certainly a new way of thinking to me. And so was the way she had decorated her cottage. My eyes could not move quickly enough. Herbs and grasses tied with twine hung from a piece of knotty wood that stretched the length of the room. Flowers in mason jars perfumed the air . . . . On the wall next to the door was a framed picture of some sort of large bird, and next to it was a map of south Florida. A stack of books cluttered her kitchen table, and bookshelves lined the wall above her couch. This place was a library and a nature museum wrapped into one. I said, "You sure do have a lot of books."

"Mind food," she said as she fixed us two tall glasses of sweet tea made pretty with lime wheels. "Do you read, Miss Avocet?"

"Yes, ma'am. I love to. Books help me to forget."

She pulled two plates down from her cupboard. "Forget what?"

"Not really forget," I answered, and I picked up a seashell and put it to my ear so that I could hear the ocean. "The words just take me someplace else."

72. Fowler, Connie May. **Remembering Blue**. New York: Doubleday, 2000. 290p.

When first encountered, husky Nick Blue is working for a logging company in North Florida in the Tallahassee area, having left his ancestral home on Lethe, a mythic island off the state's Gulf Coast, to escape a family curse. During this time he meets and marries a shy convenience store clerk, Mattie O'Roarke, who learns that Nick comes from a long line of Greek-American fishermen convinced they are descended from dolphins and therefore fated to die at sea—the so-called "Blue curse." When a fellow logger is killed, Nick realizes death can occur anywhere at anytime, so he returns with Mattie to Lethe and his seafaring roots. At first the gregarious Blue family intimidates Mattie but as her love for Nick deepens—he's a tender lover and caring husband—she begins to feel at home, to fit in, to blossom. But then the fates strike and Mattie loses Nick to the sea. Steeped in allusions to classical mythology, Connie May Fowler's fourth novel "is a pleasure to read even though the reader knows that a tragedy is lurking" (*LJ*, Jan. 2000, pp. 158-59).

73. Fowler, Connie May. **Sugar Cage**. New York: Putnam, 1992. 319p.

In **Sugar Cage**, Connie May Fowler's ambitious first novel, eight characters whose lives intersect in post-World War II Florida tell their stories in their own voices, which are as varied as the characters themselves. For instance, there's Eudora Jewel, a lusty widow, ruminating about her provocative behavior ("I am not a bad woman. My morals are as airtight as should be expected. They don't live up to Mrs. Rose Looney's standards. I'd have to practice total abstinence to make her happy. But I am not a floozy. I care deeply for my men friends"), and then there's Inez Temple, a black maid, who obsesses about the eponymous sugar cage ("Some days, it's true, I was haunted by a twinge of guilt. Because maybe if I had not been so helpful that morning, maybe if I hadn't poured sugar into that water, there would have been no cage. Now I know what Mama and Grandmama would have said. They would have said, The cage was always there, Inez—you just happened to see its deceiving bars"). The novel's action, which includes a hurricane, a baseball game between prison inmates and visitors, a pro-segregation rally, deaths by cancer and heart attack, a body snatching, and sundry mystical occurrences, takes place partly in St. Augustine and environs and partly in the sugarcane fields and swamps around Lake Okeechobee. "A poetically rendered book" (*BLGF*, 1992, p. 58).

74. Francis, Dorothy. **Conch Shell Murder**. Waterville, ME: Five Star, 2003. 245p.

Dorothy Francis's debut novel for adults—she's best known as a YA mystery writer—is an entertaining thriller that takes place in

Key West and features Katie Hassworth, a schoolteacher-turned-private eye. The case involves the murder of a prominent citizen beaten to death with a conch shell: "She slumped, her head a pulpy melon dangling wetly over the chair arm and dripping blood onto the pristine carpet." Naturally there's a lengthy list of likely suspects, including Key West's good-looking mayor who may or may not be up to his sexy eyebrows in political corruption. "Local lore, history, food, and fauna and flora add interest without overburdening a smoothly written and suspenseful tale" (*PW*, Mar. 24, 2003, pp. 61-62).

75.  Frank, Pat. **Alas, Babylon**. Philadelphia: Lippincott, 1959. 253p.

In Fort Repose, a fictional river town in Central Florida north of Orlando, harried survivors of a nuclear attack on the U.S. have no electricity, little food, and are plagued by threats of disease, radiation poisoning, and lawlessness. All of which forces their leaders—Randy Bragg, Doctor Dan, and others, including the town librarian—to find new methods or reinvent old ones for coping with existence in what is a very grim present and even more frightening future. "The genius and appeal of this [classic apocalyptic novel] arise from its absorbing combination of danger, adventure, humor, and romance" (*BLGF*, 1992, p. 21). Note: Enormously popular when first published at the end of the 1950s, **Alas, Babylon** has been reprinted at least twice, in 1976 by Bantam Books and in 1993 by HarperPerennial.

From **Alas, Babylon**:

They found Dan in Randy's office, with Helen trimming his hair. Randy told them about the two squirrels [he had shot to flavor that night's stew] and then he said, "Dan, I've been thinking about the fish. I've never seen fishing this bad before. Could anything big and permanent have happened? Could radiation have wiped them out, or anything?"

Dan scratched at his beard and Helen brushed his hand down and said, "Sit still."

Dan said, "Fish. Let me think about fish. I doubt that anything happened to the fish. If the river had been poisoned by fallout right after The Day the dead fish would have come to the surface. The river would have been blanketed with fish. That didn't happen then and it hasn't happened since. No, I doubt that there has been a holocaust of fish."

"It worries me," Randy said.

"Salt worries me more. Salt doesn't grow or breed or spawn. You either have it or you don't."

76. Gannon, Michael. **Secret Missions**. New York: HarperCollins, 1994. 365p.

Historical fact: In 1942 a Nazi submarine landed four German saboteurs on a deserted beach in Florida near Jacksonville. Michael Gannon, a prominent historian who's written extensively about World War II and specifically U-boat action off the U.S. Atlantic Coast, uses this event to construct an exciting—albeit imaginary—tale of espionage involving a devious German agent loose in Florida and a Roman Catholic priest who learns about the agent's presence while hearing a confession, but, being bound by sacramental seal, cannot reveal this vital information to American authorities. "Gannon's detailed knowledge of German U-Boat activity during World War II plays an important role in this hard-to-put-down novel. The priest and the spy ride a collision course that carries them down the east coast of Florida, across to Tampa, to Eglin Field [now Eglin Air Force Base] in the Panhandle, and back to a violent climax off the Florida east coast. **Secret Missions** is rich in plot, character, historical, and technical detail" (*FHQ*, Jan. 1995, p. 411).

77. García, Cristina. **The Agüero Sisters**. New York: Knopf, 1997. 288p.

The author's nuanced story concerns two middle-aged Cuban-born half-sisters who represent contrasting perspectives on the Cuban experience during the Castro era. For many years Reina Agüero, a master electrician, has lived a simple, nostalgic existence in pinched Havana; on the other hand, Constancia Agüero Cruz has made it big as an affluent exile first in New York and then Miami, where she drives a pink Cadillac and owns a thriving cosmetic business that caters, ironically, to Cuban women. When the sisters reunite after a 30-year separation, their different social, cultural, political, and economic assumptions create strains, but in the end Reina and Constancia come to realize that their shared blood, their sisterhood, renders them immutably more alike than different. "Born in Havana and raised in the U.S., García does soaring, zesty justice to the vagaries of both malfunctioning Cuba and daydreaming South Florida" (*Time*, May 12, 1997, p. 92).

78. Garcia-Aguilera, Carolina. **Bloody Waters**. New York: Putnam, 1996. 274p.

A former Miami private investigator who emigrated from Cuba in 1960, Carolina Garcia-Aguilera has created a winning mystery series built around the character of Guadalupe "Lupe" Solano who, not surprisingly, is a Cuban-born PI now living in Miami. A review of **Bloody Waters**, which inaugurated the series, accurately notes that Garcia-Aguilera "incorporates standard mystery formula with great success by adding her own subtle twists" (*LJ*, Feb. 1, 1996, p. 102), an observation that applies to all the Lupe novels to date, which include *Bloody Shame* (1997), *Bloody Secrets* (1998), *Miracle in Paradise* (1999), *Havana Heat* (2000), *Bitter Sugar* (2001), *One Hot Summer* (2002), and *Luck of the Draw* (2003). Readers who enjoy Edna Buchanan's Miami-based thrillers starring Britt Montero (see entries 25-26) will also find Garcia-Aguilera's Lupe Solano good company.

79. Garrett, George. **The King of Babylon Shall Not Come Against You**. New York: Harcourt, Brace, 1996. 336p.

In 1993 journalist Billy Tone returns to his hometown, fictional Paradise Springs in Central Florida, to research a book about various crimes and destructive acts—two murders, a fire, a bank embezzlement, a kidnapping, a possible suicide—that occurred there

25 years earlier, just days before the assassination of Martin Luther King Jr. on April 4, 1968. Tone talks extensively with residents who either participated in or witnessed these apparently random occurrences, including an African-American lawyer, a newspaper editor, a retired sheriff, a developer, a minister, an elderly professor, and the town librarian, who was only four at the time. Their recollections and comments form a fascinating portrait of life, past and present, not only in Paradise Springs but by extension Florida and indeed all of the American South. "As Tone interviews locals on their memories of the events and uncovers the web of connections leading up to the crimes, it becomes increasingly clear that the truth he seeks to reveal has to do with his own complicity—not with the crimes he studies but with the South itself and with the accumulated psychic debt of history" (*LJ*, Feb. 15, 1996, p. 176). A poet, playwright, and fiction writer, George Garrett is best known for his novels set in Elizabethan England.

80.   Gear, Kathleen O'Neal & W. Michael Gear. **People of the Lightning**. New York: Forge/Tom Doherty, 1995. 414p.

Part of the authors' acclaimed First North Americans series of historical sagas, which now numbers more than a dozen titles (*People of the Wolf, People of the Fire, People of the River, People of the Sea, People of the Owl, People of the Moon*, etc.), **People of the Lightning** takes readers back roughly 8,000 years to a Native American society that thrived in what today is the Titusville area of Florida's central east coast. The Gears, a husband and wife team and both trained archaeologists, bring that time and culture to life through a fictional narrative based on scholarly evidence described in their foreword. The story centers on animosity between two rival clans, one led by Cottonmouth, who's as nasty as his name, and the other by Musselwhite, an esteemed female warrior whose husband, Diver, has been captured by Cottonmouth. Believing Diver to be dead, Musselwhite marries Pondwader, a 15-year-old albino who, because of his white hair, eyes, and skin, is also known—and feared—as the Lightning Boy. **People of the Lightning** is a riveting, informative, thought-provoking novel that will be of particular interest to students of Florida's pre-Columbian history.

From **People of the Lightning**:

Wasp and the other warrior emptied Pondwader's packs onto the grass, and sorted through the contents. Pondwader tipped his chin, focused on the night sky, as if praying to Sister Moon.

The skinny Woodduck cursed and straightened up. Furiously, he kicked the contents of the packs, sending bags of food, wooden bowls, water gourds, sailing across the clearing to tumble through the grass.

Woodduck crouched before Pondwader and said, "Come along, Lightning Boy. Your death awaits you. We are only its messengers."

He gripped Pondwader's arm and jerked him to his feet. Out of sheer cruelty, he twisted the arm, brutally shoving it up behind Pondwader's back. Pondwader stood still and white.

"Trying to be brave boy?" Woodduck asked. "We shall see how long that lasts under Cottonmouth's torture. He has very persuasive techniques . . . ."

A hiss was followed by the crack of breaking bone, and Woodduck shrieked and staggered. His wide eyes looked disbelievingly at the bloody dart embedded in his ribs. A horrified wail erupted from his mouth. He took three running steps before toppling.

81. Glassman, Steve. **Blood on the Moon: A Novel of Old Florida**. Brooklyn, OH: Quality Publications, 1990. 324p.

Set in 19th-century Florida against the backdrop of bitter conflicts between white settlers and Native Americans occasioned by the Second Seminole War (1835-42), Steve Glassman's novel focuses on the years Charles Louis Napoléon Achille Murat spent in the state. Achille Murat (1801-47), a genuine eccentric, was Napoleon Bonaparte's nephew and, before his uncle's defeat at Waterloo in 1815, Crown Prince of Naples. He moved to Florida a few years after Napoleon's death in 1821, living first in St. Augustine and then at Lipona, a large plantation 15 miles east of Tallahassee where, in Glassman's fictionalized narrative, he enjoyed the company of two wives: Jenny, white, beautiful, cultured—and legitimate; and Ophelia, black, beautiful, cultured—and morganatic. While the story's main emphasis is on relationships in the Murat household and especially the intense rivalry between the two women, it also includes accounts of some major historical occurrences, such as the Indian Key Massacre in 1840. "Although Mr. Glassman has taken considerable literary license with many of the political and military events that occurred during this early period in Florida history, he nonetheless has written a book which even the most serious historian should enjoy. In the process, he tells a good story" (*FHQ*, Jan. 1991, p. 401). Note: The resourceful Glassman, a professor of English at Embry Riddle University in Daytona Beach, Florida, is also the author of a mystery novel, **The Near Death Experiment** (see entry 82), and coeditor (with Maurice O'Sullivan) of an anthology entitled **Orange Pulp: Stories of Mayhem, Murder, and Mystery** (see entry 209) and a collection of essays, *Crime Fiction & Film in the Sunshine State: Florida Noir* (1997).

82. Glassman, Steve. **The Near Death Experiment**. Miami, FL: Tropical Pr., 2001. 271p.

Someone is tampering with Florida's frozen orange juice concentrate, potentially a disaster for the nation's OJ drinkers as well as the state's lucrative citrus industry. In Steve Glassman's thriller, a college professor, Rupert J. "Bru" Bruton, Ph.D., and a librarian-cum-girl Friday, Melba T. Appleyard, work together "to uncover the white-collar criminals behind the contamination of the orange juice crop that is causing a national epidemic. Bru calls Melba the only librarian he knew who had the nerve to break a rule" (*Florida Libraries*, Fall 2001, p. 18). Not only does the novel offer readers a suspenseful mystery loaded with quirky characters, it presents basic information about Florida's citrus business in an interesting, nontechnical manner.

From **The Near Death Experiment**:

"God dammit, Bru. Don't do this. Let the authorities handle it. Remember, you told me just a couple of days ago that you'd learned that violence never accomplished anything."

"Sure. Just say go lock up a multibillionaire. As far as that goes, explain in a mild-voiced way about orange juice contamination. That ought to impress the authorities almost as much as it did the sheriff yesterday, who by the way was probably right in the skepticism she showed. I came home last night and somehow I just didn't feel good about my scene with Goins [a villainous citrus baron]. I had to have a near death experience to get it. Professor Khoury warned me about running off half cocked. I did that yesterday. I didn't have the evidence. I just thought I had it after I talked to Arbuthnot's friend. He told me he knew for a fact that Arbuthnot was planning to contaminate o.j. He's the only evidential link I have and I scared him into hiding. It's a long way from knowing these guys are behind the KiDS epidemic and proving it.

"Yesterday, I naively thought," Bru continued, "I had the whole thing taken care of. The old man told me he'd pull those polluted cans from the nation's supermarkets. Instead he sent his daughter over to kill me."

83. Graham, Heather. **Picture Me Dead**. Don Mills, Ontario: Mira, 2003. 352p.

Heather Graham may not be Florida's greatest writer but she's certainly among the most industrious, with approximately 100 novels to her credit published under three different names: Heather Graham, Heather Graham Pozzessere (her married name), and Shannon Drake (a pseudonym). The Miami-born Graham, who's been churning them out since the early 1980s, is also versatile, equally adept at writing mysteries, romances, and historical fiction. Typical of her briskly paced crime novels is **Picture Me Dead**, which involves a Miami serial killer, an enigmatic cult in the Everglades, drug trafficking, and touchy (in more ways than one) interaction between veteran homicide detective Jake Dilessio and rookie police officer Ashley Montague, a young lady blessed with both a photographic memory and an aptitude for forensic art. "The fast action is neatly punctuated by red herrings and false clues. Never mind the clichés (the obsessive cop determined to catch his partner's murderer; the religious cult that's really a front for illegal activities)—Graham's tight plotting, her keen sense of when to reveal and when to tease, and her eye for the Florida landscape will keep fans turning the pages" (*PW*, Feb. 24, 2003, p. 53).

84. Graham, Heather. **Runaway**. New York: Delacorte, 1994. 455p.

In an Author's Note prefacing **Runaway**, Heather Graham writes, "I have always wanted to do a series of books about Florida. It is much more than a place to me; it is home." So begins Graham's multivolume generational saga featuring the McKenzies, a Florida family descended from Sean McKenzie, an Irish immigrant who came to America in the late 18th century and married Geneva Tweed, a Charleston, South Carolina, lady of means. Their only son, Jarrett, was born in 1802. After Geneva's death, Sean married a woman of mixed blood (white mother, Native American father) named Mary McQueen, also known as Moon Shadow. Their only son, James—aka Running Bear—was born in 1808. Set in Florida during the 1830s when hostilities between Indian tribes and white settlers grew increasingly bitter, **Runaway** tells the story of the two half brothers and Jarrett's mysterious second wife, Tara, who's being pursued by creepy characters for a crime—murder—she swears she did not commit. Subsequent volumes in the McKenzie series are *Captive* (1996), *Rebel* (1997), *Surrender* (1998), *Glory* (1999), and *Triumph* (2000).

From **Runaway**:

They rode through wild, beautiful country. When they come upon marshland where they could ride abreast, James informed her that he had told his family and people to keep on moving with the daylight, as the tribe—encumbered by children and belongings— would move more slowly than she, Jarrett, and he needed to go. He meant to go deep into the interior of the state, far south, and into the swampland of the Everglades. "You'll be safe there," he said. "I promise you. And Jarrett will find a way to clear you. I know that he will."

Tara began to believe it herself. Night fell. She spent the darkness in the swamp, high on a hammock of land, in her husband's arms. They built no fire. She felt his warmth, and it was enough. She slept amazingly well, guarded by her husband and brother-in-law.

The temperature remained blessedly low as they rode the next day. They rode for hours, then came upon a stretch of river where they paused, for it was filled with beautiful birds. Jarrett pointed them out to her. Cranes, egrets, herons, the unbelievably pink flamingos.

"The land remains beautiful," she said.

"And deadly," Jarrett warned. "Take care. This is cottonmouth country through here. And for every gator nose you see, I promise you there is a second nearly submerged nearby. Keep your distance."

85. Gramling, Lee. **Ghosts of the Green Swamp**. Sarasota, FL: Pineapple Pr., 1996. 296p.

A sixth-generation Floridian who lives in Gainesville, Lee Gramling inaugurated the publisher's Cracker Western series in 1993 with two novels, *Trail from St. Augustine* and *Riders of the Suwannee*, and later contributed three more: *Thunder on the St. Johns* (1994), *Ninety-Mile Prairie* (2002), and **Ghosts of the Green Swamp**. Gramling's stories follow the tried-and-true Western formula popularized by Zane Grey and Louis L'Amour, which features action-packed yarns peopled by gunslingers, cattlemen, sodbusters, saloonkeepers, Injuns, and other rough-and-tumble characters who operate under a rude code of frontier justice. Florida westerns, however, differ from the traditional genre by virtue of their subtropical setting. For instance, in **Ghosts of the Green Swamp** Gramling's hero, Tate Barkley, fights the bad guys in a vast, sinister wetland that contains dangers no cowboy west of the Mississippi ever faced. Note: See Herb and Muncy Chapman's **Wiregrass Country** (entry 32) and Jon Wilson's **Bridger's Run** (entry 295) for other examples of Pineapple Press's Cracker Westerns.

86.  Granberry, Edwin. **A Trip to Czardis**. New York: Trident Pr., 1966. 194p.

In 1932 Edwin Granberry (1897-1988) published a masterful short story called "A Trip to Czardis" about a backwoods woman bringing her two young sons to the fictional Florida town of Czardis to say final goodbyes to their father, in prison there awaiting execution for murder. Winner of the prestigious O. Henry Prize for best short story of the year and frequently anthologized, "A Trip to Czardis" achieved lasting popularity, but readers often expressed a desire to know about the murder itself and the circumstances that led up to it, facts not revealed in the story. Though it took 34 years, Granberry eventually produced a novel of the same name that provides the story behind the story—a sorrowful, ironic tale of sterility, seduction, suicide, and misplaced honor in which an innocent man, Jim Cameron, is condemned to die for a murder that never happened. Note: Granberry's famous short story is included in **Florida Stories** (see entry 184) and **Orange Pulp** (see entry 209). Note also: The author's much earlier but equally tragic novel, *The Erl King* (1930), also takes place in Florida.

From **A Trip to Czardis**:

In the moonlight he saw her eyes scald with tears. She grasped his hand, and he heard a distracted whisper uttered in anguish: "I'm not asking for love—it's a child I need."

"You're drunk, Mrs. Logan."

"Never mind—you're not a boy, Mr. Cameron. Let me talk to the man I think you are. I left the world for Ponce Logan. The life I've had with him here on the ranch I wouldn't exchange for the fame of Paderewski. But a cancer is eating his heart out. It's as if the gods had poured into one mold all that's manly in body and spirit, and then mocked him. It isn't love Ponce and I lack, Mr. Cameron—it's a child."

Cameron again saw Logan's ashen face in the sunset, heard him saying: "*I didn't know until we were married. Five years later, she still doesn't know. She blames herself.*"

"When did he tell you this?"

"It's not a thing a man tells the woman he loves. The means for a child can be bought in a hospital—it was proposed to me recently in New York. I would feel like an animal in a laboratory. I care who the father is."

"You're mad, Mrs. Logan. Your husband's my friend."

87. Griffith, Leon Odell. **A Long Time Since Morning**. New York: Random House, 1954. 247p.

A Florida native who wrote both fiction and nonfiction, Leon Odell Griffith (1921-84) began his career as a journalist with the *Pensacola News-Journal* and later worked for several other Panhandle newspapers. The first (and best) of his two novels, **A Long Time Since Morning**, tackles big issues—racial tolerance and bigotry, good and evil, love and hate, life and death—as acted out within the microcosm of a small 1950s North Florida town. The main characters, who come across as real people, include Hugh Lee, conflicted publisher of the local newspaper; his sensitive wife, Anne, who's pregnant; her intimidating old father, Captain Mason, who tells the couple, "I have hated best those I loved"; Sheriff Mack McSwain, a racist and sadist; and misbegotten Mabel Gramby, whose poems were—tragically—ignored by Hugh Lee. "The story rises with the morning sun over a typical North Florida community, somewhere between Pensacola and Jacksonville. It reaches an embattled climax amid the frumpery of a luncheon gathering. It fades away with the reconciliation of man (good and bad) and his fate (bad and good) in the descending shadows of dusk" (*NYTBR*, Sept. 5, 1954, p. 11).

From **A Long Time Since Morning**:

Mabel Gramby's body had caught in the lygustrum at the corner of the house beneath the window of her second-story bedroom.

The fall had not killed her; as Mack McSwain said, she was dying when she jumped. On her left arm was a thin cut but it was from the gash across her right wrist that the blood had dripped upon the green leaves of the lygustrum. The drops on the leaves below the body looked as if they were spots of red tile paint which had splattered from a careless painter's brush.

She had fallen or jumped head downward and her head had caught first in the lygustrum but the plant limbs had given and so it looked as if she had not jumped at all but had simply crawled upon the twigs and stretched out for an afternoon nap.

She was dressed except for panties but the fall had knotted her dress about the waist; all of her legs and a part of her stomach were exposed. One shoe remained on her foot. The other had been lost in the motion of the fall; it lay on the ground beneath her. One of her hands was over her mouth as if frightened she still had managed to hold back a scream.

88.   Grippando, James. **Beyond Suspicion**. New York: Harper Collins, 2002. 336p.

Trial attorney James Grippando began writing legal thrillers while a junior partner at the powerhouse Miami law firm of Steel Hector & Davis (now merged with Squire, Sanders & Dempsey, a Cleveland-based firm), launching his literary career in 1994 with **The Pardon** (see entry 89), a novel that immediately marked him as a young man with bestseller potential. **Beyond Suspicion**, his seventh novel, is technically a sequel to **The Pardon**, though it can be read and fully appreciated without reference to the earlier work. Both titles feature Grippando's most durable character to date: Jack Swyteck, a sturdy, industrious, intelligent Miami defense lawyer who, like his creator, knows the Florida criminal justice system inside out. In **Beyond Suspicion**, Swyteck wins a life insurance case for an old flame who's later found dead—in Jack's bathtub!—which of course automatically accords him prime-suspect status. "Grippando writes in compact prose, quickly moving from one situation to the next. The legal situations are clearly written and understandable, and the characters well rounded" (*LJ*, Sept. 1, 2002, pp. 212-13).

89.  Grippando, James. **The Pardon**. New York: HarperCollins, 1994. 320p.

Jack Swyteck—James Grippando's series hero and son of invented Florida Governor Harry Swyteck—is a young criminal defense lawyer who just happens to know unequivocally that a prisoner slated to die in the state's electric chair is innocent. But despite such compelling doubt about the man's guilt, the governor, a staunch law-and-order politician, refuses to stop the execution. Later, when a vengeful psychopath manipulates a first-degree murder charge against Jack, the question arises: If Jack should be found guilty, will the governor execute his own son? "Between the chilling opening scene of the hours before an inmate's execution and the climactic meeting between Jack and his nemesis, author Grippando, a Miami attorney, rachets [sic] the tension up every few pages. **The Pardon** is a promising, cleverly plotted, and taut first novel" (*BL*, Sept. 1, 1994, p. 23). Note: Jack Swyteck stars in several other Grippando novels, including **Beyond Suspicion** (see entry 88), *Last to Die* (2003), *Hear No Evil* (2004), and *Got the Look* (2006). The prolific Grippando has also written a number of non-Swyteck mysteries set in South Florida, among them *The Informant* (1996), *The Abduction* (1998), *Found Money* (1999), and *A King's Ransom* (2001).

90.  Gruber, Michael. **Tropic of Night**. New York: Morrow, 2003. 432p.

While engaged in fieldwork in Nigeria, a white American anthropologist, Jane Doe (yes, that's her name), studies a native tribe known for its menacing voodooistic practices, and eventually both she and her husband, DeWitt Moore, an African-American writer who has accompanied her on the trip, fall victim to virulent strains of African sorcery. Ill and disoriented, Jane returns to the U.S. where she recuperates at her parents' home on Long Island. Meanwhile,

DeWitt, under the mesmerizing spell of an evil shaman, becomes obsessed with the need to punish white America; as a result, the couple's marriage, already shaky, splinters apart. Then when her pregnant sister is murdered in a sacrificial manner Jane learned about in Africa, she senses her own life is in danger. She flees to South Florida, hiding out in Miami under an assumed name, hoping to escape the vengeful DeWitt. Soon, however, one pregnant Miami woman after another is killed in the same ritualistic fashion as her sister: DeWitt is closing in. At this point, Jimmy Paz, a suave black Cuban-American detective with the Miami PD, enters the story, and together he and Jane confront DeWitt and the supernatural forces he commands. "First-time novelist Gruber keeps his far-flung locations, complicated characters and anthropological information perfectly balanced in this finely crafted, intelligent and original work" (*PW*, Jan. 27, 2003, pp. 233-34). Note: The engaging Jimmy Paz returns to investigate similar crimes in Michael Gruber's second and third equally suspenseful thrillers, *Valley of Bones* (2005) and *Night of the Jaguar (2006)*.

91.  Hailey, Arthur. **Detective**. New York: Crown, 1997. 406p.

The fecund Arthur Hailey, who has penned page-turning novels about airports, hotels, and the banking, newspaper, and automotive industries, here turns his attention to the police, specifically Miami's finest. His protagonist, homicide detective and former Roman Catholic priest Malcolm Ainslie, is caught up in a serial murder case with troubling loose ends, the first involving a former lover, city commissioner Cynthia Ernst, and the second a startling confession by a convict on death row, Elroy "Animal" Doil. Like all Hailey's novels, **Detective** offers readers an absorbing and rapidly unfolding plot, reasonably believable characters, requisite dollops of sex, and abundant detail about the whys and wherefores of the business or organization under scrutiny—in this case, big-city law enforcement. "It's a measure of Hailey's skill as a storyteller that he gives up the killer way before the end but still manages to maintain the suspense" (*PW*, May 19, 1997, p. 64).

From **Detective**:

At the outset, standing at the multi-table complex, Adele Montesino began casually, "I apologize for the excessive heat. We've been promised that air conditioning will be restored soon; meanwhile anyone who wants to shed some clothing may do so within reason, though of course that's easiest for the men—if less interesting."

Amid mild laughter, several men removed their jackets.

"I am here today to seek three indictments against the same person," Montesino continued. "The first is for murder in the first degree, and the accused is Cynthia Mildred Ernst."

Until this moment the jurors had seemed relaxed; now, abruptly, their tranquillity disappeared. Startled, sitting upright in their chairs, some gasped audibly. The foreperson, leaning forward, asked, "Is that name a coincidence?"

Montesino responded, "No coincidence, Mr. Foreman." Then, facing all the jurors, "Yes, ladies and gentlemen, I *am* speaking of Miami City Commissioner Cynthia Ernst. The two people she is charged with feloniously killing are her late parents, Gustav and Eleanor Ernst."

92.  Haldeman, Joe. **The Coming**. New York: Berkley/Ace Books, 2000. 220p.

Award-winning science fiction writer Joe Haldeman's instructive fantasy takes place in Florida during the year 2054. There's a great commotion after Dr. Aurora "Rory" Bell, an astronomy professor in Gainesville, receives a cryptic, two-word message from a craft in outer space headed for earth: "We're coming." Are extraterrestrial beings really on the way or is it a hoax? Are the words intended as a greeting, a warning, or a threat? Lots of people—Rory's composer husband; Gainesville's mayor; Florida's panicky governor; even the U.S. president—get involved in speculating about the terse message, and ultimately their behavior reveals some fundamental truths about the human species. "Haldeman's latest sf thriller provides food for thought as well as fast-paced action" (*LJ*, Dec. 2000, p. 196).

93.  Hall, James W. **Buzz Cut**. New York: Delacorte, 1996. 352p.

James W. Hall began his literary career in the late 1960s as a writer of poetry, encouraged by Peter Meinke, his English professor at Florida Presbyterian College (now Eckerd College) in St. Petersburg and a nationally known author (poetry and short stories). But after years of trying to eke out a living as a poet, Hall turned to writing mysteries set in Florida, aiming to emulate the success of such masters of the genre as John D. MacDonald (see entries 171-174) and Elmore Leonard (see entries 156-158). Hall's first effort, *Under Cover of Daylight* (1987), introduced his engaging single-name series character, Thorn, a Key Largo maker of hand-tied bonefishing flies and occasional sleuth. The novel, which received enthusiastic reviews, sold well, and since that time Hall has produced a modest shelfful of meticulously crafted Thorn thrillers, including **Tropical Freeze** (see entry 95), *Mean High Tide* (1994), *Gone Wild* (1995), **Buzz Cut** (1996), *Red Sky at Night* (1997), and *Body Language* (1998); in two other titles, *Blackwater Sound* (2002) and *Off the Chart* (2003), the popular Thorn shares top billing (and more) with Alexandra Rafferty, a sexy police photographer. Arguably **Buzz Cut** is Thorn's most exciting outing to date. In it, he must outwit Butler Jack, a brilliant psychopath who hijacks a Miami-based luxury cruise ship using all manner of deadly cunning: The stun-gun devices attached to his fingers are especially unnerving. "This is a real page-turner" (*LJ*, May 15, 1996, p. 84).

94.  Hall, James W. **Hard Aground**. New York: Delacorte, 1993. 360p.

Best known for his novels built around the exploits of a rugged yet sensitive Florida crime-solver named Thorn (see entries 93 & 95), James W. Hall offers up a somewhat different protagonist in **Hard Aground**. Hapfield "Hap" Tyler, 38, is a laid-back Vietnam vet who builds sailboards and gives tours of Mangrove House, the historic Biscayne Bay home of his famous grandfather, Commodore Randolph Tyler, a fictional version of the real-life Commodore

Ralph Middleton Munroe, patriarch of a 19th-century pioneer Florida family that settled in Coconut Grove (now part of Miami). The story takes off when Hap's brother, Daniel, an eminent archaeologist, is murdered just as he's about to reveal a startling secret concerning the Tyler clan and a long-lost Spanish galleon laden with Mayan gold and precious stones. Among the potential culprits are Daniel's girlfriend and her mother, an unscrupulous U.S. Senator. "Hall has made a career of looking beneath Florida's sunny surface and exposing its gamy, rotting underpinnings" (*BL*, June 1994, p. 1778). Note: Hall has written several other non-Thorn novels, among them *Bones of Coral* (1991), *Rough Draft* (2000), and *Forests of the Night* (2005). The latter, an exciting tale involving the Cherokee nation and set mostly in North Carolina, appears to signal a shift in emphasis for Hall, who recently expressed a desire to move beyond the stereotypical contemporary Florida mystery, which tends to highlight the state's most negative aspects—violent crime, rapacious developers, environmental atrocities, etc.—for comic or shock effect.

From **Hard Aground:**

Martina stared thoughtfully at Hollings. She took a long breath and said, "What I don't like is, the fingerprints telling the cops to be looking for one person, and this Hap Tyler is describing somebody else."

"How's that? I don't get it."

"Nothing."

"I'm not following you here."

"I don't like it," she said. "I don't like it, that someone could blow everything."

Martina looked down at Hollings's hand circling her navel.

"Okay," Hollings said. "We'll shoot him. If it'll make you feel better, we'll just drive over there and kill Tyler's ass."

Martina put her hand on Hollings's hand, pressed it to her navel, then nudged it lower.

She said, "The guy's probably already given the cops my description. The damage is done."

"He can identify you, yeah, but he can't testify against you unless he's alive. That's one of the cornerstones of the American judicial system. You got to be alive to testify against somebody."

95. Hall, James W. **Tropical Freeze**. New York: Norton, 1989. 319p.

In **Tropical Freeze** the resourceful Thorn (see also entry 93) agrees to help attractive Darcy Richards search for her big brother, Gaeton, who's mysteriously disappeared. Gaeton, a childhood friend of Thorn's, is a former FBI agent now working for Benny Cousins, a well-heeled security consultant in the Florida Keys. Short, fat, and sweaty, Benny is actually a ruthless gangster Thorn will have to tangle with before the case concludes. In the interim, Darcy energizes Thorn's love life while various Keys characters enliven the plot with splashes of local color. "If the action is sometimes unbelievable, it really doesn't matter: Mr. Hall's lyrical passion for the Florida Keys, his spare language and unusual images haunt us long after the story has faded" (*NYTBR*, Oct. 15, 1989, p. 38).

96. Hall, Rubylea. **Davey**. New York: Duell, Sloan & Pearce, 1951. 288p.

Florida-born Rubylea Hall (1910-73) wrote four substantial novels set in her native state: Her masterpiece, **The Great Tide** (see entry 97); *Flamingo Prince* (1954), based on the life and times of the charismatic Native American leader, Osceola; *God Has a Sense of Humor* (1960), an account of the struggles of a family in the Florida Panhandle circa 1900; and **Davey**, a poignant story about the life of an undersized but courageous young boy growing up on a poor sharecropper's farm in the 1920s in rural West Florida. Hall, a keen observer of the human condition, drew on her early experience as a country schoolteacher to create the memorable title character in **Davey**. "Touched by overtones that every adult will remember from his own childhood, **Davey** will be a pleasure to young and old alike. Ralph Ray Jr. adds a series of excellent illustrations that capture the full magic of the 'Cypress Country'" (*NYTBR*, Oct. 21, 1951, p. 34).

97.   Hall, Rubylea. **The Great Tide**. New York: Duell, Sloan & Pearce, 1947. 535p.

St. Joseph was an actual settlement on the Gulf of Mexico near Apalachicola in the Florida Panhandle that went from boom city in the mid-1830s to ghost town a decade later, the community destroyed by the one-two punch of a virulent yellow fever epidemic followed by a devastating hurricane. Rubylea Hall's long, satisfying saga, **The Great Tide**, places her formidable heroine, Miss Carolina "Caline" Cohran, in the thick of St. Joseph's short, turbulent existence, which is illuminated by the author's extensive knowledge of the area's history and her use of contemporary accounts. Caline—a seductive, strong-willed, calculating, sometimes manipulative woman—arrives in thriving St. Joseph as the bride-to-be of wealthy Douglas Blackwell, whom she marries not for love but money and position. Complicating matters, the man Caline does love, macho Studd Seven, is her husband's best friend. "Characterizations are excellent, the story moving and interesting, but it is the background—the description of the way of life of that time which makes this a great novel" (*LJ*, Sept. 1, 1947, p. 1194). Note: **The Great Tide** was reprinted in 1975 by the Great American Publishing Company in cooperation with the St. Joseph Historical Society. Note also: St. Joseph, site of Florida's first constitutional convention (1838-39), was eventually replaced by the city of Port St. Joe, currently the seat of Florida's Gulf County.

From **The Great Tide**:

"You'll be a riot in St. Joseph," Studd said, as they moved on. "If that crazy town doesn't go wild over you, I'll miss my guess."

"Is it really a crazy town?" Caline wanted to know, accepting the piece of chicken he passed to her. The more she heard about St. Joseph and the more she thought about it, the more excited she grew over the prospect of going there to live.

"It's the greatest little city in Florida right now," he boasted. He stopped and pointed a greasy finger at her. "And the time's not far off when it will be the greatest in America—in the world!"

Caline laughed. "I'd say you were counting your chickens before they hatched. But I know it must be a grand place. It seems to be a part of Douglas—he lives it, breathes it, and shouts about it to everyone who will listen."

"It's like that," Studd said, "it becomes a part of every man who has had anything to do with the foundation and development of it, and it becomes a part of everyone who lives there."

98. Harrison, Sam. **Birdsong Ascending**. New York: Harcourt Brace Jovanovich, 1992. 315p.

Sam Harrison's debut novel, **Walls of Blue Coquina** (see entry 99), received critical praise for its perceptive treatment of a sensitive subject. His second (and apparently last) novel, **Birdsong Ascending**, confirmed Harrison, a Florida native, as a 45-year-old writer with exceptional literary potential. Set in Calhoun, a fictional town near Sanford in Central Florida, the story unfolds at an unhurried pace, the narrative concerned mainly with the memories, longings, loves, and regrets of middle-aged Frank Birdsong, heir to a large citrus grove destroyed by a winter freeze in the mid-1980s and now in the process of transforming into a golf course and mobile home park. His persistent dream of climbing the town's water tower, a rite of passage he failed ignobly to achieve while in high school, becomes a potent metaphor for adult self-doubt and guilt. **Birdsong Ascending** has "all the smoldering moodiness of a Tennessee Williams play—with a bizarre twist ending" (*BL*, Jan. 1, 1992, p. 810).

99. Harrison, Sam. **Walls of Blue Coquina**. New York: Harcourt Brace Jovanovich, 1990. 239p.

Bobby Sauls, a 72-year-old geezer, is waiting to die as he sits on his porch looking out on a road once made of coquina and beyond it to the waters of the Gulf of Mexico on the North Florida coast. Bobby is also waiting for something big to happen—the enigmatic "something" he's been expecting all his life. Largely an interior drama that takes place within Bobby's mind, the novel slowly and plaintively reveals the pertinent facts: He and his wife own a number of modest tourist cottages where they live along with their grandson and pregnant granddaughter and her husband. One day a biker, Psychic Ike (he's into clairvoyance), rents one their cottages and tells Bobby, "Something very powerful and beautiful is going to happen here." While waiting, Bobby ruminates about significant events in his life, such as driving an ice truck down the road made of blue coquina; having an affair with a tall, dark woman; his cold wife finding out and the wall between them getting even colder; their son returning from Vietnam with a wounded soul and finishing the job at home with a shotgun. "Harrison's elaborate exploration of a dying man's need to believe in some transcendental experience while attempting to tie up the loose ends of his life is thoughtful and compelling throughout" (*PW*, Mar. 2, 1990, p. 76). Note: Coquina, Spanish for "tiny shells," is a type of limestone consisting of marine shells and coral that for centuries was used in Florida as a building material, mainly for forts and roads.

100. Hawes, Louise. **Waiting for Christopher**. Cambridge, MA: Candlewick, 2002. 240p.

The story line in this empathetic YA novel (for ages 12+) centers on a questionable action by Feena, a lonely 14-year-old girl who's recently moved from Connecticut to Florida with her divorced mother, an apathetic parent at best. When Feena observes a toddler named Christopher being abused and then apparently abandoned by his mother at a shabby amusement park near her home, she rescues—or is it kidnaps?—the little boy, hiding him away in a secret place. Feena enlists the help of Raylene, a classmate and new friend, to care for Christopher, and together the girls shower him with the love and attention he failed to receive from his mother. "Hawes' simple, eloquent words reveal complex truths of family love and sorrow. Feena's own mother appears indifferent until Feena sees her desperate need; and in the climactic moment of the story, even Christopher's abusive mother is humanized. Instead of neat solutions, there's just the painful question: How much can anyone do to help?" (*BL*, July 2002, p. 1838).

101. Heller, Jane. **Infernal Affairs**. New York: Kensington, 1996. 288p.

When dowdy, chubby, graying, over-imbibing, libido-challenged Barbara Chessner, a hapless real estate agent in the fictional Florida town of Banyan Beach, learns her husband plans to leave her for a 24-year-old cupcake, she gets smashed and makes a pact with the devil: Presto, she wakes up blond, beautiful, sexy, and successful. Then, to her horror, she finds out exactly what the devil expects in return. "A bunch of wacky characters, including a persistently on-the-scene dog, share this frothy scenario, which lacks subtlety in plot and prose but succeeds on the strength of Heller's fast-paced dialogue and humor" (*PW*, Jan. 22, 1996, pp. 57-58). Note: Jane Heller, a former book publicist, has written at least a dozen romantic suspense novels. Readers who enjoyed **Infernal Affairs** will also want to try *Sis Boom Bah* (1999), which involves feuding sisters in Florida.

102. Heller, Jean. **Handyman**. New York: Forge/Tom Doherty, 1995. 352p.

Not for the squeamish, this heart-pounding thriller about a cunning and sadistic serial murderer takes place in Tampa, Florida, and begins with a gruesome scene "so graphic and disgusting that the reader may want to take a shower and a Valium before going further" (*BL*, Oct. 15, 1995, p. 388). The tension builds as "handyman" Eugene Rickey—equally skilled at fixing things and raping, torturing, and killing women—meticulously stalks new victims, including a local TV news anchorwoman and a comely architect. "Highly recommended, but read only with the lights on" (*LJ*, Nov. 1, 1995, p. 106). Note: Jean Heller, an award-winning Florida newspaper journalist, currently reviews new books for the *St. Petersburg Times*.

From **Handyman**:

"You want some company? We could talk, and nobody would have to know about it. You're not expecting anybody today, are you?"

Cynthia thought about it. "No, I'm not," she said. "I'd like that."

"Be there in half an hour. Maybe we'll go to Ybor City for lunch to cheer you up. Carmine's, maybe, for black beans and yellow rice, or Cafe Creole for gumbo. Or someplace else. Your choice. Think about it."

Cynthia smiled as she replaced the receiver. When Liz got nervous or excited, she tended to ramble on. But her intentions were from the heart.

She turned away from the phone, and it rang again. It was probably Liz with something more she felt she had to say before the thought got away. Cynthia picked up the receiver.

"What else?" she asked with a laugh.

"Hello, bitch. I see you got my note."

Cynthia froze. An adrenaline rush kicked her in the gut, and she felt her heart leap. Bands of fear tightened around her chest, forcing her to breathe in short, shallow gasps, and her head began to swim as though she'd had too much to drink, although she still perceived the moment through the eyes of cold sobriety.

"How did you get my number?" It wasn't a question she would have predicted asking in this sort of situation, but it was something she wanted to know. How could this demon possibly have discovered her unlisted number?

"You've got a stack of bills piled up on that little table in the family room, including your phone bill, so I just helped myself," the man's voice responded. It was a young voice. It wasn't an unkind voice, but it wasn't friendly, either. It was flat. Cool. Unemotional. Unremarkable.

**Ernest Hemingway** (see entry 103) wrote many of his books in a two-story Spanish colonial home he owned in Key West, Florida. Located at 907 Whitehead Street, the Hemingway House today is a museum open to the public and is one of the city's most popular tourist attractions. Visitors can view Hemingway's studio where his old Royal typewriter still resides, as if waiting for the great writer to return from Sloppy Joe's, his favorite Key West watering hole.

103. Hemingway, Ernest. **To Have and Have Not**. New York: Scribner's, 1937. 262p.

Though his star has dimmed in recent years, Ernest Hemingway (1899-1961) remains one of American literature's iconic figures. In 1928 Hemingway moved to Key West, Florida's southernmost city, and lived there off and on for the next dozen years—years that were among the most productive of his literary life. It's hardly surprising then that Key West became the central locale for his only novel set in the U.S., **To Have and Have Not**. Considered a minor work in the Hemingway canon, **To Have and Have Not** presents an authentic portrayal of small-time commercial fishermen trying to scratch out a living in the exotic Florida Keys during the Depression years of the 1930s. The main character and narrator, Harry Morgan, a jaded charter boat captain, is forced by hard economic times to risk his life and single most important material asset—his boat—to smuggle guns, rum, and ultimately dangerous people between Florida and Cuba. There's no sugarcoated ending to this sad, realistic story, which is indubitably a work of merit and worth reading despite its modest repute among Hemingway scholars. Note: The plot of the popular 1944 film adaptation of **To Have and Have Not** deviates markedly from that of the novel. Directed by Howard Hawks, the film memorably stars Humphrey Bogart and a young Lauren Bacall.

From **To Have and Have Not**:

So there it was. I was broke. I'd lost five hundred and thirty dollars of the charter, and tackle I couldn't replace for three hundred and fifty more. How some of that gang that hangs around the dock would be pleased at that, I thought. It certainly would make some Conchs [Key West natives] happy. And the day before I turned down three thousand dollars to land three aliens on the Keys. Anywhere, just to get them out of the country.

All right, what was I going to do now? I couldn't bring in a load because you have to have money to buy the booze and besides there's no money in it any more. The town is flooded with it and there's nobody to buy it. But I was damned if I was going home broke and starve a summer in that town. Besides I've got a family. The clearance was paid when we came in. You usually pay the broker in advance and he enters you and clears you. Hell, I didn't even have enough money to put in gas. It was a hell of a note, all right.

104. Hendricks, Vicki. **Miami Purity**. New York: Pantheon, 1995. 208p.

Sherri Parlay, 36, formerly of Cleveland, Ohio ("the armpit of the world"), had been a topless dancer in Miami, Florida, for two years when she accidentally killed Hank, her "old man," by nailing him with a boom box to the head after he beat her up: "He had a terrible mean streak, but we were good together—specially when we got our clothes off." Upon release from prison Sherri decides to quit dancing and get a "regular day job," even though her "dancer's ass [was] still tight as could be." That job is at the Miami-Purity Dry Cleaners, where she quickly gets it on with the manager, twentysomething Payne Mahoney: "I took a look at that baby face, and those Jagger lips, and I got hot," confesses Sherri, panting. Payne's mother, owner of the dry cleaning establishment, tries to pry the lovers apart, but all she gets for her trouble is dead. "Ms. Hendricks proposes a world in which the first thought after murder is sex and the second is inheriting the victim's car. Few crime novelists have improvised more chilling carnage from the mundane trappings of the workplace—plastic bags, dry cleaning machines" (*NYTBR*, July 30, 1995, p. 7). Note: Vicki Hendricks, an experienced teacher of creative writing in South Florida, has several other sex-cum-crime novels to her credit: *Iguana Love* (1999), **Voluntary Madness** (see entry 105), and *Sky Blues* (2002). These are also set in Florida and just as orgasmic as **Miami Purity**.

105. Hendricks, Vicki. **Voluntary Madness**. London, England: Serpent's Tail, 2000. 219p.

After the main characters—naive, blond ex-waitress Juliette, 22, and diabetic, alcoholic writer Punch, 44—get intimately acquainted in the Florida Atlantic Coast city of Fort Pierce, they head south to Key West where the pair intends to generate juicy material for Punch's in-progress novel by raising lots of hell. When Juliette's money from her deceased father's life insurance is gone, the lovers vow to go out with bang, killing themselves during Key West's manic Fantasy Fest, an annual X-rated revelry. But the plan goes awry when Punch unintentionally kills a custodian during a break-in at the Hemingway House on Whitehead Street, where the randy couple decides it would be novel (get it?) to have sex. There are more wild antics before the sad denouement, which contains several unexpected twists. Called "Florida's queen of noir" by fellow novelist Barbara Parker, Vicki Hendricks unquestionably has the right touch for concocting imaginative erotic thrillers.

106. Herlihy, James Leo. **Midnight Cowboy**. New York: Simon & Schuster, 1965. 253p.

Only at the very end of this gritty tale of two losers in New York City does the action switch to Florida as they travel through the state on a bus bound for Miami. But the *idea* of Florida as a blissful haven emerges much earlier in the story as an important subtext and eventually the driving force behind the novel's melancholy conclusion. Joe Buck, described by author James Leo Herlihy as a "six-foot tarnished cowboy," migrates to the big city looking to become a high-paid stud, selling his services to rich women. Luckless and down-and-out, Joe hooks up with a crippled street hustler named Ratso Rizzo, a pathetic "little blond runt" who fantasizes about one day going to Florida, his mental vision of Eden, of paradise on earth. In the end the two misfits, who have formed a touching bond, finally arrive in the Sunshine State—but only one of them achieves paradise. Note: In 1969 **Midnight Cowboy** was made into a critically acclaimed film with Jon Voight in the role of Joe Buck and Dustin Hoffman as the unforgettable Ratso Rizzo.

From **Midnight Cowboy**:

Ratso could talk about the Bronx, and he could talk about Manhattan, and he could talk about nearly anything under the sun. But his best subject was Florida, and though he had never been there, he spoke more positively and with greater authority on this topic than on any other. He often studied folders in color put out by transportation companies or perused a stack of travel clippings collected from newspapers; he also owned a book called *Florida and the Caribbean*. In this splendid place (he claimed) the two basic items necessary for the sustenance of life—sunshine and coconut milk—were in such abundance that the only problem was in coping with their excess. For all that sunshine you needed wide-brimmed hats, special glasses and creams. As for coconuts, there were so many of these lying about in the streets that each Florida town had to commission great fleets of giant trucks to gather them up just so traffic could get through. And of course coconuts were the one complete food: This was common knowledge.

107. Hersey, John. **Key West Tales**. New York: Knopf, 1994. 227p.

Toward the end of his life, John Hersey, author of such modern fiction and nonfiction classics as *A Bell for Adano* (1944) and *Hiroshima* (1946), moved to Key West where he died in 1993 at age 78. Fittingly, his last book, published posthumously, is entitled **Key West Tales** and comprises 15 excellent short stories that catch the flavor of Florida's endlessly fascinating southernmost city. The tales cover a wide range of themes—loss of innocence, friendship and intimacy, attitudes toward retirement, death and dying—and half deal with historical subjects; for instance, "Did You Ever Have Such Sport?" describes John James Audubon's wanton killing of birds while visiting Key West in 1832. Others, such as "Get Up, Sweet Slug-a-bed," a long story about a feisty gay professor dying of AIDS and his mysterious male caregiver, are concerned with contemporary issues. "This is the last of his [Hersey's] work, and we can be sad about that, but still able to rejoice in the final bright gift he has given us" (*NYTBR*, Feb. 13, 1994, p. 22).

108. Hiaasen, Carl. **Hoot**. New York: Knopf, 2002. 272p.

Carl Hiaasen, one of present-day Florida's brightest literary stars, has earned a huge following among the reading public with a spate of adult novels that satirize the state's most pressing problems in a darkly comic and highly entertaining manner. They include **Tourist Season** (see entry 110), *Double Whammy* (1987), *Skin Tight* (1989), **Native Tongue** (see entry 109), *Strip Tease* (1993), *Stormy Weather* (1995), *Lucky You* (1997), *Sick Puppy* (2000), *Basket Case* (2002), and *Skinny Dip* (2004). **Hoot**, on the other hand, represents new territory for Hiaasen: A novel aimed primarily at young people (ages 10+), though many adults will also find it good reading. Certainly **Hoot**'s plot has ageless appeal: When the construction site of a new Florida pancake restaurant threatens the habitat of some miniature owls, several ecologically aware youngsters, led by a homeless waif nicknamed Mullet Fingers, employ ingenious protest tactics to save the birds. "Popular author Hiaasen's first foray into children's literature is a delight" (*BL*, Nov. 1, 2002, p. 516). Note: In an interview concerning **Hoot**, Hiaasen explained, "I wanted to write a book my 10-year-old stepson could read. That meant no outrageous sex or blatant use of the 'f word.' It was something new to try and certainly challenging" (*Tampa Tribune*, Feb. 7, 2002). Note also: A film version of the novel debuted in 2006; producers include Hiaasen and Jimmy Buffet (see entry 28); Buffet also appears on screen in a supporting role. Note also: *Flush* (2005), Hiaasen's second novel for young readers, also deals with an environmental issue, this time the malodorous practice of dumping human waste in waters off the Florida coast.

**Carl Hiaasen** (see entries 108-111) is a Florida native who currently lives in the Florida Keys. After graduating from the University of Florida with a journalism degree in 1974, he went to work for a small Florida daily, *Cocoa Today*, where he wrote feature stories. One he remembers well was "Garbage Man for a Day." Shortly thereafter it was on to the *Miami Herald* as a columnist and eventually fame as one of Florida's most popular—and wicked—novelists.

109. Hiaasen, Carl. **Native Tongue**. New York: Knopf, 1991. 325p.

Among Carl Hiaasen's favorite targets for lampoonery are Florida's many scheming developers and despoilers of the environment. Francis X. Kingsbury—formerly Frankie King, a mobster now in the federal witness protection program and main character in **Native Tongue**—is both a schemer and a despoiler. As the owner of the Amazing Kingdom of Thrills, a disreputable theme park located in the Florida Keys, Kingsbury generates an array of activist opposition, including Hiaasen's greatest creation, recurring character Clinton Tyree, aka Skink, a half-insane, one-eyed former governor of Florida turned ecoterrorist who lives off the beaten track in a junked car and eats road kill. "Late in the book a character laments his predicament as 'an irresistible convergence of violence, mayhem and mortality.' If he had added nonstop hilarity, he would have had a perfect description of this book" (*LJ*, Sept. 1, 1991, p. 230). Note: The quixotic Skink also appears in *Double Whammy* (1987), *Sick Puppy* (2000), and *Skinny Dip* (2004).

110. Hiaasen, Carl. **Tourist Season**. New York: Putnam, 1986. 272p.

**Tourist Season**, Carl Hiaasen's first solo novel, remains one of his best. (A *Miami Herald* newspaper staffer since 1976 and columnist since 1982, Hiaasen coauthored three thrillers—*Powder Burn*, *Trap Line*, and *A Death in China*—with fellow *Herald* writer Bill Montalbano in the early 1980s.) The story line in **Tourist Season** is cunningly simple: Skip Wiley, an angry columnist for the fictional *Miami Sun* and no doubt Hiaasen's alter ego, believes the "real Florida" is being destroyed by greedy promoters, bankers, entrepreneurs, developers, contractors, lawyers, and the like who entice legions of the nation's hoi polloi to crowd into the state, thus overpopulating and degrading what once was "paradise." Wiley's solution? Recruit a band of thugs to scare off Florida's tourists and newcomers by randomly killing a few of them in ways sensational enough to generate maximum media attention—for example, feed a tourist to a famished crocodile. In his final column, Wiley justifies this strategy with an impassioned screed against unrestrained development in the state: "Let me fill you in on what's been going on the last few years: the Glades have begun to dry up and die; the fresh water supply is being poisoned with unpotable toxic scum; up near Orlando they actually tried to straighten a bloody river; in Miami the beachfront hotels are pumping raw sewage into the Gulf Stream; statewide there is a murder every seven hours; the panther is nearly extinct; grotesque three-headed nuclear trout are being caught in Biscayne Bay; and Dade County's gone totally Republican." The indignation expressed here is not feigned, but represents Hiaasen's deeply held pessimism about Florida's future. Note: An earlier, less fierce novel with a similar theme is John Keasler's **Surrounded on Three Sides** (see entry 140).

111. Hiaasen, Carl & others. **Naked Came the Manatee**. New York: Putnam, 1997. 201p.

Originally serialized in late 1995 in the *Miami Herald*'s Sunday *Tropic* magazine, **Naked Came the Manatee** is a crime novel set in Miami consisting of 13 chapters, each contributed by a different South Florida writer, including such well-known scribblers as Dave Barry, Les Standiford, Paul Levine, Edna Buchanan, James W. Hall, Evelyn Mayerson, Vicki Hendricks, Elmore Leonard, and Carl Hiaasen, who had the job of pulling the story's many circuitous threads together at the end. As might be expected, numerous characters inhabit the book (among them the titular manatee, a gentle beast known as "Booger") and there are plot twists and turns galore. "Mystery fans will enjoy the interplay between familiar characters like Buchanan's *Miami News* crime reporter Britt Montero, Levine's brawny lawyer Jake Lassiter and Standiford's building contractor-turned-sleuth John Deal. The story is less important than the pleasures to be gleaned from observing very good writers at play, penning their sardonic love letter to Miami and its environs" (*PW*, Jan. 13, 1997, p. 53-54).

112. Hill, Richard. **Riding Solo with the Golden Horde**. Athens, GA: Univ. of Georgia Pr., 1994. 143p.

Richard Hill's novel provides a realistic portrait of a young jazz musician in 1950s Florida while also offering a hard look at racial conditions and attitudes that existed in the state at that time. A high IQ senior at fictional Boca Chica High School, Vic Messenger can make a saxophone sing and soon he's staying out all night, attracted by a cool world ripe with hard-to-resist temptations, particularly drugs and a sexy singer named Boop. Trying to pull Vic in another direction is his music teacher at school, who wants the talented kid to continue his formal education, possibly at Julliard. "Using song titles for chapter headings and employing headlines and magazine advertisements like jazz riffs, Hill has created a moody, believable novel that reads like the prose analogue of a tight jazz arrangement" (*PW*, June 13, 1994, p. 51).

113. Hoag, Tami. **Dark Horse**. New York: Bantam, 2002. 435p.

Emotionally scarred by a bad experience while working as a law enforcement officer in Palm Beach County, Florida, Elena Estes finds refuge at a friend's horse farm in the area. But in no time she becomes enmeshed in a mystery: What has happened to young Erin Seabright, a groom at the farm who's gone missing? "Elena agrees to investigate and soon lands knee-deep in the muck of the horse world, where she finds horses murdered for insurance money, sleazy dealers, debauched playboys, charismatic trainers, and one infuriating cop" (*BL*, Aug. 2002, p. 1886). An experienced storyteller who's written more than two dozen popular novels, Tami Hoag makes good use of her extensive knowledge of matters equestrian in this suspenseful whodunit.

114. Hoffman, Alice. **Turtle Moon**. New York: Putnam, 1992. 255p.

After her divorce, Lucy Rosen and her rebellious 12-year-old son, Keith, move from New York's Long Island to sunny Florida to start life anew in fictional Verity, a midsize town where Lucy gets a job writing obituaries for the local newspaper. The story, which involves a murder, a missing baby, Lucy's new love (a policeman), the burial of a small alligator, a bevy of enigmatic characters, and a fair number of bizarre occurrences, takes place in the month of May, annually a giddy time in Verity. The omniscient narrator explains: "Every May, when the sea turtles begin their migration across West Main Street, mistaking the glow of streetlights for the moon, people go a little crazy." **Turtle Moon** is a genuinely enchanting tale told with verve by a popular American novelist who "writes quite wonderfully about the magic in our lives and in the battered, indifferent world" (*NYTBR*, Apr. 26, 1992, p. 1). Note: Alice Hoffman's equally fine novel, *The Ice Queen* (2005), in which the main character is struck by lightning, also has a Florida locale.

From **Turtle Moon**:

As they walk back to the building, their rubber thongs beat a rhythm on the blacktop and the scent of the white flowers follows them. No one ever tells you how hot it can get in Florida during the month of May before you move down. No one mentions that sharks' teeth as big as a man's thumb can be found in the gutters after a storm or that the night air brings on spells of homesickness and bad dreams. When they get upstairs, Keith goes to his room and slams the door behind him. Lucy cleans out the bathtub, twice, with Comet and scalding hot water, then gathers the used towels together. When she first started writing the obituary column at the *Sun Herald*, she'd had a hard time; now it comes easy to her. She thinks in short, trim sentences of death and disease. Young alligator, dead of unknown causes, natural or unnatural, survived by no one, mourned by a single, sullen boy who would never in a million years allow anyone to know how often he cries himself to sleep.

115. Hoffman, Jilliane. **Retribution**. New York: Putnam, 2004. 420p.

This legal nail-biter begins with a heinous crime: In 1988 Chloe Larson, a bright, good-looking young woman, is poised to begin a promising career as an attorney in New York City when she's savagely raped, tortured, and left for dead by a sadist in a clown mask. After recovering physically but still fragile psychologically, Chloe moves to South Florida where she changes her appearance (from blond to brunette) and name (to C.J. Townsend) and goes to work as a prosecutor in the state attorney's office in Miami-Dade County. In 2000 C.J. takes on the case of a serial murderer, dubbed "Cupid" by the press (he cuts the hearts out of his victims). When the man accused of being Cupid speaks in court, C.J. realizes—to her horror—that he is the rapist who attacked her 12 years earlier. Should she reveal this unnatural connection with the defendant and remove herself from the case due to conflict of interest? Or should she keep her secret and prosecute the source of her nightmares to the fullest, though conceivably this could, if discovered, result in his going free on a legal technicality? And what if William Bantling, the defendant, is actually innocent of murder? "What might have been a run-of-the-mill slasher thriller is raised to a new level by the skilled writing and obvious real-life expertise of first-time author Hoffman, a former Florida assistant state attorney" (*LJ*, Oct. 1, 2003, p. 122). Note: The talented Jilliane Hoffman's second novel, *Last Witness* (2005), is a sequel to **Retribution**.

116. Hogan, Linda. **Power**. New York: Norton, 1998. 243p.

Dedicated to the endangered Florida panther ("May their kind survive") and set in the Lake Okeechobee region of the state, Linda Hogan's poignant novel is narrated by Omishto, a 16-year-old Native American girl whose Aunt Ama (she's actually a cousin) deliberately and illegally kills a panther, not out of fear or hunger or self-defense but deep spiritual conviction and regard for tribal tradition. Omishto, who refuses to condemn Ama, must chose between the ancient ways of her people, the Taiga (a tiny fictional Florida tribe), or the radical path taken by her mother, a thoroughly modern woman in full flight from her aboriginal heritage. Linda Hogan, a Chickasaw Indian, "is known principally as a poet, and the current work [**Power**] reflects that vocation in her lyrical, almost mystical use of language" (*PW*, Apr. 20, 1998, p. 48).

From **Power**:

In the mornings, I wake newly born, full of life, yet unable to tell what I hold as if my body is a sacred container of stories, of storms recalled, of the smooth teeth of animals and the words of ancestors. There is something sharp inside me, and unformed, that will smooth itself as I grow older.

I think, it is snowing somewhere north of here. In another place there's rain. A thief is running from a crime. There are countless houses being built. Planets are turning in the sky like eggs in a woman's body. Farther out is the world of stars, black holes, other universes, but there is no more cat, no more Ama, no more anything that would give us strength, even though I know it is coming back, all of it is coming back, because time is like waves of water, with darkness becoming light, light turning into darkness. The world is like an ocean wave carrying the cast-off debris of our lives before it turns and comes back.

117. Holleran, Andrew. **The Beauty of Men**. New York: Morrow, 1996. 272p.

What must it have been like to be an aging, in-the-closet homosexual man in a provincial, censorious Southern community near the end of the 20th century—a man whose glory days had been spent living and loving with abandon in worldly New York City and environs in the 1970s and early 1980s and whose best friends and lovers have now all died of AIDS or AIDS-induced suicide? A modern gay classic, Andrew Holleran's **The Beauty of Men** is the sorrowful story of Lark, a prematurely worn-out 47-year-old man who's no longer sexually attractive and whose circumscribed life in a small Florida town revolves around visits to his bedridden mother in a local nursing home and hurried, anonymous sex in public restrooms. "Written in the third person, this wrenching novel is at its heart a stream-of-consciousness meditation on loneliness, aging, and death" (*LJ*, June 15, 1996, p. 91).

118. Hood, Mary. **Familiar Heat**. New York: Knopf, 1995. 451p.

At the core of this unconventional love story is Faye Rios, a newlywed whose laconic Cuban-born husband, "the Captain," operates a charter boat out of a coastal Florida town. One day Faye is taken hostage during a bank robbery and raped, after which the unfeeling Captain curtly dumps her. Later, Faye suffers severe injuries and loss of memory in an automobile accident, but her convalescence becomes a time for emotional healing and self-discovery. Mary Hood, a fine storyteller and stylist, "has written a delightfully assured novel, with much to say about the inexplicable nature of love" (*LJ*, Aug. 1995, p. 117).

119. Hubbard, Susan & Robley Wilson, editors. **100% Pure Florida Fiction: An Anthology.** Gainesville: Univ. Press of Florida, 2000. 219p.

"Nutritious, delicious and literary, too—the 21 stories by Florida writers collected in **100% Pure Florida Fiction** (all published since 1985) are of consistently high caliber" (*PW*, Apr. 3, 2000, pp. 64-65). The collection includes stories from every region of the state and features both established and promising authors. Among the best known are Alison Lurie, Peter Meinke, Enid Shomer, and Joy Williams. "From alligators and the Everglades to condominiums and theme parks, this showcase of modern Florida fiction evokes the true character of our diverse state" (*FL*, Aug. 2000, p. 14).

120. Hudson, Joyce Rockwood. **Apalachee.** Athens, GA: Univ. of Georgia Pr., 2000. 400p.

The Apalachee, a prosperous pre-Columbian Native American tribe that lived in what today is the Florida Panhandle, suffered mightily from the coming of the Europeans, who inflicted disease, slavery, religious coercion, and physical brutality on the indigenous people. By the early 18th century, when Joyce Hudson's meticulously sourced story takes place, the surviving Apalachee were hopelessly caught between Spanish and British forces fighting for hegemony in colonial America. The main character, Lucia, an Apalachee woman and wife of a man being groomed to be chief, is captured by a hostile tribe allied with the British and sold as a house slave to the owner of a Carolina plantation. "Spanning the years from 1704 to 1715, this melancholy book chronicles multiple conflicts between Spanish and English, the details of plantation existence and the ultimate destruction of the Apalachee way of life" (*PW*, Mar. 27, 2000, p. 54). Note: Appended background material, including a substantial bibliography, underscores author Hudson's dedication to historical accuracy.

121. Hurston, Zora Neale. **The Complete Stories**. New York: HarperCollins, 1995. 328p.

Unquestionably Florida's preeminent African-American writer, Zora Neale Hurston (1891-1960) produced a significant body of memorable fiction, including the 26 short stories that make up this compilation. Written over a period of 30 years (1921-51), the stories, which include seven that were previously unpublished, "allow us to examine the evolution of Hurston's skills at fiction-making," observe Henry Louis Gates Jr. and Sieglinde Lemke in their informative introduction. Therefore, in addition to its intrinsic value as a comprehensive source of Hurston's short fiction, this collection serves as an important complement to her four novels: *Jonah's Gourd Vine* (1934), **Their Eyes Were Watching God** (see entry 123), *Moses, Man of the Mountain* (1939), and **Seraph on the Suwanee** (see entry 122).

122. Hurston, Zora Neale. **Seraph on the Suwanee**. New York: Scribner's, 1948. 311p.

The last of Zora Neale Hurston's novels, **Seraph on the Suwanee**, "is the story of a poor-white Florida family that gradually achieves upward economic and class mobility" (*FHQ*, July 1991, p. 117). Jim and Arvay Meserve begin their lives together in the early 1900s in Sawley, a fictional West Florida Cracker town located on the Suwannee River and known for producing lumber and turpentine. (Note that "Suwanee" is a variant spelling of Suwannee.) Later they move to Polk County in Central Florida where the hardworking Jim gets a good job supervising black fruit pickers at a large citrus grove. The Meserves eventually have three children, including Earl, who's retarded and causes his parents much grief. But as time goes by the couple grows apart, due largely to Arvay's inability to come to terms with change; though a good woman—she's the seraph, or angel, of the title—Arvay is psychologically unable to leave Sawley, her hometown. In the end, however, she achieves a degree of self-knowledge and reconnects with her husband, at one point exclaiming, "Jim, you're the boldest and the noblest man that ever forked a pair of pants. You'se a monny-ark, Jim, and that's something like a king, only bigger and better. I'm proud enough to die." As this quote indicates, Hurston's characters speak in their native vernacular, which adds credibility to the story but on the other hand might put off or intimidate some readers. Note: The novel was reprinted in 1991 by Harper Perennial in a trade paperback edition; the complete text also appears in the Library of America's volume, *Zora Neale Hurston: Novels and Stories* (1995), pp. 597-920.

A writer as well as folklorist and anthropologist, **Zora Neale Hurston** (see entries 121-123) grew up near Orlando, Florida, in the town of Eatonville, the first incorporated African-American community in the U.S. She went on to attend Howard University, earn an undergraduate degree at Barnard College, and do graduate work at Columbia University. Later she became the leading female member of the Harlem Renaissance, a movement based in New York City's Harlem that produced an outpouring of creative literature by young black writers in the 1920s.

123. Hurston, Zora Neale. **Their Eyes Were Watching God**. Philadelphia: Lippincott, 1937. 286p.

**Their Eyes Were Watching God**, Zora Neale Hurston's second novel, is widely regarded as her finest work of fiction and is unequivocally a literary tour de force. The semi-autobiographical story focuses on Janie Crawford, a beautiful, sensitive, thrice-married African-American woman seeking love and empowerment in the racist, sexist world of early 20th-century Florida. Janie finally finds the right man in Vergible "Tea Cake" Woods, but the catastrophic Lake Okeechobee hurricane of 1928, described in graphic detail near the end of the book, sets in motion a series of fateful events that doom the couple. The fact that the novel contains much black dialect might discourage some readers; also, over the years some critics (both black and white) have argued that Hurston's use of dialect fosters negative racial stereotypes. Others, however, believe that by allowing her characters to speak in their true voice, Hurston's story achieves greater authenticity and vitality. In 1990, at the annual Zora Neale Hurston Festival of the Arts in Eatonville (Hurston's Florida hometown), Pulitzer Prize-winning novelist Alice Walker was unstinting in her admiration for the book: "**Their Eyes** speaks to me as no novel, past or present, has ever done" (*PW*, Jan. 12, 1990, p. 31). And in 2005, Oprah Winfrey, who has declared **Their Eyes Were Watching God** her favorite love story of all time, sponsored an ABC TV motion picture adaptation with Halle Berry as Janie that attracted a viewership estimated at 25 million. Note: The novel was reprinted in 1990 by Harper Perennial in a trade paperback edition; and in 1991 the University of Illinois Press published a handsome new edition illustrated by Jerry Pinckney with a foreword by Ruby Dee (another Hurston fan who wrote and starred in the play *Zora is My Name!*); also the complete text of **Their Eyes Were Watching God** is available in the Library of America's volume, *Zora Neale Hurston: Novels and Stories* (1995), pp. 173-333.

From **Their Eyes Were Watching God**:

"Janie, I'm pretty sure that was a mad dawg bit yo' husband. It's too late to get hold of de dawg's head. But de symptoms is all there. It's mighty bad dat it's gone on so long. Some shots right after it happened would have fixed him right up."

"You mean he's liable tuh die, doctah?"

"Sho is. But de worst thing is he's liable tuh suffer somethin' awful befo' he goes."

"Doctor, Ah loves him fit tuh kill. Tell me anything tuh do and Ah'll do it."

"'Bout de only thing you can do, Janie, is to put him in the County Hospital where they can tie him down and look after him."

"But he don't like no hospital at all. He'd think Ah wuz tired uh doin' fuh 'im, when God knows Ah ain't. Ah can't stand de idea us tyin' Tea Cake lak he wuz uh mad dawg."

"It almost amounts to dat, Janie. He's got almost no chance to pull through and he's liable to bite somebody else, specially you, and then you'll be in the same fix he's in. It's mighty bad."

"Can't nothin' be done fuh his case, doctah? Us got plenty money in de bank in Orlandah, doctah. See can't yuh do somethin' special tuh save him. Anything it cost, doctah, Ah don't keer, but please, doctah."

124. Hyman, Ann. **The Lansing Legacy**. New York: McKay, 1974. 278p.

Once one of Florida's richest and most powerful families, the fictional Lansings of fictional Port Charles (a city much like Jacksonville) are suddenly beset by crushing problems. The clan's beautiful and talented granddaughter, Rachel Lansing, has been living a perfect exile existence in Rome until she's urgently called home by her unstable sister, Ruth. Rachel, who narrates the tale, finds the family overwhelmed by difficulties, personal and financial: Her sister is either on drugs or mentally ill or both; her grandfather's former nurse quite possibly has been murdered; her brother Cal's lack of business acumen appears to be responsible for the Lansings' declining economic fortunes; and, to top it off, Al Voss, a nefarious tycoon, is scheming to acquire the Lansing Corporation, which would completely ruin the family. This "thriller with Gothic elements" concludes with "a gripping final episode" (*LJ*, July 1974, pp. 1852-53).

125. Irving, Clifford. **Final Argument**. New York: Simon & Schuster, 1993. 356p.

A black man, Darryl Morgan, waits on Florida's death row to be executed for the murder 12 years earlier of wealthy Solomon Zide, but now it seems a key witness lied and Morgan might be innocent. Ted Jaffe, a well-known Sarasota lawyer, was the state prosecutor who secured Morgan's conviction, but he fears a new trial and what it might reveal. Why? "Culminating in an edge-of-the-seat courtroom showdown with plenty of surprises, this superior thriller is a top example of the [legal mystery] genre" (*PW*, Mar. 1, 1993, pp. 39-40).

126. Jekel, Pamela. **River Without End: A Novel of the Suwannee**. New York: Kensington, 1997. 442p.

Emanating from the mammoth Okefenokee Swamp in Georgia, the Suwannee River twists through North Florida, finally emptying into the Gulf of Mexico near Cedar Key. In this long, readable, carefully researched historical novel, Pamela Jekel, who has written similar river sagas set in other parts of the country, portrays the Suwannee as "a river road of history and legends." **River Without End** concerns the Suwannee's central role in the fierce 19th-century struggle between the Seminole Indians, a beleaguered tribe fighting to preserve its very existence, and white settlers and soldiers in Florida. The story, which covers the years 1818-1913, recounts official efforts to relocate the Seminoles west of the Mississippi River and the subsequent wars of resistance led by the indomitable Asi-Yaholo (aka Osceola) and his descendants. The author's sympathies clearly lie with the rebellious Native Americans while whites are often depicted as forked-tongued oppressors. But as one reviewer correctly points out, "Jekel is no tract writer, though; lyricism, sensuality, and an eye on the big picture inform her work" (*PW*, May 19, 1997, p. 68).

127. Johnson, Denis. **Fiskadoro**. New York: Knopf, 1985. 229p.

This provocative futuristic novel thrusts the reader into the chaos of life after a devastating nuclear war. Set in the mid-21st century during a state of Quarantine in the Florida Keys (the only portion of the U.S. that survived the attack), the story centers mainly on the thoughts and actions of three diverse characters: Anthony Cheung, a musician preoccupied with the past; Marie Wright, Cheung's ancient grandmother, who is mute but mentally sharp; and the eponymous Fiskadoro, a teenager who because his memory has been destroyed by drugs will most likely be best able to deal with the post-Quarantine world, though what form that will take is not known. **Fiskadoro** is serious fiction, as author Denis Johnson's acknowledgments suggest: "A good deal of the inspiration for this story came from the works of Ernest Becker, Bruno Bettelheim, Joseph Campbell, Marcel Griaule, Alfred Metraux, Oliver Sacks, and Victor W. Turner." Adult and mature YA readers looking for an intellectually stimulating literary experience will find the novel challenging and potentially rewarding. Eva Hoffman's *New York Times* review catches the essence of **Fiskadoro**: Johnson's "startlingly original book is an examination of the cataclysmic imagination, a parable of apocalypse that is always present and precedes redemption in a cycle of death and birth, forgetting and remembering. It is a complex and finally problematic vision. To convey it, Mr. Johnson constructs a fictional cosmos that is hard to enter, but whose resonant power becomes increasingly evident" (*NYTBR*, May 26, 1985, p. 7).

From **Fiskadoro**:

Here, and also south of us, the beaches have a yellow tint, but along the Keys of Florida the sand is like shattered ivory. In the shallows the white of it turns the water such an ideal sea-blue that looking at it you think you must be dead, and the rice paddies, in some seasons, are profoundly emerald. The people who inhabit these colors, thanked be the compassion and mercy of Allah, have nothing much to trouble them. It's true that starting a little ways north of them the bodies still just go on and on, and the Lord, as foretold, has crushed the mountains; but it's hard to imagine that such things ever went on in the same universe that holds up the Keys of Florida.

128. Johnston, Velda. **The White Pavilion**. New York: Dodd, Mead, 1973. 217p.

Family secrets and suspicious characters abound in this tantalizing murder mystery set on fictional Dolor Island (actually Amelia Island) in northeast Florida near the Georgia state line. Jennifer Langley, the story's heroine and narrator, is working in an antique store in New York City when she receives a letter from her rich Aunt Evelyn who has a grand house on the island: "I've begun to think of putting my affairs in order, as your grandfather would have phrased it. To that end, I want someone to make an inventory and evaluation of the contents of this house—furniture, silver, your grandfather's collection, and so on. I hesitate to trust an outsider to even handle some of these things, let alone give me an accurate appraisal. With the expertise you must have gained in such matters by now, you should be just the person to do the job." Recalling unhappy childhood memories of the house on Dolor Island and her less than affectionate aunt, Jennifer is reluctant to accept the assignment but finally agrees out of a sense of family duty—a decision that will place her life in peril.

129. Jones, John Paul Jr. **Cold Before Morning: A Heart-Warming Novel about a Florida Pioneer Family**. Tallahassee, FL: Father & Son Publishing, 1992. 229p.

A fictional version of the lives of the author's Scottish grandparents, James and Betty McCredie, residents of the small Central Florida town of Micanopy during the years 1854-1913, **Cold Before Morning** "is a well-written account of a little-known place and period of Florida history" (*FHQ*, Oct. 1992, p. 250). More specifically, it's the down-to-earth story of a frontier family and how its members coped with everyday situations, including such calamities as confrontations with Native Americans, the American

Civil War, a yellow fever outbreak, and disastrous citrus freezes. John Paul Jones Jr.(1912-2001), a longtime journalism professor and dean at the University of Florida and founding editor of the popular magazine *Florida Living* (now *Florida Monthly*), also wrote *What Tomorrow Brings* (1996), a sequel to **Cold Before Morning**. Both books bring Florida history alive and are recommended for both adults and young people.

From **Cold Before Morning**:

The patrols were torture. By day the McCredies waded in snake and alligator infested water, some of it waist deep, or through sawgrass over their heads that cut their faces, arms and legs. By night they slept in trees and it was not uncommon for a soldier to fall from his perch in the middle of the night and land with a splash in the swamp water below and then thrash around, cursing the army, the Indians and the world in general.

One day, David McCredie was on patrol with a party of militiamen who were pushing and cutting their way along the Okaloacoochee River. After several days, during which men were dropping every day from exhaustion and returning to Depot Number One, they came upon a small Seminole village where the unsuspecting villagers were cooking a meal. They were ordered to go in firing and in the fighting that followed two Seminoles were killed and the rest of the villagers captured.

Among those captured was an Indian called Tigertail who said he was seventy-five years old. He and the other captives were told they would be sent to the reservation in Oklahoma.

David told his brothers what happened. "This old man said he wouldn't go. He said he would die right there by the 'black water.' The cap'n rounded em up and put guards all around. 'Watch old Tigertail,' he said. They tried to watch him but durin' the night he pounded up a glass bottle and ate the glass. They found him dead there in the sand, bleedin' at his mouth."

David paused. "I was sick to my stomach when I seen him. That poor old man killed hisself cause he didn't want to leave his home."

130. Jordan, River. **The Gin Girl**. Livingston, AL: Livingston Pr. at the Univ. of Alabama, 2003. 236p.

The sweat and swelter of Florida's subtropical climate pervades this exceptionally fine first novel as its characters struggle with big human issues such as race, memory, love, and death. Mary, the story's central figure, is a woman of mixed heritage (white mother, Native American father) who grows up on a marshy, undeveloped Gulf Coast island in the Panhandle area. After high school she leaves home and for a long time drifts from town to town, working as a barmaid, drinking too much, and generally experiencing the wider world. When she has, in her words, "enough miles on me to die," Mary returns to the island where she spent her youth, seeking to renew a relationship with Joe, a childhood boyfriend who's also part Native American, only to learn that he died under mysterious circumstances years before. Mary's insistent questions about Joe's demise create much consternation in the small, close-knit community, but eventually an old blind black woman who milks snakes for a living helps Mary find the truth, not only about Joe's death but her own life. "The plot moves as slowly as the air in the swamps, but those who crave atmosphere rather than action will find much to savor in this humid thriller" (*BL*, Oct. 15, 2003, p. 394). Note: River Jordan, a native of Panama City, Florida, is also the author of *The Messenger of Magnolia Street* (2006), another atmospheric novel set in a small Southern town; she also writes plays and is a charter member of the West Florida Playwright's Project.

131. Kamal, Ahmad. **Full Fathom Five**. New York: Doubleday, 1948. 255p.

Set in post-World War II Florida, Ahmad Kamal's suspenseful novel explores the close relationship between two Greek-American brothers, Aleko and Paul Paradisis, workers in the sponge business on the state's Gulf Coast. When Paul, the younger and more sensitive of the two, returns from the war a changed man, Aleko adopts tough-love measures to shape up his brother, but his harsh approach leads to unwelcome consequences for both men. Awe-inspiring descriptions of sponge fishing add a special dimension to the story: "**Full Fathom Five** is the Gulf of Mexico come to life, its mysterious glistening quiet, its tempestuous treacherous storms, its fascinating creatures, some fierce, some friendly, who live beneath the water" (*NYTBR*, Sept. 12, 1948, p. 16). Though written more than half a century ago, Kamal's tale possesses timeless appeal.

132. Kaminsky, Stuart M. **Vengeance**. New York: Forge/Tom Doherty, 1999. 254p.

Indefatigable Stuart Kaminsky, a Chicago-born writer now living in Sarasota, Florida, has produced more than 50 crime novels and a number of nonfiction titles (for example, *Behind the Mystery: Mystery Writers Interviewed*, published by Hot House in 2005). In addition, he has served as president of the Mystery Writers of America, was recently named a Grand Master by that organization, and is an authority on American motion pictures and television. Currently he juggles four ongoing mystery series: The oldest and most voluminous (20+ titles) stars Toby Peters, an old-time Hollywood gumshoe; the others feature Porfiry Rostnikov, a Russian detective; Abe Lieberman, a Chicago cop; and Lew Fonesca, a Florida process server. Fonesca, Kaminsky's most recent creation, is a low-key, middle-aged guy who moved from Chicago to Sarasota while grieving the death of his beloved wife, a hit-and-run victim. In **Vengeance**, Fonesca's initial outing, he must track down two missing Floridians, the first a rich man's trophy wife who's apparently run off with a lover and the other a teenage girl who in all likelihood has been abducted by her abusive father. "As always, Kaminsky's sense of place is faultless, and he skillfully captures a parade of lively, credible characters, including psychiatrists, truck drivers, pimps, teenagers, and social workers" (*PW*, Aug. 2, 1999, p. 76). Note: Lew Fonesca has subsequently appeared in several equally well-received mysteries, including *Retribution* (2001), *Midnight Pass* (2003), and *Denial* (2005).

133. Kaminsky, Stuart M., editor. **Mystery in the Sunshine State: Florida Short Stories by Florida's Mystery Writers**. Sarasota, FL: Pineapple Pr., 1999. 374p.

No person is better qualified than Stuart Kaminsky (see entry 132) to put together an expertly chosen collection of Florida crime stories. Consisting of 22 selections, each by a different author, **Mystery in the Sunshine State** includes short stories by such familiar contemporary Florida pros as E.C. "Gene" Ayres, Nancy Bartholomew, Edna Buchanan, Carolina Garcia-Aguilera, John Lutz, T.J. MacGregor, and Les Standiford. Other contributors might not be as well known—David Ash, David Beaty, Stanley Ellin, Jeremiah Healy, Harold Q. Masur, Robert J. Randisi, Erik Wiklund—but their stories are also of high quality and merit inclusion. In addition, Kaminsky's introduction provides an informed perspective: "The stories in this collection are generally in contrast to the established tradition of the noir mystery set in the big city. Those stories take place largely at night in the cynical jungle of the city, the shadows in the darkness. In many Florida tales, it is not only the darkness that should be feared but also the bright sunlight. The Florida mystery can be violent. Florida's killers kill on the highways and beaches in broad daylight. There is no hiding from evil in these Florida tales."

134. Karl, Herb. **The Toom County Mud Race**. New York: Delacorte, 1992. 151p.

Aimed mainly at car-crazy teenagers who don't normally read fiction (or much of anything), this ripsnorting YA novel offers an action-packed plot, high-school age protagonists (male and female) with grease under their fingernails and rough-and-tumble adventure in their hearts, a much cherished 1969 Chevy pickup ("the toughest and meanest mudslinging machine in the county"), and an unusual setting—a remote, smelly, very muddy Florida cypress swamp. "The characters, spouting their down-home, ungrammatical dialogue, ring true, while the short chapters, each one a cliffhanger, and the fast pace of the action make this a natural for reluctant readers" (*BL*, June 15, 1992, p. 1826).

135. Kaserman, James F. **Gasparilla, Pirate Genius**. Fort Myers, FL: Pirate Publishing International, 2000. 328p.

José Gaspar, also called Gasparilla, has achieved enduring fame as a swashbuckling pirate who frequented Florida's coasts from the Keys to Tampa Bay in the late 18th and early 19th centuries—this despite the fact that he probably never existed. James Kaserman, an educator and businessman who lives in Fort Myers, portrays the legendary Gasparilla as a man of principle "who wanted to be a pirate king but who also accepted the need for democracy," which led him to establish a "Confederation or Brotherhood of Pirates," an early manifestation of present-day organized crime. This unique novel combines pirate derring-do with business theory and some bona fide Florida history. Note: Kaserman has also written *The Legend of Gasparilla: A Tale for All Ages* (2002), a version of **Gasparilla, Pirate Genius** intended for young readers.

136. Katzenbach, John. **In the Heat of the Summer**. New York: Atheneum, 1982. 311p.

John Katzenbach's first novel, **In the Heat of the Summer**, received effusive praise from reviewers when published in 1982, and three years later a film version, retitled *The Mean Season*, appeared starring Kurt Russell and Mariel Hemingway. The plot concerns a newspaper reporter, Malcolm Anderson, and his coverage of a sensational front-page story set in motion when a pretty teenage girl is found shot to death in Miami with a note in her pocket proclaiming "Number One." When the so-called "Numbers Killer" begins phoning—and taunting—Anderson after each subsequent murder, the reporter finds himself gradually drawn into the culprit's tormented world, which not only clouds his journalistic objectivity but puts his own life at risk. (Similar issues are explored in Suzy Wetlaufer's novel, **Judgment Call**, also based in Miami; see entry 282.) Katzenbach, formerly a reporter for the now defunct *Miami News* and later the *Miami Herald*, has written three other novels set in South Florida: *The Traveler* (1986), *Just Cause* (1992), and **The Shadow Man** (see entry 137).

137. Katzenbach, John. **The Shadow Man**. New York: Ballantine, 1995. 468p.

Are elderly Berlin Jews who survived the Nazi concentration camps and now live in Miami and Miami Beach being systematically hunted and eliminated by a merciless killer known only as *der Schattenmann*—the Shadow Man? Retired Miami PD homicide investigator Simon Winter, himself a Jew, hears this story from Sophie Millstein, a panic-stricken neighbor who believes she's just caught a glimpse of the elusive Shadow Man, a figure with "eyes like razors." Winter dismisses Sophie as a hysterical old woman—until she's found the next day murdered in her bed. Winter becomes further convinced of the Shadow Man's existence after talking with other Holocaust survivors and, with the help of Walter Robinson, an African-American detective, and Espy Martinez, a Hispanic prosecutor, sets out to apprehend the fiend. "Katzenbach's latest thriller starts off at 90 miles an hour and never slows down, leaving readers breathless at the stunning climax. With solid writing, a plot that's full of menace, and plenty of suspense, this one seems destined to be a hit" (*BL*, Mar. 15, 1995, pp. 1283-84).

From **The Shadow Man**:

He was alone as he ran, save for the specter ahead of him, dodging across the width of Ocean Drive [in Miami Beach], leaving behind the meager lights of the restaurants and bars that were only a short time earlier jammed with people.

Winter breathed in hard, and listened to the ocean.

It was off to his left, running parallel to his course as he pursued the Shadow Man. He could hear the waves beating their eternal tattoo against the shore.

He swept past the last of the night spots, slicing now next to high rises like so many huge monumental blocks that obscured the beach and ocean from the street. He could feel a stitch forming in his side, but he ignored it and ran on, letting the pounding of his feet fill him, keeping his eyes on the man ahead, who had settled now into a steady, fierce pace of his own.

I will run him into the ground, Winter told himself.

I will chase him until he turns gasping for air, exhausted.
And then I will have him, because I am stronger than he.

He bit down hard on his lip and then let air burst out from his lungs in a great gasp.

138. Kaufelt, David A. **American Tropic**. New York: Poseidon Pr., 1986. 463p.

A long, ambitious saga with a broad historical sweep, **American Tropic** begins in the early 16th century when three refugees from the Spanish Inquisition—a prostitute, a scholar, and a nobleman—arrive in the New World in what today is the state of Florida. The novel follows the lives of this motley trio and their offspring and succeeding generations through Florida's turbulent history from the long period of Spanish dominion to eventual U.S. statehood and modern times. In addition to invented characters, the story includes appearances by some of Florida's most famous personages, such as Hernando de Soto, Andrew Jackson, Julia Tuttle, Henry Flagler, and Osceola. In his preface, David Kaufelt, a well-known Florida writer who has lived in Key West for many years, notes that while **American Tropic** "is very much a work of fiction, I have tried, during its conception, to be true to history." And, despite occasional unevenness in the narrative, the book succeeds admirably in dramatizing Florida's post-Columbian past within the strictures of a historical novel. "Kaufelt offers the history of Florida from discovery to 1961 in a book that is reminiscent of the works of James Michener but without the verbosity and excessive detail" (*LJ*, Feb. 1, 1987, p. 92).

139. Kazan, Elia. **Acts of Love**. New York: Knopf, 1978. 374p.

Remembered primarily as a stage and film director, Elia Kazan (1909-2003) also wrote a number of popular novels, **Acts of Love** being among the lesser known. A Greek immigrant, Kazan knew and loved Tarpon Springs, a picturesque community on Florida's Gulf Coast populated mostly by Greek Americans and famous for its once thriving sponge industry. It's not surprising then that

Kazan's only Florida novel is set in Tarpon Springs. The story, which takes place soon after the end of World War II, centers on an intractable conflict between patriarchal Costa Avaliotis, a former sponge diver and now owner of a thriving bait shop, and Ethel, his sexually liberated daughter-in-law. Obstinate Costa and independent Ethel are caught in a cultural showdown between traditional Greek and modern American mores—a confrontation that ends with a shocking "act of love."

From **Acts of Love**:

Working by himself, slowly, carefully and with pleasure, Costa redid the front of the old store. Above the narrow porch, which fronted the place, he had painted in prominent letters: COSTA AVALIOTIS, HEADQUARTERS FOR TOURISTS, so announcing to all passers-by that the old man who'd killed his daughter-in-law with his bare hands was there, selling sponges, shells, sharks' teeth, all manner of curios and novelties. You could come in and, for the price of a trinket, have a long look at this murderer, finding him, as everyone did, ever so gentle. You could even allow yourself to admire him for taking the law into his own hands and wonder if you'd have had the courage to do what he did.

140. Keasler, John. **Surrounded on Three Sides**. Philadelphia: Lippincott, 1958. 219p.

Years before Elmore Leonard, Carl Hiaasen, S.V. Date, Tim Dorsey, et al. began entertaining readers with darkly comic tales portraying the Sunshine State as a lost paradise, John Keasler (1921-95) was doing a bit of the same in the old *Miami News* (where he was a columnist for 34 years) and in his fiction, particularly **Surrounded on Three Sides**. A broad-brush satire, the novel involves a public relations man's futile schemes to dissuade hordes of people, developers, and attractions from coming to and overwhelming— that is, ruining—his quiet Florida community, mythical Flat City (which closely resembles the real Plant City, Keasler's hometown). "This is a very funny novel about human gullibility" (*LJ*, Oct. 1,

1985, p. 2765). Those who find **Surrounded on Three Sides** to their liking will also want to read Hiaasen's **Tourist Season** (see entry 110), which has a similar theme. Note: **Surrounded on Three Sides** was reprinted in 1999 by the University Press of Florida in a paperback edition. Note also: Keasler is the author of *The Christmas It Snowed in Miami* (1962), a delightful book for children as well as adults who love the holiday season.

141. Kendrick, Baynard. **The Flames of Time**. New York: Scribner's, 1948. 374p.

Philadelphia native Baynard Kendrick (1894-1977) wrote some 30 novels, most of them mysteries set in Florida featuring two series detectives: Duncan Maclain, a blind sleuth who in 1970 metamorphosed into a TV gumshoe named Mike Longstreet; and Miles Standish "Stan" Rice, a deputy sheriff and later investigator for a Florida state attorney's office who practiced his craft in once popular but now little read whodunits such as *The Iron Spiders* (1936) and *Death Beyond the Go-Thru* (1938). Today Kendrick's most significant literary legacy is a historical novel, **The Flames of Time**, which takes place during the years 1787-1812 and concerns the mounting opposition to Spanish rule in the Florida territory. The narrative centers on the actions of Artillery Armes, a stalwart hero who fights hard for U.S. annexation of the territory while still finding time to indulge in a bit of chaste romance. "Mr. Kendrick's story is fast-paced, sure, exciting—a highly readable novel as well as an accurate, multi-colored canvas of the time" (*NYTBR*, June 6, 1948, p. 6). Note: Kendrick also wrote several nonfiction books, including the award-winning *Florida Trails to Turnpikes, 1914-1964* (1964), a history of how the state's roads and highways got built during the period when the automobile became ubiquitous.

142. Kincaid, Nanci. **As Hot as It Was You Ought to Thank Me**. Boston: Little, Brown/Back Bay, 2005. 336p.

Nanci Kincaid specializes in Florida coming-of-age stories aimed mainly at a young adult audience. For instance, her first novel, the well-received *Crossing Blood* (1992), takes place in Tallahassee and is narrated by an adolescent white girl struggling with her feelings about race and especially the boy next door, who happens to be black. Kincaid's latest novel (her fourth), **As Hot as It Was You Ought to Thank Me**, takes place in the fictional Florida town of Pinetta and is narrated by an adolescent white girl struggling with her feelings about sexuality and especially a charming young chain-gang prisoner in town to help clean up in the wake of a destructive tornado. Though Kincaid's plots and characters tend to be formulaic, her books are written with verve and have a surprisingly realistic edge, including hard lessons learned. "Kincaid brings a wonderfully engaging authorial sensibility to her story, while her obvious affection for her characters—and theirs for each other—is downright irresistible" (*BL*, Dec. 15, 2004, p. 707).

143. King, Cassandra. **The Sunday Wife**. New York: Hyperion, 2002. 400p.

When Ben Lynch, a man of the cloth in a big hurry for worldly success, lands the position of pastor at the socially prominent Methodist church in the fictional Florida town of Crystal Springs, he's as pleased as Joshua with a new trumpet. Unfortunately, his wife, Dean (short for Willodean), finds the role of devoted minister's wife increasingly unsatisfactory, feeling smothered by the demands of both her husband's ambition and his holier-than-thou congregation. Over time she meets and becomes friends with Augusta Holderfield, a wealthy freethinker in the town who encourages Dean to do what she wants, to please herself instead of worrying about being the perfect "Sunday wife." By story's end, Dean realizes freedom is easier said than done—and achieving it often has a very high price. "All aspects of institutional religious hypocrisy, intolerance, ultraconservatism, and general self-righteousness are fair game as Dean discovers who she really is. King, who is married to novelist Pat Conroy (*Prince of Tides*), has proven herself to be an extraordinary author in her own right" (*LJ*, Aug. 2002, p. 143).

144. King, Jonathon. **The Blue Edge of Midnight**. New York: Dutton, 2002. 259p.

Max Freeman, a 12-year veteran of the Philadelphia PD consumed with guilt over shooting a juvenile robber to death, takes early retirement, moves to South Florida, and becomes a recluse, hiding away from the world in a one-room shack on stilts in the eastern Everglades not far from the bright lights of Miami-Dade, Broward, and Palm Beach Counties and their many suburban communities that are continually pushing back the perimeter of the endangered wetland wilderness. One moonlit evening while in his canoe, Max discovers the body of a murdered child and immediately he's a prime suspect—not only for this crime but recent killings of three other children from towns abutting the Glades. To clear his name, Max hunts for the real killer, dubbed by the press the "Moonlight Murderer"; it's at this point the story jumps into high gear and never lets up until literally the final page. "Especially fine are the passages showing the different faces of Florida as Freeman travels between his austere cabin and the plush penthouse apartment of his Palm Beach lawyer, Billy Manchester. A scene in which Freeman seeks out a group of furtive Everglades natives in their natural habitat reeks with atmosphere" (*PW*, Feb. 25, 2002, p. 45). Note: **The Blue Edge of Midnight** is Jonathon King's first novel but happily not his last. An experienced journalist originally with the *Philadelphia Daily News* and more recently the *South Florida Sun-Sentinel*, King is a rising star among Florida's crowded stable of crime fictionalists, having produced three more topnotch thrillers starring Max Freeman in short order, namely *A Visible Darkness* (2003), **Shadow Men** (see entry 145), and *A Killing Night* (2005). In 2006 he abandoned Freeman (we hope only temporarily) for a new protagonist, journalist Nick Mullins, who's a sniper's target in *Eye of Vengeance*.

From **The Blue Edge of Midnight**:

I [Max Freeman] climbed into the stern of the shallow skiff and Brown crouched on a broad seat built about a third of the way back from the bow. Using a cypress boat pole almost as long as the skiff itself, he pushed us down my access trail and onto the river.

"It'll be faster goin' up the canal with two," he said, heading upstream.

The old man seemed like a magician with the boat, poling and steering his way up my river at a speed that I could match only on my best days in the canoe. Sometimes he would stand erect, working the pole its full length but suddenly slip to his knees to duck a cypress limb and never miss his rhythm. I watched him bend down and noted the short leather scabbard on his belt where he'd holstered his curved knife. It was then that I remembered my 9mm. I'd left it on the table.

145. King, Jonathon. **Shadow Men**. New York: Dutton, 2004. 270p.

In **Shadow Men**, Jonathan King's third novel, former Philadelphia cop Max Freeman, first encountered in **The Blue Edge of Midnight** (see entry 144), has become a fully certified private investigator in Florida. Continuing to live alone in a rude cabin in the Everglades, Max takes on a very cold but intriguing case: In the early 1920s a father and his two sons mysteriously disappeared while working on the Tamiami Trail (Florida's early roadway through the Everglades connecting Miami in the east and Naples in the west), and now years later a descendant wants to know what happened to them. What seems a simple, straightforward question grows in complexity—and criminality—the deeper Max digs. As in his other novels, King provides a well-written, fast-paced, cleverly plotted story enhanced by convincing characters, authentic local color, and measured portions of easily digestible Florida history and geography. "A haunting and evocative novel featuring a first chapter that ranks among the most frightening in crime fiction" (*BL*, May 1, 2004, p. 1485).

146. Kling, Christine. **Surface Tension**. New York: Ballantine, 2002. 291p.

A recent profile of Christine Kling neatly sums up her first novel, **Surface Tension**, as "the story of a female tugboat captain who responds to a mayday call from a ship captained by a former lover and is drawn into a web of deceit and underage prostitution" (*FM*, Oct. 2004, p. 14). There's also a quite beautiful woman on board the distressed vessel who's quite dead—and the former lover, Neal Garrett, is nowhere to be found. Based in Fort Lauderdale, Kling's tugboat captain, the exotically named Seychelle Sullivan, is a strong, comely heroine with the instincts of a natural amateur sleuth. In Seychelle's second outing, *Cross Current* (2004), she saves a Haitian girl from thugs, creeps, U.S. immigration authorities, and death at sea. Increasingly confident concerning her investigative prowess, Seychelle next tackles the case of a murdered gambling mogul in *Bitter End* (2005).

147. Kotker, Norman. **Billy in Love**. Cambridge, MA: Zoland Books, 1996. 160p.

A paperback original, Norman Kotker's "quirky novel of senior citizen love and lust" (*BL*, Oct. 1, 1996, p. 322) takes place at a Florida retirement community called Daymoor, where flirtatious musician Billy Symmes and wealthy widow Joyce Tarlow meet and decide to marry—but obstacles arise due to money, Joyce's hucksterish son, and Billy's capricious indiscretion with a hooker. Interior musings by the main characters reveal complex webs of motives, desires, and fantasies. The result is an "often poetic riff on old burdens and new chances" (*PW*, Sept. 9, 1996, p. 78).

148. Kudlinski, Kathleen. **Night Bird: A Story of the Seminole Indians**. New York: Viking, 1993. 60p.

Told from the point of view of an 11-year-old Seminole Indian girl named Night Bird, this brief but touchingly rendered tale involves the U.S. government's brutal efforts in the mid-1800s to get rid of Florida's Seminoles, either by removing them to Oklahoma (not yet a state) or killing them. The question for Night Bird and her dwindling tribe: Should they agree to go west into the unknown or retreat further into the dense, swampy Everglades? Though intended mainly for readers ages 7-12, **Night Bird** is not written in a condescending or juvenile manner, nor is the subject matter of interest only to young people. Black-and-white drawings by James Watling nicely complement Kathleen Kudlinski's text.

149. Lardner, Ring. **The Ring Lardner Reader.** Edited by Maxwell Geismar. Scribner's, 1963. 696p.

By the late 19th century railroads had opened up coastal Florida to travel and tourism and the state soon became a winter mecca for America's wealthy elite, drawn by the sun and beaches, the reputed health benefits of the peninsula's springs and climate, and the growing number of first-class hotels built by moguls Henry Flagler and Henry Plant. Inevitably the middle class—always eager to ape the rich and powerful—followed and by the 1920s the Sunshine State was awash with provincial business and professional men and their wives in search of the Florida experience. Ring Lardner (1885-1933), one of the country's premier humor writers then and now, satirizes the pretensions of Florida's bourgeois visitors in two classic short stories, "The Golden Honeymoon" and "Gullible's Travels," both included in **The Ring Lardner Reader.** Written in 1922 and first published in *Cosmopolitan*, "The Golden Honeymoon" tells the story of Charley and Lucy, a small-town couple from New Jersey who decide to spend their 50th wedding anniversary in St. Petersburg, Florida. Sparks fly when by chance they meet Mr. and Mrs. Frank Hartsell, who hail from Hillsdale, Michigan: It seems Lucy and Frank were once engaged until, according to Charley, the story's overly competitive narrator, "I stepped in and cut him out, fifty-two years ago!" In similar fashion Mr. Gullible narrates "Gullible's Travels," which originally appeared in the *Saturday Evening Post* in 1916. It's the story of "a social-climbing Chicago woman who drags her husband to Florida for the winter, hoping to meet some of the famous Four Hundred 'society leaders'" (*BLGF*, 1992, p. 66). The long-suffering Gullible has a keen eye for pomposity and affectation, which he describes in a colloquial idiom that's as delightful today as when first written nearly a century ago. And it's not a stretch to suggest that these two charming short stories offer savvy readers more nourishing Florida history than many a dry textbook. Note: "The Golden Honeymoon" and "Gullible's Travels" are also available in *The Portable Ring Lardner*, edited by Gilbert Seldes and published by Viking Press in 1946. Also "The Golden Honeymoon" is anthologized in Kevin M. McCarthy's carefully chosen **Florida Stories** (see entry 184).

From "Gullible's Travels" in **The Ring Lardner Reader**:

First, we went to St. George Street [in St. Augustine] and visited the oldest house in the United States. Then we went to Hospital Street and seen the oldest house in the United States. Then we turned the corner and went down St. Francis Street and inspected the oldest house in the United States. Then we dropped into a soda fountain and I had an egg phosphate, made from the oldest egg in the Western Hemisphere. We passed up lunch and got into a carriage drawn by the oldest horse in Florida, and we rode through the country all afternoon and the driver told us some o' the oldest jokes in the book. He felt it was only fair to give his customers a good time when he was chargin' a dollar an hour, and he had his gags rehearsed so's he could tell the same one a thousand times and never change a word. And the horse knowed where the point come in every one and stopped to laugh.

150. Lardo, Vincent. **McNally's Dilemma**. New York: Putnam, 1999. 320p.

Before his death, Lawrence Sanders (1920-98), author of nearly 40 crime novels during a productive career, wrote seven lighthearted Florida mysteries starring Palm Beach playboy and sleuth Archibald "Archy" McNally, perhaps best described as an American version of Bertie Wooster, British writer P.G. Wodehouse's famous creation. So popular were Sanders' McNally books—*McNally's Secret* (1991), *McNally's Luck* (1992), *McNally's Risk* (1993), *McNally's Caper* (1994), *McNally's Trial* (1995), *McNally's Puzzle* (1996), and *McNally's Gamble* (1997—that his publisher (Putnam), with the approval of his estate, tapped Vincent Lardo to continue the series. Lardo's first effort, **McNally's Dilemma**, finds the dapper Archy sorting out a tangled case involving high-society adultery, blackmail, and murder. Since then, Lardo has added a number of new titles to the McNally list, including *McNally's Folly* (2000), *McNally's Chance* (2001), *McNally's Alibi* (2002), *McNally's Dare* (2003), and *McNally's Bluff* (2004). Note: **McNally's Dilemma** prompted a class-action lawsuit on behalf of consumers when Putnam erroneously listed the deceased Sanders as the author on the title page and jacket (though in small print on the copyright page Lardo was credited with writing the book); settlement of the suit rendered purchasers of the book and audio edition eligible for a cash refund.

151. Largo, Michael. **Southern Comfort**. 4th ed. Miami, FL: Tropical Pr., 1999. 240p.

Ask almost any reader familiar with Florida literature about the novels of Michael Largo and the response is likely to be Who? That's too bad, because Largo is a talented writer who not only knows how to deliver a compelling story but has something consequential to say about the world as observed in steamy Florida. **Southern Comfort**, which is both a character study and a grim tale of murder, clearly stands out as the best of his three novels to date. Earl Tucker—a gruff, laconic, alcoholic, illiterate, gator-poaching Cracker (some would use the more pejorative term "redneck")—lives in very modest circumstances with his wheelchair-bound wife, Ellen, in Central Florida's Withlacoochee River back country. Though unlikable in many respects, Tucker emerges as a strong protagonist, an individualist who confronts life and its troubles on his own implacable terms. A key plot point in the novel occurs when several army reservists engaged in survival training in the woods are murdered after they mess around with two local flirting teenage sisters. The killers—the girls' father and brothers—also go after Tucker, believing that he too was up to no good with their kin. "A profusion of detailed description celebrates life while, thematically, Largo explores the mystery of death as transformation. There are echoes of Flannery O'Connor and Eudora Welty" (*LJ*, June 15, 1977, pp. 1403-04). Note: **Southern Comfort** was first published in 1977 by New Earth Books, a small press in New York City; the Tropical Press edition (1999) is a revised reissue. Note also: Earl Tucker returns in Largo's second novel, *Lies Within*, a thriller set in South Florida and published by Tropical Press also in 1999.

From **Southern Comfort**:

"Do they know you gator, do they have your name?"

"If they did, I'd be arrested. They're cracking down. They have a lot of warrants out all over gator country. Ellen read to me that a few weeks ago federal men gave out close to fifty warrants."

"The buyers don't seem to care."

"Why should they. No one touches them."

"Two sets!"

"Keep that light steady you bastard, keep it steady. He fired and one died instantly. The other moved for the water but Jeff followed it with the light. Tucker fired a couple of times and the alligator died with its jaw in the river. It was solid land so Tucker got out of the skiff to roll the jackets off. Jeff spread the legs for easier cutting. He also held the light, following the knife.

"We made two hundred [dollars] so far," Jeff said, as they got into the skiff.

"No matter how many times I see gators skinned and rolled, I always find it strange to see them without their hides."

"It looks like they have gator shoes and gloves on." He shined the light.

The carcasses were in the long grass. In the night the flesh was grey and pink. The hides can be taken without making any blood. Blood was only where the bullet went in.

152. Largo, Michael. **Welcome to Miami**. Miami, FL: Tropical Pr., 2000. 254p.

Quite different in tone and substance from Michael Largo's **Southern Comfort** (see entry 151) and *Lies Within* (1999), **Welcome to Miami** is a satire involving a Cuban refugee in the U.S. Emilio Garcia Abierto arrives in Florida in 1980 as part of the massive influx of Cuban immigrants known as Marielitos, but his reason for leaving his homeland is not to escape political oppression or experience Yankee-style freedom and democracy; rather, Abierto, a dedicated Communist and staunch supporter of the Cuban revolution, comes to Miami with orders from Castro (or so he believes) to spy on and sabotage the city's Cuban exile community, which he disparages as a bunch of *gusanos* (worms). A pathetically ineffective operative, Abierto lives the secret-agent life for 20 years, marrying a woman from the Cuban-American community ("to better blend in"), fathering two children, and waiting patiently for his moment to strike a glorious blow for Fidel. All the while he and his family partake fully of the fruits of American materialism, becoming addicted to fast food, video games, Disney World, etc. Largo presents Abierto's story through the eyes of a friend, a man named Max, who's trying to sell Hollywood on the idea of making a movie based on a trumped-up version of his friend's life as a Cuban agent provocateur. "An enormously appealing, madcap spy story set among the eccentrics who populate southern Florida . . . . Largo has managed to write a comic tour de force that is also a haunting meditation on loss and history" (*LJ*, Nov. 1, 2000, p. 135).

153. Latimer, Jonathan. **The Dead Don't Care**. New York: Doubleday, 1937. 261p.

In this classic thriller a case takes Chicago PI William Crane and a sidekick to the Florida cities of Miami and Key West— nowheresville in the 1930s, especially for a sophisticated, quick-witted, hard-imbibing (Scotch), superior sleuth like Bill Crane who, the omniscient narrator informs the reader, "never found that a little relaxation hindered him in his work. His best ideas came while he was relaxed. However, it was hard to make a client see this. Clients were often stupid. That's why they had to hire detectives." Some of the slang is dated—who for instance remembers the meaning of a "phony plate of spaghetti"?—but that hardly matters: True fans of the mystery genre will find **The Dead Don't Care** just as diverting today as it was in 1937. "Two private investigators who like to drink double triple Scotches manage between drinks to solve a kidnapping, a shooting and a poisoning on a Florida estate. In spots very funny; very, very tough throughout. Readers with weak stomachs had better not apply" (*Time*, Mar. 28, 1938, p. 64).

154. Lee, Chas. **Totally Trusting**. Mahomet, IL: Mayhaven, 1992. 222p.

During Christmas vacation teenager Chipley Sentinel is shunted off to her grandparents, owners of fictional Sky Springs, an exclusive resort on the west coast of Florida, while her mom and stepdad go skiing in posh Aspen, Colorado. At first Chipley's dejected by the thought of Christmas with the old folks in Florida, but she soon discovers that Sky Springs offers the adventure of her young life, as she and her Uncle Wilder, a famous cave diver, work to help save Florida's endangered sea cows, called manatees, from those who would harm the lovable, lumbering creatures. Artist Wanda Ritner's illustrations enhance the text of this suspenseful eco-thriller, intended mainly for young readers (ages 10+).

From **Totally Trusting**:

"Chipley," her uncle whispered, breaking the silence. "I need you to help me put on my scuba pack. The boys should have been out of the cave by now. I have to check on them."

"Pardon me?" Chipley wasn't sure she could trust her ears.

"I'm going down to see what's happened. They've still got a little air in reserve, but not that much," Wilder said, getting ready to stand up.

"No! You can't! Your broken arm!" She blurted out.

"What did you say?" Wilder said.

"I mean . . . I'll go." She was trying to sound rational. "I know how to dive."

"I can't let you do that. You've never been in a cave," Wilder said. "I know why you want to do it, and I love you for it, but I can't let you go. If you'll help me get my tanks on, I can make it." Chipley stood up. She had to think fast—faster than she'd ever thought in her whole life.

155. Lenski, Lois. **Strawberry Girl**. Philadelphia: Lippincott, 1945. 208p.

Soon after Ohio-born writer and illustrator Lois Lenski (1893-1974) began taking annual health-related vacations in Florida, she initiated a series of regional novels for young people, of which **Strawberry Girl** is surely the best known and loved. Winner of the prestigious Newbery Medal for the year's most distinguished contribution to American children's literature in 1946, the book tells the story of the Boyer and Slater families, poor but proud rural folk known as Crackers living in Central Florida in the early 1900s. Lenski's use of Cracker dialect and inclusion of instances of antisocial behavior—for example, Pa Slater can be "mean, and when he's drunk, you can't never tell what he'll do"—was controversial when the book first appeared but today almost everyone views the author's realistic approach as literary ingenuity. Also, Lenski's simple but appealing black-and-white drawings add an important visual perspective to the story. But it's the title character, spirited 10-year-old Birdie Boyer, who over the years has captured the hearts of readers, young and old. Note: A perfect complement to **Strawberry Girl** is Lenski's longer novel, the 223-page *Judy's Journey* (1947), a sympathetic portrayal of migrant workers in the U.S., including Florida.

From **Strawberry Girl**:

The boy's face showed surprise. "Never heard o' no sich doin's as that. We let our cows run loose all year round. Don't bring 'em up but oncet a year. What you fixin' to plant?"

"Sweet 'taters, peanuts and sich. That's sugar cane over there," explained Birdie, pointing. "Pa and Buzz planted it when we first bought the place. It's doin' real well. We'll be grindin' cane shore 'nough, come fall. Right here we're fixin' to set strawberries."

"I mean! Strawberries!" Shoestring's eyes opened wide.

"Yes, strawberries!" said Birdie. "Heaps o' folks over round Galloway are growin' 'em to ship north. Pa heard a man called Galloway started it. So we're studyin' to raise us some and sell 'em."

"You purely can't!" said the boy. "Can't raise nothin' on this sorry old piece o' land but a fuss!" He spat and frowned. "Sorriest you can find—either too wet or too dry. Not fitten for nothin' but palmetto roots. Your strawberries won't never make."

Birdie lifted her small chin defiantly.

156. Leonard, Elmore. **Maximum Bob**. New York: Delacorte, 1991. 295p.

Bob Gibbs, a Florida good old boy, is a Palm Beach County circuit court judge and the eponymous "Maximum Bob," famous for imposing harsh sentences on guilty defendants. But despite his apparent devotion to the strictest standards of justice, Bob has the moral sensibilities of a weasel in a chicken coop, ready at anytime to use his powerful position for personal gain or gratification. For instance, though married, the judge is a chronic skirt-chaser, and early in the story he scares his wife by planting an alligator in the backyard of their home, causing her to flee in horror, which in turn allows him to be alone with a comely young county probation officer whom he lusts after. As might be expected, during the course of his checkered career Bob has rubbed a lot of folks the wrong way—and now someone's trying to kill him. "A master of dialogue, Leonard captures the feel, the sound, and the action of the Gold Coast crime scene . . . . **Maximum Bob**, the story of a Cracker judge in Palm Beach County, ranges from the Gold Coast towns of West Palm Beach, Boynton Beach, and Ocean Ridge all the way to the world of Belle Glade alligator poachers" (*BLGF*, 1992, pp. 184-85).

157. Leonard, Elmore. **Pronto**. New York: Delacorte, 1993. 265p.

Born in New Orleans in 1925 and raised and educated in Detroit, Elmore Leonard has written close to 40 crime novels, about a quarter of which are set entirely or partly in South Florida, beginning with *Gold Coast* in 1980. In **Pronto**, Leonard introduces Harry Arno, a 66-year-old Miami Beach bookie who's worked for the local mob for 20 years but is now being squeezed by the FBI to rat out his boss, obese Jimmy Cap (short for Capotorto), who meanwhile has just learned via the grapevine that Harry's been ripping him off and is therefore a candidate to swim with the fishes. Harry loves Miami Beach—he's especially fond of eating Jell-O at Wolfie's delicatessen on Collins Avenue—but he's no dummy. Before Jimmy's goons can come calling, he and his ex-stripper girlfriend, Joyce Patton, take off for Italy, specifically Rapallo, a town on the Riviera chosen because Harry was stationed there during World War II but also because it was then the home of Ezra Pound, the expatriate American poet, who inexplicably fascinates Harry. (A bookie interested in Ezra Pound is pure Elmore Leonard.) In a sequel to **Pronto** entitled *Riding the Rap* (1995), Harry returns to Florida, only to be kidnapped by some thugs who hold him hostage in a dilapidated mansion in Manalapan, an upscale community south of Palm Beach. Both Harry Arno thrillers exemplify the qualities that make Leonard's fiction so successful commercially and literarily: memorable characters, pitch-perfect dialogue, strong sense of place, and darkly comic plots. Note: A film version of **Pronto** starring Peter Falk as Harry Arno appeared in 1997.

158. Leonard, Elmore. **Rum Punch**. New York: Delacorte, 1992. 297p.

Most of the action in this cleverly concocted mystery occurs in the Florida communities of West Palm Beach, Palm Beach Gardens, and Palm Beach Shores. The story begins when Jackie Burke, a middle-aged flight attendant, is nabbed by federal agents at the Palm Beach International Airport trying to smuggle $50,000 into the country from the Bahamas for an illegal weapons dealer, Ordell Robbie, who along with his sad-sack sidekick, Louis Gara, is a nasty piece of work. After being released from custody with the assistance of Max Cherry, an old sweetie of a bail bondsman, Jackie reassesses her options, which now include the dangerous idea of scamming Ordell and keeping the money for herself. "One of the things that distinguishes Elmore Leonard's fiction is the way he breaks down our expectations about characters. His bad guys are funny and vulnerable, and his good guys are capable of larceny" (*BL*, June 15, 1992, p. 1787).

From **Rum Punch**:

Ordell asked Jackie to come to the apartment in Palm Beach Shores Wednesday, after her flight was in, for what he called the Pay Day meeting.

Tonight, the weapons would be taken down to Islamorada and put on Mr. Walker's boat. He'd make delivery tomorrow and get paid and the next day, Friday, Jackie would bring all his cash over from Freeport.

Louis arrived. He said Simone was getting dressed still; told him to say she'd be a little late. Ordell said you can't enter that woman's house and not get taken to bed, can you? Louis wasn't saying. Ordell asked had he moved the TEC-9s to the storage place. Louis said early this morning and gave Ordell the padlock key. Outside of that Louis wasn't saying much; acting strange.

Jackie arrived. He introduced her to Louis, his old buddy, said, "This is Melanie," and was surprised the two women looked about the same age and wore the same kind of blue jeans. The difference in them, Melanie's were cut off at her butt, she was messier-looking and had those huge titties. Jackie had that fine slim body on her and Melanie, you could tell the way she looked at Jackie, wished she had one like it.

The first thing Jackie did, she took him out on the balcony and said, "I don't want any more surprises. We do it the way I lay it out or no Pay Day."

159. Leslie, John. **Blue Moon**. New York: Pocket Books, 1998. 256p.

Set in Key West, John Leslie's Gideon Lowry mystery series debuted in 1994 with **Killing Me Softly** (see entry 160). In **Blue Moon**, his fourth outing, Lowry—a stout, mellow, piano-playing PI—has reached the ripe old age of 60 and now normally limits his investigative work to such prosaic matters as insurance fraud. But should a friend ask him to look into a particular problem, he just can't so no, which is what happens in **Blue Moon**. Beautiful and worldly Gabriella "Gaby" Wade has agreed to marry Roy Emerson, a smooth-talking businessman, but deep down she has some nagging reservations about the guy, so she asks Lowry, a former lover and now fond friend, to run a background check on her fiancé. Lowry duly investigates and what he finds isn't comforting. At the same time, in a seemingly unrelated bit of business, he begins probing into the details of a megabucks real estate deal in Key West that increasingly has the smell of corruption about it. Could it be that Gaby's intended is behind this dubious venture and, if so, can Lowry connect the dots? "Although less frenetic and flamboyant than the Florida noir of Carl Hiaasen, James W. Hall or Elmore Leonard, Leslie's latest delivers an atmospheric, thoughtful South Florida mystery" (*PW*, June 15, 1998, p. 45).

160. Leslie, John. **Killing Me Softly**. New York: Pocket Books, 1994. 251p.

Judging from the enthusiastic reception of **Killing Me Softly** and subsequent titles in the author's Gideon Lowry series—*Night and Day* (1995), *Love for Sale* (1997), and **Blue Moon** (see entry 159)—the Key West sleuth has made a highly favorable impression on mystery fans. A Conch (Key West native), Lowry can best be described as a laid-back, overweight gumshoe nearing retirement age who has three ex-wives and suffers from colitis—that is, a character with a persona you won't forget easily. And when he's not busy with his Duval Street detective agency, he may be found playing piano at a local hotel lounge where his drink is Barbancourt rum over ice "with just a splash of soda to drag it out." In fact, it's at the bar that Lowry meets fiftyish Virginia Murphy, who persuades him to reopen the 40-year-old unsolved case of her sister's murder. Lowry's search for answers stirs up many buried and unwelcome memories in Florida's southernmost city. A big bonus for readers is the large amount of local color John Leslie inserts in the story.

From **Killing Me Softly**:

Key West had always served as a kind of hideout for drifters. Something about being out in the ocean a hundred miles from the mainland, away from America, gave people the belief they could escape. Key West was like a foreign country in many ways. Draft dodgers showed up here in the sixties; guys hiding from the IRS, the FBI, the DEA, and the WPA—wives pursuing alimony. At one time work was available on fishing boats and in the tourist joints that paid off the books, and a person could live in a shack or under a tree someplace, no questions asked.

It was a place in which to get lost. Except that everybody in town knew everybody else's dirty little secret. It wouldn't leave the rock, but the price of protection was the knowledge that everybody in Key West knew your business.

As a community we could be as hardheaded about protecting our own people's secrets as we were loose in revealing those of the strangers among us.

161. Levine, Paul. **Flesh and Bones**. New York: Morrow, 1997. 336p.

Paul Levine's series hero, Jack Lassiter, a former professional football player (linebacker, Miami Dolphins) and now a Miami trial lawyer-cum-detective who first materialized in **To Speak for the Dead** (see entry 162), makes his seventh appearance in **Flesh and Bones**. The novel's plot revolves around a South Beach fashion model who calmly walks into a trendy SoBe bar and shoots her rich father, killing him instantly. She justifies the deed by claiming daddy molested her as a child, an alleged crime revealed years later with the help of a psychiatrist who specializes in recovering repressed memories. "A wry line of patter, the obligatory Floridian environmental concerns and a drop-dead gorgeous blonde in a short black dress, high heels and lots of trouble add up to another winner in the refreshingly unpretentious Jake Lassiter series" (*PW*, Jan. 13, 1997, p. 59).

162. Levine, Paul. **To Speak for the Dead**. New York: Bantam Books, 1990. 293p.

Miami attorney Paul Levine's first novel, **To Speak for the Dead**, takes place in the city he knows best, and one of the story's conspicuous strengths is Levine's intimate knowledge of Miami's people, places, and culture. Protagonist and narrator Jake Lassiter is a wisecracking defense lawyer (and doubtless the author's alter ego) who has subsequently starred in half a dozen similar legal thrillers by Levine, including *Night Vision* (1991), *False Dawn* (1993), *Mortal Sin* (1994), *Slashback* (1995), and **Flesh and Bones** (see entry 161). In **To Speak for the Dead,** Lassiter defends orthopedic surgeon Dr. Roger Salisbury against the charge of medical malpractice in the death of a wealthy patient, Philip Corrigan. But it quickly develops that the good doctor, a flagrant womanizer, has not only been sleeping with the dead man's oversexed wife but quite possibly the two of them conspired to kill the victim. The chilling ending, which involves Dr. Salisbury, Mrs. Corrigan, and a head-to-toe plaster cast, is memorable. "A finely tuned plot from first novelist Levine, who orchestrates his tense courtroom and medical scenes with expert panache, fluid prose, and sly humor" (*LJ*, July 1990, p. 133). Note: Series character Lassiter last appeared in 1997 (in **Flesh and Bones**); since that time Levine has limited his output to a couple of non-Lassiter legal mysteries, *9 Scorpions* (1998) and *Solomon vs. Lord* (2005).

From **To Speak for the Dead**:

Finally the two women set sail for our table. One looked straight at me from under a pile of auburn hair that reached her shoulders and kept going toward Mexico. She had caramel skin and lustrous ebony eyes. The other had thick, jet black hair that only made her porcelain complexion seem even more delicate. She wore one earring shaped like a golden spermatozoan and another of ivory that could have been a miniature elephant tusk. Both women wore tourniquet-tight slacks, high-heeled open-toed shoes, and oversized cotton sweatshirts, with spangles and shoulders from here to the Orange Bowl.

"May we join you for a moment?" Miss Caramel Skin asked. The *you* was a *chew* . . . .

They already were sitting down and Caramel Skin was chattering about her ex-boyfriend, a Colombian, and what a scumbag he was. *Skoombag.* She was Costa Rican, Miss Earrings Honduran.

I shouldn't have brought Roger to Bayside, a yuppie hangout with shops, restaurants, and bars strung along Biscayne Bay downtown. It was a pickup place, and these two probably assumed we were in the hunt—two decent-looking guys under forty in suits—when all we wanted was solitude and an early dinner.

163. Lewis, Anthony. **Gideon's Trumpet**. New York: Random House, 1964. 262p.

Tony Lewis, a well-known civil libertarian and highly regarded *New York Times* columnist, chronicles the true story of Clarence Earl Gideon, a boozy drifter accused in 1961 of stealing coins in the amount of $65, a case of beer, and a few bottles of wine from a pool hall in Panama City, Florida, hardly a major heist. What made Gideon and his alleged crime significant was that, though he lacked legal representation, he was prosecuted, found guilty, and sentenced to five years in Florida's state prison at Raiford. Acting on his own, Gideon appealed and in 1963 the U.S. Supreme Court overturned his conviction, declaring in a landmark case, *Gideon v. Wainwright*, that the state must provide a court-appointed attorney for defendants too poor to hire one. The public defender system we take for granted today grew out of the Gideon case, and Lewis's fictionalized account brings the legal drama and its major players to life. Note: In 1979 **Gideon's Trumpet** was made into a television movie starring Henry Fonda as the indigent—and ultimately vindicated—Clarence Gideon.

164. Lewis, Terry. **Conflict of Interest**. Sarasota, FL: Pineapple Pr., 1997. 328p.

Tallahassee trial lawyer Ted "Teddy Bear" Stevens, an unkempt alcoholic whose life is falling apart minute by minute, takes on a murder case he hopes will save his career, but instead it only exacerbates his problems, entangling him in a serious breach of professional ethics. Can Ted escape disbarment? Salvage his self-respect? Avoid the pit of despair? Overcome the urge to end it all? Readers will remain glued to the end. "The real strength of this first novel lies in the relationship that develops between lawyer and client. The writer, a judge himself, sketches the unique alliance with candor and verisimilitude. A good, quick read for courtroom drama fans" (*BL*, Apr. 15, 1997, pp. 1407, 1410). Note: Terry Lewis's second novel, *Privileged Information* (2003), also deals with a painful legal dilemma, this time involving Paul Morganstein, Ted Stevens' law partner.

165. Lindsay, Jeff. **Darkly Dreaming Dexter**. New York: Doubleday, 2004. 304p.

Amoral Dexter Morgan, a blood-splatter specialist with the Miami PD, moonlights as a serial killer, but a discriminating one who kills only other serial killers, which in a twisted way renders him a hero in this much praised first novel. Though perceived by others as a perfectly normal, likable guy (for instance, he has a girlfriend, an engaging sense of humor, and wears bowling shirts), the inner Dexter is a creepy piece of work, a sociopath who carefully preserves one drop of blood from each of his victims on a slide as a souvenir; to date, he has over 30 slides. Moreover, because Dexter serves as the tale's narrator, readers are privy to his deepest thoughts and darkest dreams. "It's been years since there's been a thriller debut as original as this one by Lindsay, who takes a tired subgenre—the serial-killer novel—and makes it as fresh as dawn" (*PW*, Apr. 19, 2004, p. 36). Note: An equally well-received sequel, *Dearly Devoted Dexter*, appeared in 2005.

166. Long, Ellen Call. **Florida Breezes; or, Florida, New and Old**. Jacksonville, FL: Douglas Printing Co., 1882. 442p.

Though author Ellen Call Long (1825-1905) writes about real people and events in this once controversial account of life in antebellum Florida during the period between 1820 and 1845, she uses the novelist's technique of employing fictional characters— Henry Barclay, a Bostonian visiting Florida for his health, and Guy McLean, a college friend living in Tallahassee—to tell the story.

Long's 19th-century writing style will strike some 21st-century readers as stilted and long-winded, but those who stick with it will find her novel provides illuminating insights into how people in the Florida Territory thought and acted during the time prior to statehood (1845). Long, the eldest daughter of Richard Keith Call, territorial governor of Florida from 1836 to 1839 and 1841 to 1844 who later took the highly unpopular stand of opposing Florida's secession from the Union at the outset of the Civil War, wrote **Florida Breezes** in large part as a defense of her father's political legacy. In an informative preface to a facsimile edition of the book published in 1962, historian Rembert W. Patrick explains that Long "resented the criticism leveled at her father because of his loyalty to the Union in 1861, and proved herself faithful to his ideals by championing the rights of Negroes in a New South determined to relegate former slaves to a second-class citizenship. Perhaps these attitudes of hers caused residents of Florida to buy and burn her book, and thereby make it a rare item of Americana." Note: The facsimile edition mentioned above is a reproduction of the corrected 1883 printing of Long's novel. Published in Gainesville in 1962 by the University of Florida Press (forerunner of the University Press of Florida), the facsimile edition contains not only the text of the novel but some new material, including the aforementioned preface by Rembert Patrick; a substantial introduction by Margaret Louise Chapman, a Florida historian and librarian; and an eight-page name and subject index.

From **Florida Breezes**:

In Florida, negroes [sic] and Indians! The one promising me dainties, the other health! I remembered my gruff old doctor at home, and I blessed him that he sent me South. How readily we adapt ourselves to new places and to new modes, however rapidly they follow. A few weeks only have transferred me from one extreme to the other—a change not greater in the thermometer than in social surroundings. Where I had ice and snow, I have now green fields, fruits and flowers, not on gala days alone, but every day and enough for everybody—black and white—for this is the distinction here, not rich and poor; for although all may not be rich, there are none of the last—no wretchedness asking succor from cold and hunger. Everything is new—all are earnest and hopeful. Scarce a decade has passed since the Indian shared these wilds only with the deer and wolf, one not less tame than the other; but these hold their places no longer. The blacksmith's hammer, wagons, and teams, the trades and professions tell of different occupants, while beauty and elegance and hospitality, declare it not less a Paradise for the change—for the wilderness was gladdened.

167. Lurie, Alison. **The Last Resort**. New York: Holt, 1998. 321p.

Professor Wilkie Walker, a prominent environmentalist, has become withdrawn and depressed recently. Now 70 and believing he has cancer (after seeing blood in his stool), Wilkie contemplates suicide, not wanting to be a burden to his much younger wife, Jenny, who's totally devoted to his welfare and career. Jenny, in an effort to cheer up her husband (she's unaware of the cancer scare), suggests they close their New England home for the summer and spend the time relaxing in Key West, one of Florida's premier resort venues—and for some, due to its location at the end of a long sting of small islands jutting out into the Gulf of Mexico, the last resort. Wilkie agrees to go, not because he gives a fig about Key West but the idea of drowning himself in the Gulf appeals to his melancholy mood. Once in Florida, nothing works out quite the way either Wilkie or Jenny envisioned, thanks to interactions with various locals they meet, including Jacko Jackson, their handsome landlord who is HIV, and Lee Weiss, a charismatic woman who tempts Jenny to explore lesbian love. "By the end of this astringently bittersweet novel . . . we are struck by how much Alison Lurie has managed to layer into this deceptively frothy romance about men and women ending and renewing their lives in the hothouse (or vacation paradise) perched on the southern tip of our country" (*NYTBR*, July 12, 1998, p. 7).

168. Lutz, John. **Burn**. New York: Holt, 1995. 288p.

Called "one of the best in a fine series" (*BL*, Mar. 1, 1995, p. 1182), **Burn** is John Lutz's ninth mystery featuring his gimpy, cane-carrying, middle-aged Florida private eye, Fred Carver, a former Orlando policeman retired due to a bullet-shattered kneecap. In this particular case, Carver investigates claims that his client, a local contractor named Joel Brandt, is stalking a woman Brandt says he does not even know let alone care about. The more Carver digs— and he's a dogged dick—the more perplexing and psychologically tangled the situation becomes, especially when he learns that Brandt recently lost his wife and is beset by grief. In addition, Carver finds himself on the receiving end of several unnerving physical attacks by a giant assailant—and his personal life takes a jarring turn when Beth, his African-American girlfriend, discovers she's pregnant. "Lutz's eye for Florida noir (fast food joints, trailer parks and 'local criminals' who 'view tourists as game animals') is impeccable . . . this is top of the line" (*PW*, Feb. 6, 1995, p. 79).

169. Lutz, John. **Lightning**. New York: Holt, 1996. 288p.

In John Lutz's previous thriller, **Burn** (see entry 168), readers learned in an intriguing subplot that Orlando-area PI Fred Carver's lover, black journalist Beth Jackson, had become pregnant, much to the distress of both partners. In **Lightning,** the couple first debates whether or not to have the child; eventually Beth decides, against Carver's wishes, to abort the fetus, but at the last minute changes her mind. In an ironic twist, a bomb explodes just as Beth enters the abortion clinic to cancel her appointment, the blast killing two workers and causing her to miscarry. A distraught Carver then dedicates himself to tracking down those responsible for the crime. "Carver's almost inchoate ruminations about the fanaticism of anti-abortion zealots are especially well done, and fans of the balding, disabled detective won't be disappointed" (*BL*, June 1996, p. 1679). Note: Other standouts in Lutz's Fred Carver series, which began in 1986 with *Tropical Heat*, are *Kiss* (1988), *Flame* (1990), *Spark* (1993), and *Torch* (1994).

170. Lytle, Andrew. **At the Moon's Inn**. New York: Bobbs-Merrill, 1941. 400p.

A fictional account of Hernando de Soto's historic 1539-43 expedition that explored the American territory the Spanish called *La Florida*, **At the Moon's Inn** follows the conquistadors across the Atlantic to Cuba and then into present-day Florida and a number of other southeastern states as they pressed their search for gold and other treasure. Andrew Lytle, who taught creative writing at the University of Florida from 1948 to 1961, describes in vivid prose, including imagined dialogue, the adventures and misadventures of de Soto and his 700-man army, including their encounters with the native population and efforts to cope with the region's humid climate. "Mr. Lytle has an extraordinary feeling for the sound and shape of a period. He has recreated the conquistadors, their courage, ambition, religious exaltation, and cold-blooded materialism, and at the same time has told a credible and exciting tale of human endeavor and defeat" (*New Yorker*, Nov. 22, 1941, p. 110). Note: The novel was reprinted in 1990 by University of Alabama Press; the reprint edition contains a first-rate introduction by Douglas E. Jones, a de Soto scholar.

171. MacDonald, John D. **Condominium**. Philadelphia: Lippincott, 1977. 447p.

John D. MacDonald (1916-86), one of Florida's most admired and productive writers, is best known for his many Travis McGee mysteries, e.g., **The Deep Blue Good-by** and **The Lonely Silver Rain** (see entries 172 & 174), but he also produced memorable novels about the state's eternal conflict between preservation-minded environmentalists and profit-driven entrepreneurs. The most prominent of these are **A Flash of Green** (see entry 173) and **Condominium**, his longest work of fiction. The latter, a bestseller in hardback in 1977 and again in paperback in 1978, begins with the building and marketing of a shoddily constructed high-rise condominium development, called Golden Sands, on fictitious Fiddler Key, a Florida Gulf Coast barrier island that closely resembles Sarasota's Siesta Key. When a monster hurricane strikes the area, four of the buildings collapse—the condos and their inhabitants victims not only of the fury of the storm but the greed of unscrupulous developers. More than 20 major characters populate this substantial book; all are caught up in the disaster and all, one way or another, convey the author's concern, passion, and outrage. "The novel is so convincing that condominium owners and developers will read it with growing apprehension" (*LJ*, Mar. 1, 1977, p. 631). Note: In 1979 cable TV's Home Box Office presented an eight-hour film adaptation of **Condominium** (shown in two four-hour parts) with Dan Haggerty and Ralph Bellamy in lead roles.

172. MacDonald, John D. **The Deep Blue Good-by**. Philadelphia: Lippincott, 1964. 200p.

A native Pennsylvanian, John D. MacDonald moved to Florida in his early thirties in 1949 and the following year published his first novel, *The Brass Cupcake*. Forty-three books later he introduced his most famous character, Travis McGee, in **The Deep Blue Good-by**, which opens with these oft-quoted lines: "It was to have been a quiet evening at home. Home is the *Busted Flush*, 52-foot barge-type houseboat, Slip F-18, Bahia Mar, Lauderdale." Later McGee, the story's narrator, reveals he won the *Flush* in a marathon poker game. All totaled, MacDonald wrote 21 McGee novels: Each includes a color in the title; each presents a mystery worthy of McGee's talent for detection; each adds to the reader's perception of McGee as a smart, tough, philosophical, sun-seeking, gin-drinking, woman-loving romantic who supports his enviable life style by recovering lost or stolen property for clients (his fee is normally half the value of the recovered property and is always off-the-books); and, finally, each offers an immensely entertaining as well as intellectually satisfying literary experience. In **The Deep Blue Good-by**, McGee pursues Junior Allen, a smugly smiling but deadly dangerous villain who's stolen some valuable stones belonging to an attractive young lady who ends up in bed on the *Busted Flush* with a randy McGee. Note: MacDonald originally named his famous detective *Dallas*

McGee, but, according to the author's papers (at the University of Florida), the name was changed after the assassination of President Kennedy in Dallas, Texas, in November 1963. While casting about for a new name, MacDonald checked a list of U.S. Air Force bases and hit upon Travis, after Travis Air Force Base in California.

173. MacDonald, John D. **A Flash of Green**. New York: Simon & Schuster, 1962. 336p.

Some years ago in the commentary section of the *Tampa Tribune* (June 12, 1994), editorial writer Joe Guidry observed, "I wish that every new Florida resident could be given a copy of MacDonald's **A Flash of Green**. Though published in 1962, it remains the best examination of moral dilemmas raised by Florida's development . . . . Oh, **A Flash of Green** has some compulsory melodrama, and the developer's tactics are made viciously ruthless, but MacDonald conveys why we're willing to transform sandy beaches and tropical breezes into concrete and exhaust fumes." The novel, set in a Gulf Coast community near Sarasota, also has a compelling plot and nuanced characters, among them Katherine (Kat) Hubble, a fetching widow and environmental activist; Elmo Bliss, a corrupt county politician and avaricious developer full of crude wisdom ("Like my daddy used to say, a man with a plate glass ass shouldn't walk where it's slick"); and Jimmy Wing, the novel's sad central figure, a middle-aged newspaper journalist whose amoral detachment gives way in the end to active martyrdom. Note: Despite the color in the title, this is not a Travis McGee novel. Note also: **A Flash of Green** was made into a feature-length motion picture in 1984, directed by Victor Nuñez, Florida's foremost independent filmmaker; financed in part by PBS, the film aired on public television in 1986 and stars Ed Harris, Blair Brown, and Richard Jordan.

From **A Flash of Green**:

One motel operator on Cable Key had expressed the hidden fear to Jimmy Wing one quiet September afternoon. "Some season we'll get all ready for them [tourists]. We'll fix up all the signs and raise the rates and hire all the waitresses and piano players and pick up the trash off the beaches and clean the swimming pools and stock up on all the picture postcards and sun glasses and straw slippers and cement pelicans like we always have, and we'll set back and wait, and they won't show up. Not a single damn one." He had peered at Jimmy in the air-conditioned gloom of the bar, and laughed with a quiet hysteria. "No one at all."

And this hidden fear, Jimmy realized, was one of the reasons—perhaps the most pertinent reason—for the Grassy Bay project. Once you had consistently eliminated most of the environmental features which had initially attracted a large tourist trade, the unalterable climate still made it a good place to live. New permanent residents would bolster the economy. And so, up and down the coast, the locals leaned over backward to make everything as easy and profitable as possible for the speculative land developers. Arvida went into Sarasota. General Development went into Port Charlotte. And a hundred other operators converged on the "sun coast," platting the swamps and sloughs, clearing the palmetto scrub lands, laying out and constructing the suburban slums of the future.

When master mystery writer **John D. MacDonald** (see entries 171-174) died on December 28, 1986, more than 70 million copies of his 77 books had been sold worldwide, and his Travis McGee character had become one of the most celebrated detectives in modern fiction. In a recent article in the *Wall Street Journal* (Oct. 22, 2005), Leonard Cassuto observed, "It's been 20 years since MacDonald, who died in 1986 at the age of 70, wrote the last of the 21 Travis McGee novels. But the books all remain in print and, what's more, eminently relevant . . . . The prescient social vision of the McGee series continues to shape contemporary crime fiction."

174. MacDonald, John D. **The Lonely Silver Rain**. New York: Knopf, 1985. 232p.

The 21st—and last—of John D. MacDonald's Travis McGee novels, **The Lonely Silver Rain** begins serenely enough: "Once upon a time I was very lucky and located a sixty-five-foot hijacked motor sailer in a matter of days, after the authorities had been looking for months. When I heard through the grapevine that Billy Ingraham wanted to see me, it was easy to guess he hoped I could work the same miracle with his stolen *Sundowner*, a custom cruiser he'd had built in a Jacksonville yard. It had been missing for three months." McGee, who over the years had developed a profitable cottage industry as a "salvage consultant" working out of Fort Lauderdale, soon found Ingraham's yacht, but it's what was on board—three brutally murdered teenagers—that thrusted him into the maelstrom of a violent drug war raging over the cocaine trade in Florida. Though the bad guys target McGee for death, he survives, just missing being killed by a letter bomb and later a professional hit man. MacDonald had planned to write one more McGee mystery (tentatively titled *A Black Border for McGee*), but he died before it could be completed. Still, a strong feeling of weariness with life, of resignation, of finality, pervades **The Lonely Silver Rain**, as if the author intuited the end was at hand.

175. MacGregor, T.J. **Mistress of the Bones**. New York: Hyperion, 1995. 347p.

Prolific Florida author Trish Janeshutz MacGregor, who's been steadily cranking out mysteries since 1977, writes (or has written) under three names: Trish Janeshutz, Alison Drake, and T.J. MacGregor. Her plots often involve some aspect of parapsychology, astrology, or New Age phenomena, thus affording her a distinctive niche among Florida's many contemporary crime writers. For instance, in an early Trish Janeshutz novel, *In Shadow* (1985), a beautiful and brainy young chemist at a Miami university is murdered soon after concocting a drug that enhances psychic powers. Among MacGregor's most popular paranormal thrillers are those featuring the crime-solving husband-and-wife team of

Quin St. James and Mike McCleary; titles include *Storm Surge* (1993), *Blue Pearl* (1994), and **Mistress of the Bones**. In the latter, the murder victim—a retired bail bondsman living in the Florida Keys on mythical Tango Key in a house reputed to be haunted—had become sexually obsessed with a beautiful Cuban woman who died in that house . . . 300 years earlier.

176. Mackle, Elliott. **It Takes Two**. Los Angeles: Alyson, 2003. 274p.

Set in Fort Myers, Florida, in 1949 when Jim Crow segregation reigned and homosexuality was verboten in Florida, Elliott Mackle's first foray into fiction deals with local hate crimes and how these events impact the lives of Lee County detective Spencer "Bud" Wright and his lover and narrator of the story, Dan Ewing, manager of the fictional Caloosa, touted as "the third largest hotel between Sarasota and Miami." Published as an original paperback by a press specializing in gay material, **It Takes Two** received scant attention in the mainstream review media, but its saucy style, genuinely interesting plot, and honest depiction of social attitudes about race and sex in postwar Florida commend the novel to both adult and mature YA readers. Note: The author, scion of one of the legendary Mackle brothers, major Florida developers during the period 1950-70, knows the state and its prejudices well (see entry 285 for another reference to the Mackle brothers).

From **It Takes Two**:

Arguing about love with your partner is foolish, of course. And this wasn't the first time Bud had tried to butt out of whatever he thought we were doing. Like everybody else he'd been taught that men don't sleep two to a bed. He'd allowed me to stay with him at the rooming house exactly twice, both times when his landlady was out of town. We'd also used rooms at the hotel, the cabin of the Caloosa's fishing boat, even a blanket on an empty beach.

Later, he'd almost always swear that we'd made love for the last time. Actually, he didn't say "made love." He said "messed around" or "mixed it up." Aside from when the lights were off, he didn't use any such words for what he felt. He said, simply, that we were buddies. And tried letting it go at that.

I wasn't exactly in love with Bud that morning anyway. On the other hand, I wasn't taking his hands-off protestations too seriously. Life in the Navy taught me that words often short-circuit what some men are naturally inclined to do. In such cases, direct action beats Hollywood dialog all to hell.

177. Mandel, George. **Crocodile Blood**. New York: Arbor House, 1985. 429p.

Be warned: Some reviewers hated this strange fantasy while others praised it as creative fiction. After five white, alligator-poaching youths brutally gang-rape a Seminole Indian girl in the Everglades, she's tossed into a swamp where a giant crocodile mates with her. Half dead, the girl, Majosee Cowaya, is rescued by Old Junn, a black man, but later the criminal justice system allows the rapists to go free and Majosee, now pregnant, is condemned to banishment by her grandfather and tribal chief, Chitto Jumper. That's not, however, the end of the saga: Majosee's offspring is endowed with "crocodile blood" and spawns a race of monstrous creatures called "bahaymas" that unleash a campaign of bloody vengeance against the rapists and those who failed to punish them. George Mandel's literary style and construction—20 "collages" divided into three "panoramas"—is as unconventional as the story. One reviewer advised, "Strictly for sleaze freaks" (*LJ*, Nov. 15, 1985, p. 111), whereas another concluded, "Skeins of dream and vision tangle with the thread of reality in this tour de force, forming a powerful, surreal story of aberrant human nature and the madness it can engender" (*PW*, Sept. 20, 1985, p. 104).

From **Crocodile Blood**:

Hoarse with emotion, Chitto spoke in American to include Cowaya [Majosee's black husband] in what pertained to him. "You went up in the swamp alone, Majosee, no respect for elders who told you no. Now you talk in judgment time, no respect for law say you be quiet. You ask what about us to judge the pale faces who took onto you. You who went first to their own kind, expect they punish for rape. They who been raping us, our land, our spirit, our power, for centuries."

His righteous soul, blinding him with tears, firmed him for final verdict. He raised his voice to the furious height of his anguish, crying, "One like you she lay herself down for them pale faces, like to lay with death, she been doomed to hide in the wilderness from swamp fire and hurricane. She—"

"Old man, you hide from war," she interrupted in a rage, unfamiliar to his years of Majosee, screaming, "your fear of pale faces you call wisdom now!"

"Be lost in the swamps then," he bellowed in a wretched wail of sandstorms, "after her to hide from the beasts for judgment!"

"I'll survive to show you war! Old men, if I live the world will die!"

"Majosee!" His voice shattered. "For justice you went to the white. For baby riddance you went to the black. Majosee," he wept, "Majosee, for judgment . . ." his voice collapsing, Chitto threw it as high as he could to force out ". . . go now to the crocodiles!"

178. Mathews, Richard & Rick Wilbur, editors. **Subtropical Speculations: An Anthology of Florida Science Fiction**. Sarasota, FL: Pineapple Pr., 1991. 304p.

This impressive collection of 16 short stories by Florida-connected science fiction writers includes both previously published and original works, most of which have a Florida locale. Among the reprinted tales are such genre classics as "Beak by Beak" by Piers Anthony, a prominent sf and fantasy maven; "All the Universe in a Mason Jar" by another sf standout, Joe Haldeman; "You Triflin' Skunk" by Hugo Award-winner Walter M. Miller Jr.; and "Desirable Lakeside Residence" by the late Andre Norton, one of the few women who's achieved major success as a science fiction writer. Authors contributing new stories include Don F. Briggs, Charles Fontenay, Jack C. Haldeman, Joe Taylor, and coeditor Rick Wilbur. Note to the editors: A second anthology along the same lines as **Subtropical Speculations** would be most welcome.

Naturalist, explorer, and writer **Peter Matthiessen** (see entry 179) was born in New York City in 1927 and educated at Yale University. Research for his books has taken him to such places as Tibet, the Amazon jungle, Siberia, New Guinea, and East Africa. And Florida, where Matthiessen turned a century-old vigilante murder in the Everglades into a trio of acclaimed novels.

179. Matthiessen, Peter. **Killing Mister Watson**. New York: Random House, 1990. 372p.

One of Florida's most infamous—and intriguing—real-life murder cases occurred in 1910 near Chokoloskee Island in the remote Ten Thousand Islands region of the western Everglades when an ornery, red-bearded man named E. J. "Ed" Watson was shot to death vigilante-style by his neighbors, who believed him to be a serial killer. Indeed, solid (albeit circumstantial) evidence suggested that the ill-tempered Watson, who operated a sugarcane farm and syrup business on his own small island, had over the years murdered more than 50 people, most of them itinerant workers he had hired. Interweaving historical fact and creative conjecture, famed writer Peter Matthiessen recounts the particulars of Watson's life, death, and alleged crimes through invented recollections of ten contemporaries who knew the man and bits of his story. Not only do Matthiessen's diverse and often contradictory voices provide a believable profile of a complex man, they paint a realistic picture of existence in that isolated, sparsely populated area of Florida during the early years of the 20th century. "What a marvel of invention this novel is. Whether writing from the perspective of a historian, a sheriff or a postmaster's wife, Peter Matthiessen's ear is perfectly attuned to the vocabulary and cadences that give age and personality to human speech" (*NYTBR*, June 24, 1990, p. 7). Note: **Killing Mister Watson** is the first of three novels Matthiessen wrote about the Watson case. The second, *Lost Man's River* (1997), continues the narrative from the point of view of Watson's son, Lucius; and the third, *Bone by Bone* (1999), is told in Ed Watson's own words (as revealed out of Matthiessen's fertile brain). Simply put, the Watson trilogy is a remarkable literary achievement.

From Matthiessen's Author's Note at the beginning of **Killing Mister Watson**:

A man still known in his community as E.J. Watson has been reimagined from the few hard "facts"—census and marriage records, dates on gravestones, and the like. All the rest of the popular record is a mix of rumor, gossip, tale, and legend that has evolved over eight decades into myth.

The book reflects my own instincts and intuitions about Mister Watson. It is fiction, and the great majority of the episodes and accounts are my own creation. The book is in no way "historical," since almost nothing here is history. On the other hand, there is nothing that could not have happened—nothing inconsistent, that is, with the very little that is actually on record. It is my hope and strong belief that this reimagined life contains much more of the truth of Mister Watson than the lurid and popularly accepted "facts" of the Watson legend.

180. Mayerson, Evelyn Wilde. **Miami: A Saga**. New York: Dutton, 1994. 464p.

As the title indicates, the city of Miami is the central character in this informative and readable novel, which spans more than 100 years of the community's history, from the 1880s to Hurricane Andrew in 1992. The plot follows the lives of five ethnically varied families whose fortunes over several generations parallel Miami's transition from frontier hamlet to vibrant metropolis. Evelyn Wilde Mayerson, a well-known South Florida author and Miami resident since the age of three, "convincingly weaves together the fates of black and white settlers, Seminoles, carpetbaggers, winter visitors and Latinos, whose combined energies, ambitions and foibles coalesce in the electric, international atmosphere of the city today" (*PW*, Jan. 17, 1994, p. 398). Note: Prior to publication, **Miami: A Saga** had the working title of *Dade County Pine*, and at least one early review—*LJ*, Feb. 15, 1994, p. 185—appeared under that title.

181. Mayerson, Evelyn Wilde. **No Enemy But Time**. New York: Doubleday, 1983. 404p.

Hilary McIntyre, a bright, inquisitive, bookish, frequently perplexed adolescent girl who lives in a hotel on Miami Beach and wants desperately to be grown up, is the focus of this poignant coming of age story that takes place during the war years of 1941-45. Half Irish and half Jewish, Hilary loves her parents—they work in the hotel managing the kitchen—and cherishes some of the other adults in her life, but their behavior often mystifies her; for example, what is she to think when she witnesses her father ardently kissing a woman clearly not her mother? Hilary loathes her own body—ears too big, breasts too small—and spends considerable time trying to understand sex, which she learns about mainly by reading such (then) racy novels as Hemingway's *For Whom the Bell Tolls*: Exactly what *were* Robert Jordan and Maria doing in that sleeping bag?? And of course there's always the looming Nazi threat, which sets Hilary to wondering where she and everyone she knows might hide in case the Germans come to Miami Beach? "Probably the Everglades," she thinks, "where Jimmy Tiger had his alligator camp. There, concealed under straw-thatched chickees, they could sit with the Seminoles and help them stitch multicolored skirts, while Jimmy Tiger let out the alligators to eat up the Nazis." An absolutely wonderful book for both adult and YA readers.

182. McBain, Ed. **Gladly The Cross-Eyed Bear**. New York: Warner, 1996. 326p.

Attorney Matthew Hope lives and works in the fictional Florida Gulf Coast community of Calusa (a thinly disguised version of Sarasota) where he's now recovered from a coma and other traumatic injuries suffered in his previous case (described in **There Was a Little Girl**; see entry 183). After this experience he's decided to limit his practice exclusively to civil law—it might be duller than the criminal variety but normally not as risky to life and limb—and so it's not surprising that in **Gladly the Cross-Eyed Bear** (Hope's 12th outing) he's litigating a tangled matter involving copyright and patent infringement. His client, Lainie Commins, is a young, attractive, slightly cross-eyed toy designer who's locked in a bitter dispute with her former boss, high-powered toy manufacturer Brett Toland, concerning who owns the rights to Gladly, a cuddly, cross-eyed teddy bear that's proved to be a hot commercial property. Hope's case is going swimmingly until someone—Lainie Commins?—shots and kills Toland on his yacht. "McBain, as he has for more than 40 years, keeps his readers riveted through this entire, satisfying tale" (*PW*, July 8, 1996, p. 77). Note: Ed McBain (a pseudonym for Evan Hunter, who was born Salvatore Lombino but legally changed his name to Hunter) is best known for his many 87th Precinct police procedurals set in New York City, but his Matthew Hope novels are every bit as engrossing. The series, a welcome addition to the Florida mystery genre, totals more than a dozen titles. Regrettably there will be no more: Evan Hunter died in July 2005.

183. McBain, Ed. **There Was a Little Girl**. New York: Warner, 1994. 323p.

On the very first page of this intricately constructed thriller the protagonist, Florida lawyer-cum-sleuth Matthew Hope, is shot twice outside a seedy bar in a poor, African American area of Calusa (read Sarasota)—an assault that puts him in a coma for most of the rest of the book. Two private investigators who work with Hope plus a Calusa police detective attempt to discover who perpetrated the attack and why. Working backward, they begin piecing together a fascinating story that has its roots in the death (murder or suicide?) three years earlier of a beautiful circus performer who, though an adult woman, was only three feet tall—the "little girl" of the title. "This is an amazingly accomplished, richly enjoyable three-ring circus of a book directed by a ringmaster at the top of his form" (*NYTBR*, Oct. 2, 1994, p. 27). Note: **There Was a Little Girl** is the 11th novel in Ed McBain's Matthew Hope series that began with the publication of *Goldilocks* in 1978 and includes such winners as *Beauty and the Beast* (1982), *Cinderella* (1986), *Puss in Boots* (1987), *Three Blind Mice* (1990), *Mary, Mary* (1992), **Gladly the Cross-Eyed Bear** (see entry 182), and *The Last Best Hope* (1998).

184. McCarthy, Kevin M., editor. **Florida Stories**. Gainesville: Univ. of Florida Press, 1989. 326p.

Editor Kevin McCarthy has assembled a first-rate anthology of 17 previously published short stories by such accomplished writers as Stephen Crane, Harry Crews, Edwin Granberry, Ernest Hemingway, James Leo Herlihy, Zora Neale Hurston, Donald Justice, MacKinlay Kantor, Ring Lardner, John D. MacDonald, Theodore Pratt, Marjorie Kinnan Rawlings, Isaac Bashevis Singer, Gore Vidal, and Philip Wylie. McCarthy explains in his introduction, "[W]e have chosen stories that are set in Florida or off its coast and that present some important aspect of its history or inhabitants . . . . Collectively the stories allow Florida to be seen in all its variety and richness." Informative headnotes by the editor accompany each story and add significantly to the book's value. Note: An equally worthy companion volume, *More Florida Stories*, also edited by McCarthy, was published in 1996 by the University Press of Florida. Note also: A collection with a similar title, *Florida Stories: Tales from the Tropics*, appeared in 1993; edited by John and Kirsten Miller and published by Chronicle Books in San Francisco, it includes both fiction and nonfiction selections.

185. McCarthy, Susan Carol. **Lay That Trumpet in Our Hands**. New York: Bantam, 2002. 281p.

Today, when most people think of or hear about the bad old days of Jim Crow racism in the U.S. prior to the civil rights revolution of the 1960s and 1970s, they tend not to include Florida among the Deep-South states (Alabama, Arkansas, Georgia, Louisiana, Mississippi, South Carolina) where the most virulent racist attitudes and practices prevailed. For whatever reasons—perhaps because native Northerners have for decades made up a large percentage of the state's population or because the Sunshine State has frequently, if erroneously, been touted as a "paradise"—Florida is rarely thought of as a place where the worst forms of racial intolerance such as Ku Klux Klan intimidation and lynchings occurred. Anyone who reads Susan Carol McCarthy's superb first novel, **Lay That Trumpet in Our Hands**, will immediately understand that this is a false perspective; that Florida—paradisiacal Florida—strictly enforced the same rigid forms of segregation with exactly the same stern and sometimes violent methods as the other states of the Old South. McCarthy's story, loosely based on her own experiences growing up in a small Florida town during the waning days of the Jim Crow era, opens in 1951 with the racially charged murder of a 19-year-old black orange grove worker named Marvin Cully. Cully worked for and was friendly with the McMahons, a white family who recently moved from the North to Mayflower, a small, rural Central Florida community where the family owns and operates a small citrus business. Reesa "Roo" McMahon, 12, serves as narrator, describing how she, her parents, grandmother, brothers, and a few friends take a determined stand against hatred and bigotry in their Klan-dominated town. Readers will admire (and some fall in love with) plucky Reesa, who exhibits a poignant blend of innocence, courage, fear, and maturity beyond her years. In addition, some famous historical figures, such as Thurgood Marshall and Harry T. Moore (Florida's first civil rights martyr), make cameo appearances, which enhance the story's sense of drama and realism. "Reminiscent of *To Kill a Mockingbird*, McCarthy's debut novel is an engrossing story of one white girl's coming of age during the early years of the Civil Rights Movement" (*LJ*, Feb. 1, 2002, p. 131). Note: McCarthy's second novel, *True Fires* (2004), also deals with the issue of race in a small Florida town in the 1950s.

From **Lay That Trumpet in Our Hands**:

"What in the Sam Hill were you thinking, Ren [Reesa's brother]?" I hiss at him, deliberately standing between him and his show.

"Don't want to talk about it."

"Of course you don't! Because it's probably the dumbest damn thing you've ever done in your life! Standing on a water tower, yelling at the Klan. You heard what they did to Marvin, you know they killed the Moores. What did you think they'd do to you?"

"Nothing," he mumbles. He's refusing to look at me.

"Nothing? You mean you thought nothing, or they'd do nothing?"

"I thought we were safe," he says, meeting my eyes for the first time. "Because we're white!" He hurls the words at my chest.

There it is. The ugly truth that had been circling 'round my stomach, creeping up my spine, sneaking around the edges of my mind. The bald fact that skin color—the paper-thin veil that made Marvin an easy target and gave Ren his air of invincibility—no longer matters. With the Klan's attack on two white boys, the rules have abruptly changed; their evil is no longer limited to Negroes, Jews and Catholics. The Klan's crossed its own hate line. Now, any of us, even children, can be targeted. It's a dreadful thought.

186. McCunn, Ruthanne Lum. **Wooden Fish Songs**. New York: Dutton, 1995. 384p.

**Wooden Fish Songs** is a fictionalized account of the extraordinary life of Lue Gim Gong (1860-1925), a Chinese American who became widely known as "Florida's Plant Wizard" in recognition of his cultivation of many improved varieties of citrus, including a commercially successful cold-resistant orange aptly named the Lue Gim Gong, which won a major horticultural prize in 1911. Lue (his family name) came to America from China at age 12 and in 1886 found his niche in DeLand, Florida, where he managed a five-acre citrus grove for his benefactress, Fanny Burlingame, a well-to-do spinster who converted him to Christianity and supported his research. Readers learn about both Lue the man and the plant genius through the imagined recollections of three very different women: His mother, Sum Jui, who first taught him about cross-pollination and grafting root stocks; Sheba, an uneducated descendant of slaves who worked closely with him for years in DeLand; and the aforementioned Miss Burlingame, whom Lue gratefully addressed as "Mother Fanny." The women's musings—wooden fish songs—form a vivid portrait of the self-effacing Lue and his botanical accomplishments.

From Sheba's recollections in **Wooden Fish Songs**:

While the nurseryman was yet raising the *Lue Gim Gong* trees, he put the orange up for a big prize. It won, too, just short to the time the trees was ready for selling. Yes, a big medal. One called the Wilder for the best new fruit of the year.

Nineteen and eleven that was, a date I won't soon forget. The nurseryman made sure news of the medal got floated round good, and Lue was writ up in newspapers and magazines everywhere. One look at them, Jim say, and you can see clear how plain folks, big growers, and powerful government men all was buzzing.

I tell you, they was calling the orange "a marvel," "rare and good," Lue "a genius," "a plant wizard," and more. Fact is, they bragged so big the wanting for *Lue Gim Gongs* caught and spread quicker than a fire.

People from all over the world commenced to send Lue letters, and his grove spilled over with folks coming to make admiration over him and his orange. Them river excursion boats even made his place into a stop.

187. McDonald, Cherokee Paul. **Summer's Reason**. New York: Donald I. Fine, 1994. 240p.

A former Fort Lauderdale beat and motorcycle cop, author Cherokee Paul McDonald knows his way around South Florida's criminal community, and in **Summer's Reason** his eponymous heroine, young Jesse Summer, needs every bit of that knowledge to cope with the many malefactors she encounters. Jesse, a drop-dead beautiful Lauderdale PD rookie detective who shares her beach house with several eccentric pets, soon finds herself on the trail of drug smugglers, child pornographers, and eventually a shadowy group of slimeballs engaged in the business of selling children to rich pedophiles. All of this sordidness is psychologically wrenching for Jesse, who was raped by her mother's boyfriend when she was ten and now suffers from sexual ambivalence. Heavy doses of Lauderdale local color add to the novel's appeal. "McDonald's no-holds-barred plot, mile-a-minute action, realistic police lingo, and authentic portrayal of life in the cop shop make this top-notch action thriller well worth reading" (*BL*, Oct. 1, 1994, p. 243).

188. McDonald, Joyce. **Comfort Creek**. New York: Delacorte, 1996. 194p.

The Ellerbees sink into poverty when the phosphate mining company that for years dominated their Florida town, fictional Panther Ridge, goes belly up. Pa-Daddy is unable to find a job and to make matters worse Mom abandons him and their three daughters, taking off for parts unknown to try her luck at making it as a country singer. Eleven-year-old Quinn, the Ellerbees' strong-willed middle daughter who wants to be a reporter when she grows up, narrates this moving tale of a family on the skids. Only Quinn's grandmother, Nancy Jo, refuses to be discouraged, as she quietly talks about Comfort Creek, a make-believe place where all is pleasant and peaceful. Quinn, skeptical by nature, doesn't believe a word of it—or does she? "An unusual setting and the realistic handling of economic and environmental issues further strengthen this engaging story" (*BL*, Nov. 15, 1996, p. 588). Note: Primarily intended for readers ages 10+, **Comfort Creek** is part of the publisher's excellent Yearling Books series. Note also: Joyce McDonald is the author of *Devil on My Heels* (2004), a provocative story about race, the Ku Klux Klan, migrant laborers, and a citrus farmer's liberal-minded teenage daughter in Florida during the 1950s. This novel is also mainly for a YA audience.

189. McGuane, Thomas. **Ninety-Two in the Shade**. New York: Farrar, Straus & Giroux, 1973. 205p.

In a profile of Thomas McGuane published years after **Ninety-Two in the Shade** first appeared, *Time* magazine (Dec. 25, 1989, p. 70) neatly summed up the book as "a dazzling novel of free-floating angst and male brinkmanship set in the Florida Keys." The particulars are these: Nichol Dance, a Key West fishing guide, plays a malicious joke on Tom Skelton, the intent being to run Skelton, an upstart competitor, out of business. Skelton retaliates by blowing up Dance's boat. Dance then warns Skelton that if he continues to guide, he will be killed. Naturally the macho Skelton ignores the threat, which leads to the story's existential climax: "He

[Dance] climbed into Skelton's boat with the gun in his hand and asked Skelton where he wanted it. Skelton pointed to the place [his heart] he had imagined at the shopping center some time ago. And the question of his conviction or courage was answered. But this was not theater; and Dance shot him through the heart anyway. It was the discovery of his life." Note: A disappointing film version of the novel directed by McGuane and starring Peter Fonda and Warren Oates appeared in 1975. Note also: McGuane, who lived in Key West for a number of years before moving to Montana, used Florida's southernmost city as the locale for two other works of fiction, *The Bushwhacked Piano* (1971) and *Panama* (1978). Neither of these novels is in the same league as **Ninety-Two in the Shade**, which has achieved classic status, but both are enthusiastically recommended as minor works set in Florida by a major 20th-century storyteller.

190. McLendon, James. **Deathwork**. Philadelphia: Lippincott, 1977. 327p.

A cross between fiction and nonfiction (called "faction" by author James McLendon's editor), **Deathwork** paints an unvarnished picture of capital punishment in Florida circa the early 1970s. The story's fictional narrator, Lincoln Daniels, a writer (much like McLendon himself), goes inside the old Florida State Prison at Raiford where he interviews four death-row inmates, three men and a woman, all scheduled to die in "Old Sparky," the state's electric chair, on the same day. These prisoners and others who know them, including their keepers, describe in exhaustive detail the atmosphere and procedures before, during, and immediately after a legal execution. Though now somewhat dated in terms of specifics, the book still delivers a strong psychological punch; moreover, it remains relevant today as capital punishment continues to be a hotly debated issue in contemporary American society. "First novelist McLendon's precise, emotionless prose is absolutely compelling" (*LJ*, Sept. 15, 1977, p. 1868). Note: **Deathwork** is the first title in McLendon's proposed Sun Quartet—four novels intended to explore the general theme of "man's surge for freedom." Unfortunately, only one other book in the quartet, *Eddie Macon's Run* (1980), set in Texas, was completed before the author's untimely death in 1982 at age 40. Both novels were widely read when published and eventually made into feature films.

191. Medary, Marjorie. **Orange Winter: A Story of Florida in 1880**. New York: Longmans, Green, 1931. 295p.

Of potential interest to both adult and young adult readers who want to discover more about Florida's past, this well-written historical novel deals with the realities of pioneer life in the state during the late 19th century. Hetty Hollister, the story's central character, is a spunky Midwestern teenager sent to Florida by her parents for the winter to work in an orange grove owned by her Uncle Dud (Dudley) and Aunt Han (Hannah) in the St. Johns River area near the city of Sanford north of Orlando. Everything—climate, plants, animals, customs, food—is new to Hetty, who initially wasn't thrilled about coming to Florida. But the girl is a quick learner with a positive attitude and soon she's reveling in her new experiences. In addition to mastering the rudiments of citrus farming, including tending smudge pots during cold nights, Hetty learns to cope with the unnatural daytime heat, the inconveniences of rural life, and occasional encounters with strange wild things, like alligators. Eight full-page illustrations complement the printed text. "It [the novel] will all be found very interesting, and the reader will eat her next orange with a due appreciation of much of which she was probably ignorant before" (*Saturday Review of Literature*, Apr. 2, 1932, p. 642). Note: **Orange Winter** was also published in 1931 as *Hetty's Orange Winter* by Grosset & Dunlap "by arrangement with Longmans, Green & Co." The text, including subtitle, illustrations, and pagination, are exactly the same in both editions.

From **Orange Winter**:

"You've certainly earned a vacation," said Uncle Dud when Hetty was recovering from the excitement and strain of the fire, and hobbling about the house with her knee bandaged. "A boat trip will be just the thing. I want Hannah and you to see Silver Springs and the Ocklawaha" [a long tributary of the St. Johns River].

Uncle John and Aunt Bess could not be persuaded to join the expedition. They were too content with settling their cabin. So one day in early February Uncle Dud drove Aunt Han and Hetty in the buckboard to Sanford and put them aboard the same streamer on which they traveled in November. Hetty laughed as she confided to Uncle Dud about the dark spell of homesickness with which she had watched that boat go away leaving her in Sanford. It seemed so absurd now that she had ever hated coming to Florida.

192. Medina, C.C. **A Little Love**. New York: Warner, 2000. 368p.

The four attractive, financially well-off women at the center of this relationship novel are symbols of subtle but important social changes in contemporary Hispanic-American culture. The women, all residents of Miami, are good friends and openly share their aspirations and frustrations, especially about men and sex. Isabel, a Cuban-American engineer, devotes herself almost exclusively to work since her longtime marriage to an Anglo recently ended in divorce; her cousin, Mercy, is a high-powered real estate agent who changes her lovers nearly as often as her thong underwear; Julia, a Mexican-American author, is having a hard time choosing between the great guy she's engaged to and a hot-to-trot lady flamenco dancer; and Lucinda, a native of the Dominican Republic, finds her perfect upscale existence threatened by her husband's adultery. Despite being well off materially, none of these women enjoys a truly satisfying love life. But beneath the surface **A Little Love** is about much more than romantic ups and downs; rather, it's a penetrating look at the growing impact Hispanics are having on American society and vice versa. "An awareness of the burgeoning economic power of Latinos, particularly Latinas; the crisscrossing of different Latino cultures in the U.S. without loss of identity; and the unity of Latino families across generational divides—all anchor this buoyant fiction" (*PW*, May 29, 2000, p. 47).

193. Menéndez, Ana. **In Cuba I Was a German Shepherd**. New York: Grove Pr., 2001. 240p.

Ana Menéndez's collection of 11 interrelated stories deals with Florida's Cuban exile community in and around Miami. The characters share memories, both sad and funny, of their lost homeland while attempting to adjust to their new American surroundings. For instance, in the title story Maximo, a physically small man who was a university professor in Cuba but is now something much less grand, explains to his friends, "Here in America, I may be a short, insignificant mutt, but in Cuba I was a German shepherd." Nostalgic yearning to return to a glorious past is a consuming passion among many of the author's immigrants, but as American-born Lisette reminds the older generation in "Her Mother's House," the book's final story, "The past wasn't something you could play again like an old song." Menéndez's tales are "hauntingly beautiful and bitterly truthful" (*BL*, Apr. 15, 2001, p. 1536).

194. Merle, Robert. **The Day of the Dolphin**. Translated from the French by Helen Weaver. New York: Simon & Schuster, 1969. 320p.

Originally published in Paris in 1967 as *Un Animal Doué de Raison* and set in Florida in the early 1970s, Robert Merle's controversial political thriller focuses on training two bright dolphins, Fa and Bi, for use as weapons of war by the U.S. military—in this instance, war against Red China (as the People's Republic was commonly called during the Cold War). The story also includes some sexual hanky-panky among the dolphins' trainers, but this business is peripheral to the core issue: animal exploitation by a rabid military. "Beneath the intricacies of its engrossing plot there lies a profound and timely concern with man's relation to his animal brothers and the environment they share together . . . . [Merle's novel] is a skillful fictional blend of reality and fantasy" (*NYTBR*, July 13, 1969, p. 4).

195. Michener, James. **Space**. New York: Random House, 1982. 632p.

Renowned storyteller James Michener (1907-97) first gained critical acclaim for his *Tales of the South Pacific* (1947) and later celebrity as the author of such gargantuan novels as *Hawaii* (1960), *The Source* (1965), *Centennial* (1974), and *Texas* (1985). **Space**, another typically big Michener book, is a detailed fictionalized account of America's space program from its beginnings during World War II up through the 1970s, during which time activity at NASA's Florida facilities at Cape Canaveral and the Kennedy Space Center (on Merritt Island) placed the state at the nexus of the U.S. space effort. Michener's saga was not universally well received, one influential critic, John Noble Wilford, suggesting, "The problem may be inherent in the story: It is too contemporary, the real people and events still too familiar, to lend itself to historical novelization in the manner of Mr. Michener's more notable recent books" (*NYTBR*, Sept. 19, 1982, p. 3). Though valid in 1982, the passage of time has mitigated this criticism. Because of this—and because of Michener's infectious enthusiasm for the subject and the remarkable amount of fascinating information and creative conjecture he offers—most general readers today interested in the heroic early years of space exploration will find the novel well worth their time.

From **Space**:

The five Earthbound members of the Solid Six were proud that Claggett [Randolph Claggett, fictional U.S. Marine and astronaut from Texas] had been chosen so early for a ride in space, and they haunted the control rooms at Cape Canaveral to follow his progress. The center had been redesignated Cape Kennedy in honor of the President slain less than two years earlier, but none of the professionals ever used that name; to them it would always be Canaveral.

They were living, as usual on their eastern trips, at the Bali Hai in Cocoa Beach, and when it appeared assured that Claggett and his teammate were going to make a success of their flight, Ed Cater suggested that they all drive back to the Dagger Bar for a celebration at which he and Gloria would provide the beer, and Hickory Lee the oysters. All the astronauts, especially those from landbound states, relished Florida seafood, particularly the oysters, because they could be consumed in great quantities without producing fat. As Claggett and his partner were now learning, even one extra ounce of fat in that Gemini capsule meant added problems, so that the young pilots had a phobia about pies and cakes: "They can wait till we're retired."

196. Mickle, Shelley Fraser. **Replacing Dad**. Chapel Hill, NC: Algonquin, 1993. 264p.

As **Replacing Dad** opens, George Marsh (Dad), popular principal of the only public school in Palm Key, a fictional small town in North Florida, has already left his family—Linda (Mom), sons Drew and George (the Second), and daughter Mandy—and moved in with Mandy's fourth-grade teacher. The story, told in alternating first-person chapters by Linda and 15-year-old Drew, relates how Mom, a college dropout, and the kids cope with this unexpected and embarrassing development. "Set against the backdrop of small-town Florida, the novel presents quirky and likable characters who, despite the story's somewhat predictable ending, manage to amuse and engage the reader" (*NYTBR*, Sept. 5, 1993, p. 12). Note: **Replacing Dad**, which is recommended for both adult and YA readers, is Shelley Fraser Mickle's second novel and the first set in Florida. In 1999 CBS turned the story into a TV movie starring Mary McDonnell as Linda Marsh. Mickle's third novel, *The Turning Hour* (2002), deals with teen suicide and also has a Florida locale.

From **Replacing Dad**:

Of course, I [Linda] didn't especially like having the end of my marriage appear in the paper like that. But at least it had been made to sound more matter-of-fact than like a funeral. And I was thankful for that. I think the worst thing you can do for somebody is to feel sorry for them. I didn't want sympathy, I wanted a job. I didn't want any "oh, you poor thing." I wanted a baby-sitter for George the Second. I didn't want kind whispers when I walked by. I wanted a ten-day cruise, a new car, my mortgage paid, and somebody to cut off George the First's dick and stick it up on the flagpole in front of City Hall.

197. Mikaelsen, Ben. **Stranded**. New York: Hyperion Books for Children, 1995. 247p.

Set in the Florida Keys, **Stranded** is the story of 12-year-old Koby Easton, a self-conscious youngster whose "first life" ended four years earlier when she lost a foot in an accident while riding her bicycle. Since then she's had to wear a prosthesis, which she disdainfully calls her "leggy," describing it as a "phony-looking chunk of plastic." The kids at school stare and whisper, so it's no wonder that Koby spends as much time as possible alone, swimming and sailing in the ocean near her home: In the water she doesn't have to wear leggy. Koby's other major problem concerns her parents' recent separation. Though she doesn't know it right away, her life is about to change for the better after she rescues two stranded pilot whales caught in a net not far offshore. The suspenseful conclusion, while anticipated, is satisfying for all concerned, especially Koby—and the readers who are rooting for her. Intended mainly for young people (ages 9+), Ben Mikaelsen's novel has "strong, well-developed characters, an intriguing plot in which an engaging main character is repeatedly placed in danger, and an exotic setting so clearly described that readers will feel they have been there to visit" (*BL*, Aug. 1995, p. 1949).

198. Mink, Charles. **Princess of the Everglades**. Sarasota, FL: Pineapple Pr., 1991. 212p.

It's 1926 and Kirk Quintaine's Progressive Mandolin Orchestra from North Dakota is touring South Florida playing a totally offbeat new sound called Indian Jazz that features Quintaine's twin ten-year-old daughters, Sheila and Skeezix, both mandolin virtuosos. After entertaining famous inventor Thomas Edison at his winter home in Fort Myers, a horrendous hurricane literally carries Sheila off into the Everglades, where she eventually lands in an osprey nest atop a cypress tree. Edison and his friends Henry Ford and Charles Lindbergh join Kirk in the search for Sheila, who in the meantime has been given shelter by a group of Native Americans. Then who does the woebegone girl encounter but a helpful, chubby man calling himself Alphonso Caponi, who tells her he's in the Glades looking for new "business" opportunities. "Mink deftly orchestrates his wildly improbable plot and exotic cast of characters, striking very few false notes" (*LJ*, May 15, 1991, p. 109). Recommended for both adult and YA readers.

From **Princess of the Everglades**:

"You miss your mommy and daddy, don't you, honey?"

Sheila threw her arms around the man's neck and began to cry. She was very embarrassed by the noise she made. She was not the kind of person to make these loud kinds of noises. Her throat and sinuses were wet and flabby. She was aware of the Indians drawing closer to see her cry. She could hear their feet in the underbrush. She clasped her hands around the man's neck at the clean collar of his shirt. Her tears stained his powder-blue suit. He really was a very fat man. He was a toad of a man . . . .

"You don't know who I am, do you, Sheila?"

She shook her head.

"You never saw my picture in the paper?"

"No."

"I'm quite famous in the town of Chicago. They call me a gangster there. My name's Alphonso Caponi."

"Al Capone," Sheila said.

He smiled.

199. Monroe, Mary. **The Upper Room**. New York: St. Martin's, 1985. 310p.

This powerful novel, which takes place mostly in a poor migrant labor camp called Goons on the edge of the Everglades west of Miami, is dominated by the strong but mercurial personality of Ruby Montgomery, aka "Mama Ruby," an obese, hard-drinking, sexually ravenous, violence-prone black woman who sometimes seems to be the devil incarnate while at other times deeply religious. Early in the story Mama Ruby steals her best friend's stillborn baby, bringing it, a female, back to life using her healing hands, and then flees to Goons where she raises the child, whom she names Maureen, as her own. Ruby obsessively loves and protects her adopted daughter, and as Maureen grows up she's installed in the desirable "upper room" of the house, a move intended to keep the girl happy and at home—and under Ruby's controlling gaze. But as Maureen blossoms into a beautiful young woman, she's eager to escape her mother's suffocating domination and, after a false start, makes the break, a decision that has disastrous consequences. "The dialogue and setting are reminiscent of Zora Neale Hurston [see entries 121-123], but the story has a bizarre, violent edge à la Stephen King. Fantastic and exaggerated, the novel may seem dated in its descriptions of race and sex, but it is a candid portrayal of the cold-blooded yet fascinating Mama Ruby" (*PW*, Oct. 29, 2001, p. 38). Note: **The Upper Room**, Mary Monroe's first novel and the only one with a Florida setting, was reprinted in 2001 by Dafina Books, an imprint of Kensington Publishing Corp.; "A Reading Group Guide" consisting of 10 discussion questions is appended in the reprint edition. Note also: Do not confuse the author of **The Upper Room**, Mary Monroe, an African-American writer, with Mary Alice Monroe, who is white and writes novels set in the South Carolina lowcountry.

From **The Upper Room**:

"Big Red, you got to find Mo'reen!" Ruby hollered. "Find her and tell her I forgive her. I don't care who she pregnant by. Just bring her back to me! OH LORD!"

Fast Black entered holding a mason jar filled with pot liquor in one hand.

"I remember when Mo'reen was a itty-bitty baby," she sighed. "Now here she is fixin to have a baby herself."

"By a albino. Lord. Mo'reen might end up with a all white baby," added Bobby, who had entered the house immediately after Fast Black.

Big Red drove Ruby back to her house and within ten minutes Ruby's living room was filled with concerned friends.

When Maureen walked up in the front yard, she heard all kinds of chatter coming from inside the house.

"Yellow Jack, come out of Mama Ruby's ice box!"

"Slim, quit steppin on my foot!"

"Big Red, put that gun away."

"Catty, pull down your dress."

"Loomis, stop feelin on my legs!"

"I bet a maniac done kilt Mo'reen and fed her to the gators."

"Aaarrrggghhh!"

200. Moore, Laura. **Night Swimming**. New York: Ballantine/Ivy, 2003. 432p.

Professional business brings Dr. Lily Banyon, an attractive marine biologist, back to her Florida hometown, fictional Coral Beach, where she's agreed to complete a study to determine whether a proposed development might damage the beach community's fragile offshore reef. Complications include longstanding tensions between Lily and her censorious mother, Lily's suppressed romantic feelings for Coral Beach's good-guy mayor, and chicanery by a bad-guy developer. The latter eventually compels Lily to do some hazardous underwater field work. A substantial, well-written romance, **Night Swimming** provides "a fairly satisfying tale about how things are not always what they seem" (*BL*, May 1, 2003, p. 1584).

201. Morris, Scott M. **Waiting for April**. Chapel Hill, NC: Algonquin, 2003. 352p.

The narrator of this tangled tale, young Roy Collier, must deal with a dysfunctional family's bitter memories, self-deceptions, and outright lies in his effort to discover the truth about his father. The mystery of Sanders Royce Collier began on a blustery night in December 1965 when he arrived, a total stranger, in the fictional Florida Panhandle town of Citrus. A recently discharged Vietnam vet, Sanders Collier was cocky, good-looking, well-dressed right down to his fancy cuff links, and very glib, claiming a distinguished South Carolina lineage. Soon he wed local girl June Lanier, though all the while he secretly desired her sexy younger sister, April (she of the title), who had married her high school sweetheart, Leonard, a jock. Roughly nine years after blowing into Citrus, Sanders was killed in a hunting accident—at least everyone in town said it was an accident. Sanders' son, Roy, who was only seven at the time of his father's death, grew up not knowing much about the man and nothing about his complicated romantic feelings concerning the Lanier sisters or the details of his death. But now Roy is older, and he's determined to find out who his daddy really was and how and why he came to die as he did. Scott Morris, a fifth-generation Floridian who teaches English at the University of Mississippi, "has written a wonderfully sensual story in the eloquent, understated style that readers have come to expect from Southern writers" (*LJ*, Mar. 1, 2003, p. 120). Note: This is Morris's second novel; his first, *The Total View of Taftly* (2000), takes place in Mississippi and was heralded by some critics as great fiction and panned by others as an eccentric failure.

202. Murphy, Dallas. **Apparent Wind**. New York: Pocket Books, 1991. 261p.

A light crime novel laced with antic humor and a pro-environment message, Dallas Murphy's romp has aptly been described as a "flamboyant comic nightmare about real-estate development run amok in south Florida" (*NYTBR*, Jan. 20, 1991, p. 27). Upon his early release from prison, affable con man Dennis "Doom" Loomis finds himself the unexpected owner of a soggy, dilapidated town on fictional Omnium Key in the Florida Keys, the property inherited from his murdered father, also a scam artist. The plot, which pits Doom and some weirdo pals against a couple of avaricious land developers, includes all manner of mayhem from dummy corporations to inventive disguises to bombings to strangulations. In the end, however, it's the offbeat characters that steal the show.

203. Myers, Anna. **Flying Blind**. New York: Walker, 2003. 192p.

Mainly for young readers (ages 9+), Anna Myers' informative story is set in the early years of the 20th century and deals with Florida's once formidable plume trade, an evil enterprise that devastated large portions of the state's wild bird population, especially egrets, in the quest for showy feathers to adorn women's hats. Accompanied by his adopted son, Ben, and a talkative macaw named Murphy, amiable "Professor" Elisha Riley travels around the country declaiming Shakespeare and selling a medical cure-all. When they get to Florida, Riley and his motley little family learn about the plume business and then set out to find a way to save the birds without driving every plume hunter into despairing poverty. "The characters don't disappoint, and there's plenty of action and suspense to drive the plot as the trio searches for the right resolution to egret slaughter" (*BL*, Sept. 15, 2003, pp. 240-41).

204. Newell, David M. **If Nothin' Don't Happen**. New York: Knopf, 1975. 252p.

The cover of this humorous, often hilarious book promises "An old-timey sampler of Florida cracker tales from the Withlacoochee River country"—and happily that's exactly what the reader gets. Told in Cracker vernacular by David Newell's irrepressible raconteur, Billy Driggers, the 29 tall tales sport such intriguing titles as "Mumps, Mixed-up Medicine and the Three Mysteries" and "My Temptation and the Little Gal in the Pierce-Arrow," but the focus is squarely on the everyday "doin's" of the Driggers and Epps clan, which includes Ma Driggers, Billy and his brother Tarley, and their Uncle Winton Epps, as they go about their business of huntin', fishin', lovin', moonshinin', and occasional farmin' in the backwoods of West Central Florida. The stories are sometimes earthy but, as author Newell notes in his introduction, Billy never uses cuss words or obscenities, not because he doesn't know them but "like your true Florida cracker he watches his language around womenfolk, preachers and polite society in general. That's the way Ma Driggers brought up her boys." **If Nothin' Don't Happen** and its equally entertaining sequel, *The Trouble of It Is* (1978), are enhanced by black-and-white drawings by artist Mark Livingston.

From "Gossip & Warnin's & the Lame Dog" in **If Nothin' Don't Happen:**

Way back in the Hammock there lived an old couple who folks called Uncle Dan and Aunt Shug. I never did know if they had ary other name, but I'm here to say they was near 'bout the sloppiest folks I ever seen. One time when I were helpin' Uncle Wint hunt a lost dog we come by their place and went inside because it were a right cold December day. It seemed like Uncle Wint were a real old friend and him and Uncle Dan shaken hands and when Aunt Shug come in from the kitchen she hollered out, "Well, I'll be danged if'n it ain't old Winton Epps! How you doin', Winton?" And she give Uncle a big hug and kiss. I don't know how he stood it because she were a lookin' sight—long, straggly, tangled-up hair, no teeth and the saggin'est bosom you ever seen in your life.

"If I felt any better I'd have to take somethin'. Must be this cool weather. I whinnied a couple of times yesterday," Uncle said, sort of flippin' up one of them hound-ear bosoms. "You don't mind if I flip 'em up, do you, Shug?"

"Flip 'em up, Winton, if it gives me pneumonia," Aunt Shug said, grinnin' till her nose 'bout touched her chin. "I'm so glad to see you that I'd even let you snap my pistol."

205. Ney, John. **Ox and the Prime-Time Kid**. Sarasota, FL: Pineapple Pr., 1985. 216p.

John Ney's Ox books—*Ox, The Story of a Kid at the Top* (1970), *Ox Goes North* (1973), *Ox Under Pressure* (1976), and **Ox and the Prime-Time Kid**—relate the adventures of Ox Olmstead, a megarich boy from Palm Beach, Florida's most conspicuously affluent community. Ox, who has a penchant for making uninhibited, politically incorrect comments about the American way of life, has reached the ripe old age of 17 in **Ox and the Prime-Time Kid**. In this caper he reluctantly agrees, as a favor to his father, to help young Mark Cartwright, a lonely, neurotic, drug-abusing brat, find

Mark's missing mother, who lives somewhere in Florida. After roaming hither and yon around the state in Ox's Ferrari, they finally track down the elusive mom. But then Mark disappears, and Ox is forced to enlist the assistance of some menacing Miami drug lords to retrieve him. "Previous books about Ox were aimed at the young adult market, but older readers too will enjoy Ney's wry depiction of the boys' trip, and his perceptive insights into adolescence" (*PW*, Oct. 11, 1985, p. 56).

206. Nolan, Peggy. **The Spy Who Came in from the Sea**. Sarasota, FL: Pineapple Pr., 1999. 129p.

In an effort to infiltrate and terrorize the U.S. homeland during World War II, German U-boats deposited spies on deserted beaches on Long Island in New York and in Florida near Jacksonville. Peggy Nolan uses this bit of wartime history as the major plot point in **The Spy Who Came in from the Sea**, a novel aimed largely at young readers (ages 10-14) but also suitable for adults who enjoy reading about the period. In 1943, 14-year-old Frank Hollahan, Nolan's protagonist and narrator, moved with his mother from Philadelphia to Jacksonville, where Frank's father shipped out for service overseas. While exploring a remote stretch of beach near his new home, Frank spots a strange man—surely a spy!—emerging from the sea. However, when he breathlessly tells his eighth-grade classmates about the spy, the news is ignored: Frank's inclination for telling tall tales has already been well established at his new school. (He of course sees it differently: "Funny how you can get a reputation just by trying to make things a little more interesting.") But Frank knows that this time he's not fibbing or exaggerating, and with the help of two friends—Rosemarie Twekenberry, who has a crush on Frank, and a stuttering beach hermit known as Weird Wanda—he spies on the spy and ultimately the enemy's dastardly plans are foiled. The novel "paints a rich picture of life in northeast Florida during World War II .... Author Peggy Nolan, a University of Miami graduate, taught elementary school and, after retiring, decided to chronicle her father's exploits in the FBI. The resulting first novel is an excellent, can't-put-down mystery for early teenagers" (*FHC FORUM: the Magazine of the Florida Humanities Council,* Fall 1999, p. 43).

207. Norman, Geoffrey. **Sweetwater Ranch**. New York: Atlantic Monthly Pr., 1991. 261p.

Set in the lazy Perdido River area that forms the boundary between Alabama and the Florida Panhandle, Geoffrey Norman's thriller takes awhile to take off. First, the reader meets the novel's hero, Morgan Hunt, a private investigator who lives on the river with a faithful coon dog and a pretty Cajun lady, Jessie Beaudreaux. Like many fictional private eyes, Hunt is no goody two-shoes. In fact, he's an ex-Green Beret who's served time for murder, and even after receiving a pardon he insists "I wasn't sorry" about the incident that put him behind bars. The action picks up when the lawyer who worked to obtain Hunt's pardon hires him to help a former pro football player, Big John, who runs a camp for wayward boys in rural North Florida called Sweetwater Ranch: It seems the camp is in danger of being put out of business due to a questionable lawsuit claiming Big John used excessive discipline on one of his charges, a boy who has run away. Hunt has his hands full locating the runaway accuser and battling not only his sleazy attorney but a dirty cop. "No tour of crime-fiction Florida is complete without a visit to Norman's steamy backwoods Panhandle" (*BL*, June 1994, p. 1779). Note: Morgan Hunt is also the central character in Norman's novels *Blue Chipper* (1993) and *Deep End* (1994).

208. O'Dell, Scott. **Alexandra**. Boston: Houghton Mifflin, 1984. 146p.

Aimed mainly at young adults (ages 12+), **Alexandra** takes the reader inside the sponge diving business in the predominately Greek-American community of Tarpon Springs, Florida. While helping her grandfather gather sponges (after the tragic death of her father), spunky teenager Alexandra Papadimitrios, who narrates the story, discovers that a family member is smuggling cocaine, cleverly concealing the illegal drug in, yes, the sponges. Should she tell the authorities what she knows or, out of loyalty to kin (a great virtue in Greek society), turn a blind eye? That's young Alexandra's moral dilemma. The late Scott O'Dell's many other YA novels include the much admired *Island of the Blue Dolphins* (1960), a Newbery Medal winner.

From **Alexandra**:

The day dawned clear and quiet, but now a wind was rising out of the Gulf, above the reefs at Anclote Key. We heard it in the palm trees as we sat down to supper. At first it was only a whisper, scarcely that—more like a lover's sigh.

"The wind," my mother said, "is trying to make up its mind whether to be a breeze or a hurricane."

"Like the big wind," Grandfather Stefanos said, "in . . . in . . ." He paused, trying to remember the date.

"The day after Easter in nineteen hundred and fifty-six," I said to help him out.

"Fifty-eight," my sister Daphne said, more to put me down than to help Grandfather remember.

"It was the year fifty-nine," he said and hobbled out on the porch, repeating the date. He went down the steps and stood among the palmettos and stared up at the sultry clouds that had turned from white to blue-gray just while we were sitting there at the table.

209. O'Sullivan, Maurice J. & Steve Glassman, editors. **Orange Pulp: Stories of Mayhem, Murder, and Mystery**. Gainesville: Univ. Press of Florida, 2000. 320p.

Editor Maurice O'Sullivan, an English professor at Rollins College in Winter Park, Florida, has written extensively about the state's literature, and coeditor Steve Glassman, who teaches in the humanities department at Embry-Riddle Aeronautical University in Daytona Beach, Florida, is the author of two novels set in Florida, **Blood on the Moon** (see entry 81) and **The Near Death Experiment** (see entry 82). An invaluable anthology, **Orange Pulp** contains nine examples of Florida crime fiction originally published between 1929 and 1975, including short stories by Edwin Granberry (see entry 86) and Mary Roberts Rinehart and excerpts from such older novels as **The Dead Don't Care** (see entry 153) by Jonathan Latimer and *Dividend on Death* (1939) by Brett Halliday (a David Dresser pseudonym). The next to last selection consists of previously unpublished chapters of an unfinished novel by that master of noir, Charles Willeford (see entries 290-292), and the book concludes by reprinting Don Tracy's classic novel **The Hated One** (see entry 271) in its entirety. "The scholarly introduction ['From the City of Angels to the Magic Kingdom'] charts the shifting locale of the American detective story in recent decades from California to South Florida" (*PW*, Oct. 16, 2000, p. 53). Note: O'Sullivan and Glassman have also edited *Crime Fiction & Film in the Sunshine State: Florida Noir*, a collection of 11 essays published in 1997 by Bowling Green State University Popular Press.

210. Owens, Janis. **My Brother Michael**. Sarasota, FL: Pineapple Pr., 1997. 304p.

A tempestuous family saga that "has a definite Faulkneresque flavor, but retains an aura of its own" (*Florida Libraries*, May-June 1998, p. 89), Janis Owens' debut novel is the story of two brothers, Gabriel ("Gabe") and Michael Catts, who love the same woman, Myra Sims, literally the girl next door. Indeed, these three characters grow up poor on the same street in a rural North Florida mill town during the 1950s and 1960s. Early on, Gabe, the narrator, falls in love with Myra and is crushed when she moves to Alabama to get away from an abusive father. At the same time, Michael encourages Gabe to escape the poverty of their youth by making it possible financially for him to attend a prestigious college in the North. Later Gabe comes home for a visit and—surprise—finds that Myra has returned to Florida and married Michael. Crushed again, Gabe goes back north to study for a graduate degree while Michael goes on to become the manager and then owner of the town's mill. Years later, at age 40, Gabe accepts Michael's invitation to come and stay with him and Myra in their home while he completes a book he's writing. Alas, Gabe is still infatuated with Myra and, unaware that years of mistreatment by her father have left her mentally unstable, he sleeps with and impregnates her. And that's not the end of the story. "Though Owen's [sic] fraternal melodrama can't avoid sentimentality, her fine writing and the ring of her natural voice will carry readers along like a tale told on a porch on a sultry Southern night" (*PW*, Jan. 20, 1997, p. 394). Note: Those who find **My Brother Michael** to their taste will doubtless want to read Owens' companion novel entitled *Myra Sims* (1999), which tells basically the same story but from Myra's quite different perspective. And more recently Owens has added to the saga with the publication of *The Schooling of Claybird Catts* (2003), a novel that focuses on Gabe and Myra's teenage son, Clayton "Claybird" Catts.

211. Parker, Barbara. **Suspicion of Innocence**. New York: Dutton, 1994. 347p.

A former prosecutor with the state attorney's office in Dade (now Miami-Dade) County, Barbara Parker launched her Suspicion mystery series in 1994 with **Suspicion of Innocence**, a riveting thriller about a woman the authorities suspect might have murdered her younger, flashier, and naughtier sister, who's found floating dead and disfigured in the Everglades: "Blonde hair drifted around her head. Her body rolled face up. The nose and lips were gone." Subsequent titles include *Suspicion of Guilt* (1995), *Suspicion of Deceit* (1998), *Suspicion of Betrayal* (1999), *Suspicion of Malice* (2000), *Suspicion of Vengeance* (2001), and *Suspicion of Madness* (2003). The novels brim with South Florida local color and star Miami lawyers Gail Connor, an ex-debutante, and sleekly handsome Anthony Quintana, who together form a power couple whose rocky relationship (personal and professional) figures prominently in the series' backstory. From the beginning both reviewers and readers have responded enthusiastically to Parker's style, plots, and characters. **Suspicion of Innocence**, for example, was praised as "an exhilarating debut that steams with Miami heat" (*PW*, Nov. 8, 1993, p. 57). Note: Parker's *Suspicion of Rage* (2005), the eighth title in the series, is set mainly in Cuba.

212. Pearce, Donn. **Cool Hand Luke.** New York: Scribner's, 1965. 304p.

Though better known as a film than a book, **Cool Hand Luke** is a first-rate novel, surely the best Florida prison story ever written. (Wyatt Blassingame's *Halo of Spears*, published in 1962, and Sterling Watson's **Weep No More My Brother**, see entry 280, are among the runners-up.) Donn Pearce's gritty tale takes place in the 1950s in a chain-gang prison camp in Central Florida near Tavares in Lake County where an incorrigible, calculating, daring, devil-may-care drifter named Lloyd Jackson, aka "Cool Hand Luke," constantly flouts the rules. Luke escapes, receives brutal punishment, then escapes again, and in the end is shot to death by Boss Godfrey, a callous guard in charge of the road gang. Ironically, Luke's death occurs while he's holed up in a church railing against God's—or is it Godfrey's?—indifference. In any event, Luke's spirit is finally broken, not by prison but a bullet in the head. ". . . an impressive novel. Such is the intensity of the author's vivid and galling account that one forgives an occasional sentimental tinge, just as one welcomes the flashes of poetry, the pungent prison slang" (*NYTBR*, Sept. 19, 1965, p. 54). Note: Donn Pearce wrote from personal experience, having served two years on a Florida chain gang after being convicted in 1949 of stealing $100 worth of tools in Tampa. Note also: The aforementioned film version of **Cool Hand Luke** (1967) stars Paul Newman in the title role. One bit of trivia: The film's most famous line, "What we've got here is failure to communicate," does not appear in the book but still might have been written by Pearce, one of the movie's two scriptwriters.

From **Cool Hand Luke:**

And then one night while playing poker he [Luke] managed to bluff his way into stealing a pot of a dollar and sixty-five cents. Everyone else had thrown in his hand except Bullshit Bill who was holding a pair of aces. But when Luke raised the last bet a dollar he refused to call the raise. After dragging in the nickles [sic], dimes and quarters, Luke showed his hand to Bullshit Bill. He had a pair of nothing. Smiling, he murmured softly.

Just remember, man. Wherever you go and whatever you do. Always play a real cool hand.

And from that night on he always answered to the name of Cool Hand Luke.

213. Peck, Robert Newton. **The Cowboy Ghost**. New York: Harper Collins, 1999. 240p.

Hoping to win his rancher father's approval, skinny and inexperienced 16-year-old Titus MacRobinson volunteers to help with the family's cattle drive across Florida. The grueling trek helps Titus better understand both his coldhearted father and himself. "As with many of Peck's books, the strength of the novel emerges from richly drawn characters whose evolution is unpredictable but entirely believable" (*BL*, June 1999, p. 1816). Set in the 1920s, this YA tale is peppered with cowhand slang of the period.

214. Peck, Robert Newton. **Nine Man Tree**. New York: Random House, 1998. 176p.

A prolific writer, Robert Newton Peck has turned out numerous novels for young people with a Florida setting, including *The Seminole Seed* (1983), **The Cowboy Ghost** (see entry 213), *Horse Thief* (2002), *Bro* (2004), and **Nine Man Tree**. The latter, set in the state's backcountry in 1931, tells the story of young Yoolee Tharp and his father Velmer, a mean, ignorant drunk who abuses his wife and children, and their encounters with a menacing 500-pound wild boar that kills and devours people. Yoolee, the story's narrator, is almost done in by the beast and Velmer winds up in even worse shape—dead. In an epilogue, a wise old Calusa Indian kills the animal, but only after acknowledging its legitimate place in the natural order. "A tale full of bite" (*PW*, Aug. 17, 1998, p. 73).

215. Pedrazas, Allan. **The Harry Chronicles**. New York: St. Martin's/Thomas Dunne, 1995. 256p.

Nice guy Harry Rice, owner of the Sand Bar, a local watering hole in an unfashionable area of Fort Lauderdale in South Florida moonlights as a private investigator. His current case initially entailed tracking down a stolen gun collection belonging to attractive Eloise Loftus, but in no time Harry's up to his personable eyeballs in big trouble, accused of murdering his client's husband. "An elusive naked dancer; an aging mobster and his hard-bodied, knife-wielding moll; and Harry's bartending cohorts add pizzazz. Great dialog, colorful locale, and skillful construction strongly recommended this title" (*LJ*, Sept. 1, 1995, p. 211). Note: Allan Pedrazas followed up **The Harry Chronicles**, his first novel, with *Angel's Cove* (1997), an equally engaging mystery that features some of the same characters, including protagonist Rice.

216. Pickard, Nancy. **The Truth Hurts**. New York: Simon & Schuster/Atria, 2002. 336p.

Famous Florida nonfiction crime writer Marie Lightfoot, Nancy Pickard's series protagonist first introduced in **The Whole Truth** (see entry 217), is hard at work on a book about her parents—civil rights activists who disappeared in Alabama in 1963—when an invidious creep calling himself (herself?) Paulie Barnes starts seriously harassing her, claiming in a scandal sheet that her parents were actually racists who supported segregation and rode with the Klan. The elusive Barnes also demands that Lightfoot maintain a detailed account of her present ordeal, which will, if all goes according to plan, end with her death! Should Lightfoot refuse to write what would be the ultimate snuff story, her mysterious tormentor vows to kill her friends one by one, including her black lover, Franklin DeWeese. "The campaign of terror against Lightfoot, involving psychological torture through devices like e-mail and FedEx, is wickedly well constructed and convincing" (*BL*, July 2002, p. 1828).

217. Pickard, Nancy. **The Whole Truth**. New York: Pocket Books, 2000. 264p.

Highly praised by reviewers and nominated for several awards honoring mystery writing, **The Whole Truth** is Nancy Pickard's debut novel starring Marie Lightfoot, a celebrated Florida-based chronicler of true crimes; subsequent Lightfoot titles include *Ring of Truth* (2001) and **The Truth Hurts** (see entry 216). **The Whole Truth** opens with Lightfoot attending a sensational murder trial in her hometown of Bahia Beach, a fictional city on South Florida's Atlantic Coast that closely resembles Fort Lauderdale, where she's taking notes for a book about the case, which is, as the old saw goes, stranger than fiction. The accused, Raymond Raintree, an oddly small and wizened man, has allegedly killed a six-year-old girl and then surgically removed her pineal gland. Immediately after being convicted, Raymond shocks the courtroom by shooting the judge and making a cleverly executed escape. He remains at large for most of the rest of the story, eventually threatening Lightfoot when she starts getting close to discovering this weird little man's real identity. In the end, Raymond's mother's "wish to see her son again spurs the frightening climax to this stunning synthesis of psychological suspense and commentary on our culture of celebrity" (*PW*, Jan. 31, 2000, p. 84).

From **The Whole Truth**:

. . . in many ways Florida is uniquely suited to escapees.

The traffic and the crowds make it easy to hide, to pick up rides, to blend in. There may be water all around, but where there's water there are boats to steal, hijack, or stowaway. Jump the right ship, and a runaway can be stepping off in Colombia in less than a week. For every highway that's easy to blockade, there are dozens of little back roads connecting to other little back roads, many of them through Everglades, or swamp, or thick forest where a man can lose himself for a lifetime, provided he has the survival skills to forage for himself—or he forces other people to give him what he needs. Not only that, but many of the thousands of boats that tie up to Florida docks are empty most of the time, waiting for their owners to fly down from Indiana, or just to get a weekend free. Scores of houses sit empty a good portion of the year, too, waiting for tourist renters, or in new developments that are slow to sell.

In many ways, Florida is an escapee's paradise, and a law enforcer's hell.

218. Pope, Edith. **Colcorton**. New York: Scribner's, 1944. 330p.

Edith Pope (1905-61), an accomplished Florida novelist active from the 1920s to the 1950s, was socially and professionally friendly with fellow writer Marjorie Kinnan Rawlings (see entries 232-235); both women were Scribner authors and had legendary Maxwell Perkins as their editor. Unlike Rawlings, Pope's literary star has dimmed over the years, but **Colcorton**, clearly her finest novel, is still read, mostly by students, and considered by some authorities a minor classic. The core issue in the book is miscegenation, an explosive subject especially in the South during the 1940s when the story takes place. Abby Clanghearne, an unmarried, countrified woman who lives at Colcorton, a once grand but now dilapidated mansion outside St. Augustine in North Florida, harbors an awful secret: She and her brother, Jared, are mulattoes, descended from a prominent slave trader and his black African wife—characters modeled on the real-life Zephaniah and Anna Madgigiane Jai Kingsley, owners of a large antebellum plantation on Fort George Island north of Jacksonville. Public revelation of the Clanghearnes' mixed heritage ruins Jared's life, but Abby, who's as hardy as grits, perseveres. "Pope is best at portraying strong heroines who triumph over powerful histories, such as that left by Kingsley and his African wife" (*BLGF*, 1992, p. 16). Note: The novel, a runner-up for the Pulitzer Prize for fiction in 1945, was reprinted in 1990 by Penguin Books in a paperback edition with an informative introduction by Rita Mae Brown.

From **Colcorton**:

"Miss," Abby said, "you got any books here by man name Clement Johnson?"

The woman dropped her knitting and reaching over thumbed through a file of little cards.

"Miss," Abby said. "You got any—"

"A moment," the woman whispered. "I'm looking. *Goat Song* is out. *Arcanum* is out. *Deliverance*, let's see. *New England Gothic* we simply can't keep on the shelves."

"What you mean, they're out?" Abby said fiercely. "You got em or h'ain't you?"

The woman said, "We own copies, but—"

"You got em here in the Library is all I want to know."

"I'm trying to tell you, we can't keep them on the shelves. His last book is especially popular locally because of the, partly, Florida locale. I could put your name on the waiting list. You would be, let's see, seven, eighth on the list if you care to wait that long."

Abby leaned forward and peered at the names on the card. "You mean all them people here in Augustine have read his book!"

The woman said in amusement, "These are the people who hope to read it. Really, I think everyone else in town has read the thing. It isn't a good book, either. But it's fashionable."

219. Pope, Edith. **River in the Wind**. New York: Scribner's, 1954. 392p.

In a prefatory note, Edith Pope concisely explains where fact ends and fiction begins in this historically faithful, well-written novel dealing with the Second Seminole War that raged in territorial Florida during the 1830s. Invented characters mingle with real people from history, such as General Joseph Hernandez and the great Seminole chief, Osceola, as the ugly conflict between Native Americans and whites unfolds. "Lovers of historical fiction will find in **River in the Wind** just about everything they could fairly ask: an epochal crisis impartially studied; an enchanted setting brought intensely near; lively characters; and a spirited story that rings true in all its incidental details . . . . It is not the least of Mrs. Pope's virtues that, like the late Marjorie Kinnan Rawlings, she loves the Florida she writes about" (*NYTBR*, Mar. 14, 1954, p. 4).

From **River in the Wind**:

A sound, as of an animal hurt in a trap, seemed to come from within the grove. Puzzled, William turned and walked toward it. He said to Scip, "Go back and get your gun." Drawing and priming his pistol, he walked around an oak, smelled vomit, and nearly trod on an Indian slumped at the base of the tree with his arms outstretched behind him. Slowly the Indian raised his head. From eyes to waist he was covered with blood that had dried and tightened and was being washed with a fresh flow: above this bloody mask his eyes were imploring and nearly senseless. The Judge turned abruptly away. Collecting himself, he looked again at the mutilated face; each cheek had been laid bare and the nose cut off. The Indian's wrists were tied to thongs of deerhide fastened round the tree trunk. With shaking fingers the Judge got his clasp-knife open and cut the thong. The Indian fell over.

220. Powell, Richard. **I Take This Land**. New York: Scribner's, 1962. 437p.

Once a big-name author but now little read, Richard Powell (1908-99) was born in Philadelphia and fittingly his best known work of fiction is *The Philadelphian* (1956). At the end of World War II Powell moved to Florida, settling in Fort Myers where over the next couple of decades he produced a number of popular novels set in his adopted state, including light mysteries such as *And Hope to Die* (1947) and *A Shot in the Dark* (1952), a satire about government bureaucracy called **Pioneer, Go Home** (see entry 221); and **I Take This Land**, a fictionalized account of the development of rural Southwest Florida during the period 1895-1945. Powell's macho protagonist in **I Take This Land**, Philadelphia native Ward Campion, is a railroad man (he got into the business as the result of winning a poker game), but railroads are only part of this sweeping saga: "There are brawls, booms-and-busts, and beddings aplenty as aggressive young Campion builds his Fort Taylor (Fort Myers?) and Southern Railroad and rivals Cracker Rush Lightburn in pursuit of the local schoolmarm" (*LJ*, Dec. 1, 1962, p. 4455).

221. Powell, Richard. **Pioneer, Go Home!** New York: Scribner's, 1959. 320p.

If Richard Powell's **Pioneer, Go Home!** is no longer quite the "hilarious novel" promised on the book's cover, it still resonates as an amusing satire on government bungling and red tape. The Kwimpers, a New Jersey working-class family on vacation in Florida circa the early 1950s, take a wrong turn off a road called the Gulf Coast Highway and unaccountably wind up on a pristine, albeit unclaimed, spit of land next to a deserted inlet where they become squatters and in due course apply for all sorts of welfare assistance, which ultimately precipitates a legal donnybrook. Full of mangled grammar and uncommon commonsense—at one point Pop Kwimper advises his son, "Toby, the government don't run out of money. It's only folks that run out of money"—this humorous tale paints Florida as a whimsical paradise. Note: In the early 1960s the novel was made into a feature film, *Follow That Dream*, starring Elvis Presley who at one point sings, "What a wonderful life/Living a life of ease./I got no job to worry me./No big bad boss to hurry me."

222. Poyer, David. **Down to a Sunless Sea**. New York: St. Martin's, 1996. 352p.

In this enthralling novel, Tiller Galloway, an ex-Navy SEAL, finds himself in the Florida Panhandle helping Monica Kusczk, recent widow of his old army (Vietnam) friend Bud, sell the Kusczks' underwater cave diving business. But before any sale takes place, Galloway discovers some alarming facts: Bud apparently was in hock to a drug smuggler; Bud's death, originally assumed to be accidental, was anything but; and a syndicate of rich developers is secretly hell-bent on acquiring the Kusczk property, which includes rights to an enormous—and potentially very lucrative—freshwater aquifer. What makes the novel special are the cave-diving scenes: "Poyer's descriptive powers bring the terror and beauty of the underwater caves to vivid life" (*LJ*, Oct. 15, 1996, p. 91).

From **Down to a Sunless Sea**:

He crashed softly into a soot-silted floor so narrow, he could touch both walls with his elbows. Lying there, he wrote "330 feet" on his slate, then felt for the knots on the line and added "40'." As he waited for things to clear a little, he checked his gauges and watch, bringing them so close that they touched the glass of his mask; then he patted the octopus [breathing apparatus] bungeed to his chest. The total silence when he wasn't exhaling didn't feel comforting now. It was oppressive, a reminder of how deep and far back they were, how many millions of tons of rock lay between him and the sky . . . . Suddenly, he got another spray of water from his regulator. He purged it again and it stopped.

All at once, he wanted overwhelmingly just to get out of this crack in the ground so far down, it felt like they were beneath the foundations of hell. Toll and Scovill were nuts, and here he was following them in even deeper.

223. Prather, Ray. **Fish & Bones**. New York: HarperCollins, 1992. 257p.

A bank robbery in 1971 in a small, fictional North Florida town (Sun City) changes the life of "Bones," the African-American narrator of this disarming coming-of-age story. Just 13 when the robbery took place, Bones ("not my real name") is now 34 and looking back on what happened with the wisdom of age: After the robbery, young Bones decides to go after the reward money offered for information leading to the capture of the culprit(s), but in the process he uncovers some disagreeable secrets about his town and its denizens, who include "Fish" Baker, who's not been right mentally since being beaned by a baseball five years earlier; "Mad Dog" Holden, whose dreams of pitching in the big leagues ended when his fast ball smashed into Fish's head; Fish's older brother, Mose Baker, a sullen U.S. Marine home on leave at the time the robbery occurred; and Madame Baker, a greedy hairdresser and mother of Fish and Mose. Though intended primarily for young people ages 10+, the novel has the power to engage adult readers.

224. Pratt, Theodore. **The Barefoot Mailman**. New York: Duell, Sloan & Pearce, 1943. 215p.

During the late 19th century when South Florida was still mostly pioneer territory and the area lacked any semblance of decent roads, intrepid postmen delivered mail between Palm Beach and Miami by walking barefoot up and down the beach along the Atlantic Coast. The round trip required six days to complete and covered a distance of more than a 100 miles; over a year's time a postman could put up to 6,000 miles on his leather-tough, shoeless feet. Theodore Pratt's **The Barefoot Mailman** is a fictionalized account of one such mail carrier, Steven Pierton, whose work is enlivened by the natural wonders of the beach environment and sometimes interrupted by snakes, wild pigs, beachcombing bandits, storms, ghastly heat . . . and a comely young lady. The novel—the first in Pratt's classic Palm Beach trilogy, which also includes *The Flame Tree* (1950) and **The Big Bubble** (see entry 225)—can be enjoyed as both an exciting adventure tale and a fascinating bit of Florida history. As one reviewer put it, the book is a "unique contribution to the treasury of Americana, Deep South Division. It will open the eyes of many readers who have wondered about the genesis of our American Riviera" (*NYTBR*, July 25, 1943, p. 6). Note: The barefoot mail service ended when Henry Flagler's Florida East Coast Railway reached Miami in 1893 and took over the work. Note also: A 50th anniversary edition of **The Barefoot Mailman** appeared in 1993, published by Florida Classics Library. Note also: A more recent but quite different novel drawing on the same history—John Henry Fleming's satirical *The Legend of the Barefoot Mailman*—was published in 1996 by Faber & Faber.

225. Pratt, Theodore. **The Big Bubble: A Novel of the Florida Boom**. New York: Duell, Sloan & Pearce, 1951. 230p.

Theodore Pratt (1901-69), a prolific author who once bragged that he had written more about Florida than anyone else "past, present, and possibly future," made his mark with **The Barefoot Mailman** (see entry 224), a popular, well-told tale of old Florida and the first title in his Palm Beach trilogy. But **The Big Bubble**, the final entry in the trilogy, has similar qualities, including a highly readable narrative rooted in historical fact—in this instance the frenzied Florida real estate boom that enveloped the state in the 1920s. Adam Paine, Pratt's flamboyant protagonist, closely resembles real-life architect and developer Addison Mizner, a physically and intellectually impressive man whose creative genius contributed enormously to the making of Palm Beach and Boca Raton, which are among Florida's swankiest communities. Though written more than half a century ago, **The Big Bubble** has it all for discriminating novel readers today: three-dimensional characters, an energetic and enjoyable plot, smart writing, informative history, and a luminous nude swimming pool scene that's both tasteful and as erotic as anything in present-day fiction.

From **The Big Bubble**:

Florida wallowed in prosperity. People succeeded in business because they were here and had their doors open. Often this was at the expense of Northern banks, whose depositors drew out their money to invest in the big land bubble. People outside the state couldn't comprehend why those in Florida believed in the bubble, but they did, sincerely and passionately and completely. To them it was not a bubble, but a solid, shining globe ever expanding.

Evangelists praised Miami and God in the same breath. It was virtually impossible to get away from the sound of sand-suckers, pile-drivers, riveting, cement mixing, hammering, sawing, and orators who declaimed about the glory of Florida and its blue sky and green water and unlimited future. In the town of Sanford a few faithless raised their voices and were squelched by the Kiwanis Club which sang, to the tune of, *Yes, We have No Bananas*:

> "*Yes, we have no old fossils,*
> *We have no old fossils today.*
> *In 1920 we had them aplenty*
> *But now they've all passed away.*
> *We have a live Chamber of Commerce,*
> *Rotary and Kiwanis,*
> *But now we have no old fossils,*
> *There are none left in Sanford today.*"

226. Pratt, Theodore. **Florida Roundabout**. New York: Duell, Sloan & Pearce, 1959. 250p.

In addition to novels (see entries 224-225), Theodore Pratt wrote many short pieces, and **Florida Roundabout** contains 16 of the best. All concern some aspect of the state; all are short stories except for an autobiographical piece entitled "My Turbulent Love Affair with Florida" and an essay on manatees, "Sea Serpents, Mermaids, and Sea Cows"; and all are worth reading today. The stories cover a myriad of topics and themes: In "The Owl That Kept Winking," a hunter is outwitted by a wily old bird; "Cocks Must Fight" deals with passions unleashed at an illegal cockfight; "The Pensioners" is a sad story of retirees in Florida struggling to find purpose and meaning in their twilight years; "Seminole Justice" provides a glimpse into the state's Native American culture; "Five to Seven, Palm Beach" brilliantly deconstructs a pretentious party at a Palm Beach mansion. Note: "Five to Seven, Palm Beach" is reprinted in **Florida Stories** (see entry 184), edited by Kevin McCarthy. Note also: In addition to historical novels and short stories, Pratt wrote four mysteries under the pen name Timothy Brace, including *Murder Goes Fishing* (1936) and *Murder Goes in a Trailer* (1937), both set in Palm Beach County. No wonder that in his day Pratt held the unofficial title of Florida's "literary laureate."

**Theodore Pratt** (see entries 224-226), born in Minneapolis, Minnesota, in 1901, spent his teen and college years in New York State and later lived in Europe for a time. He moved to Florida in the 1930s and knew immediately "This is for me." During an illustrious writing career he produced 35 books, 17 set in the Sunshine State. Pratt, who also wrote numerous magazine articles about Florida, died in 1969.

227. Price, Eugenia. **Maria**. Philadelphia: Lippincott, 1977. 352p.

Best known for her historical fiction featuring such Georgia locales as Savannah and St. Simons Island, Eugenia Price (1916-96) also wrote several novels set entirely or partly in 18th-century St. Augustine, Florida's oldest city; they include *Don Juan McQueen* (1974), *Margaret's Story* (1980), and **Maria**. In the latter, Maria Evans Fenwick Peavett Hudson, the title character, arrives in colonial St. Augustine in 1763 married to David Fenwick, a British soldier who soon dies of fever. Over the next 30 years the beautiful, ambitious, self-reliant Maria marries twice more, first to Joseph Peavett, a kind and wealthy older man who also dies of natural causes, and then to John Hudson, a scoundrel half Maria's age who gambles away her money before dying in disgrace in prison. Price's plots frequently incorporate Christian values, and in the end Maria comes to the realization that spiritual salvation is far more consequential than accumulation of worldly riches. "A smooth blend of story-telling art and meticulous research mark this tale of a valiant woman in 18th century America" (*PW*, Mar. 14, 1977, p. 90).

228. Pulitzer, Roxanne. **The Palm Beach Story**. New York: Simon & Schuster, 1995. 256p.

Roxanne Pulitzer, a good-looking, sexy nobody from small-town Cassadaga in upstate New York, married into Palm Beach, Florida, wealth and position, but when her spouse, publishing heir Herbert "Peter" Pulitzer, dumped her amid rumors of illicit drug use and adulterous hanky-panky, she struck back with a vengeful pen, first in a dirt-dishing autobiography, *The Prize Pulitzer: The Scandal That Rocked Palm Beach—The Real Story* (1988), and then several novels of the roman à clef variety—*Twins* (1990), *Facade* (1992), and **The Palm Beach Story**—that closely detail the intimate activities of Florida's most keenly watched upper crust. **The Palm Beach Story**, the last and arguably best of Pulitzer's fictional revelations, takes the reader inside a select few of the town's posh mansions, spending an inordinate amount of time in the richly appointed bedrooms. "Life in Palm Beach is no stroll on the sand as local society veteran Pulitzer (*Twins*) spins with an insider's authority her third juicy tale of the fables and foibles of the chronically (and sometimes thinly disguised) rich" (*PW*, Nov. 6, 1995, p. 84). Note: Readers who find **The Palm Beach Story** to their liking will also enjoy Pat Booth's wicked novel, **Palm Beach** (see entry 19).

From **The Palm Beach Story**:

The bedroom was baronial. In fact, it had been torn from an English castle, shipped to Palm Beach, and painstakingly reassembled. Each piece had a pedigree Hank had paid for handsomely and Ashton would know instinctively, but at that moment neither of them was capable of even noticing the decor. They kept their eyes on each other as if they were held by a magnetic force.

He closed the door behind them. It made a heavy solid sound, as if he were locking out the rest of the world. She felt at once terribly safe and strangely nervous. Then she felt the gentle force of his hands on her shoulders and the hungry pressure of his mouth on hers, and both the nervousness and the safety evaporated in the sheer thrill of his touch.

Without taking his mouth from hers, he began to undress her. She felt the chiffon dress float to the floor like a cloud. The filmy satin underwear followed. She stepped out of her shoes. When she was wearing nothing but the emerald necklace, he let go of her, took a step back, and stood looking at her in the dimly lit room. His eyes went up and down her body like hands. She could feel her pulse beating in her throat and her nipples growing erect under his gaze. And still he went on staring at her, caressing her with his gaze. She was accustomed to having men look at her with admiration, but this was different. She felt like a prize, not a trophy to be won, but a work of art to be cherished.

229. Quindlen, Anna. **Black and Blue**. New York: Random House, 1998. 293p.

Married with a 10-year-old son, Frances Flynn Benedetto, 38, is an emergency room nurse—and a victim of domestic violence.

Her handsome husband, Bobby, a New York City policeman, has a controlling personality and a penchant for beating his wife. As the novel opens, Fran and son Robert, assisted by a group dedicated to helping abuse victims, have left home, established new identities, and gone into hiding in Florida far, far away from the New York area. But will anywhere be far enough from Bobby, a man determined to find—and punish—his wife? "Fran changes her name to Beth Crenshaw and ends up in a dreary garden apartment in inland Florida, an hour from the ocean. She and Robert, afoot beside the Florida highway, have their Thanksgiving dinner at the Chirping Chicken and try to come to terms with their memories of the good Bobby and the bad Bobby—knowing all the while that the relentless Bobby is out there and after them: a heartbreaking game of hide-and-seek" (*Time*, Feb. 23, 1998, p. 84). Anna Quindlen, a former *New York Times* columnist, maintains the suspense throughout this emotionally wrenching story, which she tells with a seasoned writer's eye for convincing detail.

230. Rainey, John Calvin. **The Thang That Ate My Grandaddy's Dog**. Sarasota, FL: Pineapple Pr., 1997. 368p.

Talented African-American writer John Calvin Rainey's first novel concerns a black family's relocation from the urban North to the rural South. Young narrator Johnny Woodside's mother and her children leave New York to live with her in-laws on a rambling old farm in backwoods Florida, a move necessitated by her husband's conviction for drug trafficking and the state's confiscation of all the family's assets. Soon other relatives show up at Johnny's grandparents' homestead near fictional Boggy Bottom, a poor black hamlet adjacent to a large swamp and forest. For Johnny, a little city kid, the farm, the Boggy community, and the surrounding territory are full of wonders and constant new experiences where he and his siblings and many cousins "have one adventure and misadventure after another as they learn tough lessons about survival, self-respect, and common sense. The book rings with the humor and pain of ordinary life" (*LJ*, Apr. 1, 1997, p. 131). Note: Despite the cutesy title and youthful narrator, **The Thang That Ate My Grandaddy's Dog** is not a juvenile book; it contains some frank language and situations and will appeal to both adult and young adult readers. Note also: Rainey's novel received an Honor Book citation for fiction from the American Library Association's Black Caucus in 1997 and was on the shortlist for that year's Lillian Smith Award for fiction.

231. Ramus, David. **The Gravity of Shadows**. New York: Harper Collins, 1998. 304p.

When reclusive Palm Beach, Florida, millionaire Andrew Stevenson asks struggling local art dealer Wil Sumner to appraise his ultra-private collection of rare drawings for possible sale, Wil accepts with alacrity, but soon finds himself entangled in a web of intrigue and violence centering on items in Stevenson's possession that quite possibly could affect the outcome of the next gubernatorial election in Florida. Stevenson's attorney, who adamantly opposes the sale of any of his client's artwork, further complicates Wil's job, as does Stevenson's bewitching daughter, M.K. Author David Ramus, a former art dealer, enhances the story with insider information about the rarefied world of high art. "Ramus' cast is pleasing, his pacing perfect, and his spiking of the plot with dashes of political and art history most alluring" (*BL*, May 1, 1998, p. 1504).

232. Rawlings, Marjorie Kinnan. **The Marjorie Rawlings Reader**. Selected & edited by Julia Scribner Bigham. New York: Scribner's, 1956. 504p.

Marjorie Kinnan Rawlings (1896-1953), Florida's most famous and beloved writer of fiction, was born in Washington DC, her father a patent attorney for the U.S. government. In 1913 the Kinnan family moved to Wisconsin where she studied at the state university at Madison, receiving a Bachelor of Arts degree in 1918 along with a Phi Beta Kappa key. In 1928, after working for ten years as a newspaper journalist in Louisville (Kentucky) and Rochester (New York), Marjorie and her husband, Charles

Rawlings, moved to North Central Florida where for $14,400 they bought an old farmhouse and orange grove at Cross Creek, a rural hamlet located between Ocala and Gainesville. It was here, inspired by Florida's exotic environment and the area's hardy residents, called Crackers, that Marjorie Rawlings found her literary voice. She was also fortunate at that time to find the right publisher, Charles Scribner's Sons, whose extraordinarily skilled editor, Maxwell Perkins, provided her with just the right combination of professional advice and personal encouragement. A deliberate writer who died much too early, Rawlings produced a relatively small oeuvre, albeit a significant one. The purpose of **The Marjorie Rawlings Reader** is to bring together between two covers "a representative selection of [Rawlings'] best writing" (Introduction). Assembled and edited by her close friend and literary executor, Julia Scribner Bigham (Charles Scribner's daughter), the hefty volume contains Rawlings' first novel, **South Moon Under** (see entry 234), in its entirety; two chapters from her most cherished novel, **The Yearling** (see entry 235); three short stories from her celebrated collection, *When the Whippoorwill* (1940); three previously uncollected stories; and four chapters from *Cross Creek* (1942), Rawlings' phenomenally successful book of autobiographical vignettes based on her experiences in frontier Florida between 1928 and the end of the 1930s. Note: Bigham's 11-page introduction to **The Marjorie Rawlings Reader** includes much valuable information about Rawlings' career and major writings. Note also: The **Reader** was reprinted in 1988 by the San Marco Bookstore in Jacksonville, Florida. Note also: A somewhat similar book with a very similar title—*A Marjorie Kinnan Rawlings Reader*—was published in a spiral binder in 1989 by the Florida Endowment for the Humanities; edited by Dorothy Abbott, it incorporates material written by Rawlings, articles about her, and numerous photographs of the author at Cross Creek and environs.

233. Rawlings, Marjorie Kinnan. **Short Stories by Marjorie Kinnan Rawlings**. Edited by Rodger L. Tarr. Gainesville: Univ. Press of Florida, 1994.

This compilation of 23 short stories includes all of Marjorie Kinnan Rawlings' published short fiction except for a couple of minor items. Most of the stories originally appeared in the *Saturday Evening Post*, the *New Yorker*, *Harper's*, and *Scribner's Magazine* over two decades between the early 1930s and 1950s. Though best known for book-length works, particularly **The Yearling** (see entry 235) and the autobiographical *Cross Creek* (1942), Rawlings from the beginning displayed an impressive gift for short-story writing, a talent amply revealed in such classic tales as "Jacob's Ladder," "A Mother in Mannville," "Benny and the Bird Dogs" (narrated by one of Rawlings' most engaging Cracker characters, Quincey Dover), and the O. Henry Short Story Prize-winning "Black Secret" and "Gal Young 'Un." (A highly praised cinematic version of "Gal Young 'Un" came out in 1979, directed by prominent independent Florida filmmaker Victor Nuñez.) "The reader is able to follow Rawlings's development as an author, beginning with her first short story published in 1931, 'Cracker Chidlings,' which was written three years after she moved to the backwoods of north central Florida. These stories reflect both Rawlings's personal growth and perceptions of Florida's blacks and Crackers living in the early twentieth century" (*FHQ*, Oct. 1994, p. 263).

234. Rawlings, Marjorie Kinnan. **South Moon Under**. New York: Scribner's, 1933. 338p.

Marjorie Kinnan Rawlings' debut novel deals with a group of poor, white, insular Floridians who eked out a meager living in rural areas of the state in the 19th and early 20th centuries. Commonly called Crackers, these crude, clannish, often illiterate folk were mostly hunters, dirt farmers, and small cattle ranchers; quite a few were chronic moonshiners, poachers, rustlers, and the like; and almost all were excessively wary of outsiders and the ways of urban civilization and its institutions. As a result, many mainstream Floridians disparaged Crackers as "poor white trash"—forerunners of today's "rednecks." But other saw them as hardworking, God-fearing, independent-minded people who exhibited a rough dignity in the face of frequent adversity. For Rawlings, who came to know her Cracker neighbors well, the truth lay somewhere in between, as the characters in **South Moon Under** suggest. The novel, set in the 1920s in the Big Scrub area of thick pine forest along the Ocklawaha River in Central Florida, describes the life and sorrows of Lantry "Lant" Jacklin, a man utterly at home in the woods. The reader is quickly drawn into Lant's world and the issues he grapples with, which range from conflicts over liquor laws and fencing cattle to a final, devastating showdown with a mean kinsman, Cleve Jacklin. "Marjorie Kinnan Rawlings has wrought with rare conscientiousness in transferring to the printed pages the homely virtues of these people so that the printed page glows with the breath of life. Her novel is both a living document and a book of which one must say that it is distinguished art" (*NYTBR*, Mar. 5, 1933, p. 7). Note: The complete text of **South Moon Under** is reprinted in **The Marjorie Rawlings Reader** (see entry 232). Also a reprint edition of the novel was issued in 1977 by Norman S. Berg, a publisher in Dunwoody, Georgia.

235. Rawlings, Marjorie Kinnan. **The Yearling**. New York: Scribner's, 1938. 406p.

If any Florida novel deserves the designation "classic," it is Marjorie Kinnan Rawlings' **The Yearling**, a tour de force that became an instant bestseller in 1938 and won the Pulitzer Prize for fiction the following year. The story, which takes place in the latter part of the 19th century in what today is the Ocala National Forest, chronicles a year in the hardscrabble life of the Baxters, a Cracker family of three: Penny ("Pa"), Ora ("Ma"), and son Jody, who's 12, carefree, and much attached to an orphan fawn he rescued and named Flag. The book brims with vivid, realistic drama—snake bites, ruined crops due to harsh weather and foraging animals, the hunt for a cunning and deadly bear named Old Slewfoot—but none is more emotionally wrenching than the death of Flag, a heartbreaking coming-of-age ordeal for Jody. An authentic American masterpiece, **The Yearling** explores universal themes and truths that resonate with both adults and young people.

Note: Rawlings forcefully rejected the notion that **The Yearling** is a "children's" or "juvenile" book and insisted Scribner's never promote it as such. Note also: The novel has been reprinted many times and has never been out of print. Perhaps the most appealing edition produced to date is the one Scribner's published in 1939 to commemorate the book's receipt of the Pulitzer Prize: Handsomely bound in a heavy linen fabric called crash, it features full-page color illustrations by the distinguished artist N.C. Wyeth. Note also: A popular film adaptation of the novel premiered in 1946 starring Gregory Peck as Pa, Jane Wyman as Ma, and Claude Jarman Jr. as Jody.

From **The Yearling**:

In the morning Penny felt well enough to dress and hobble around the clearing, leaning on a stick. He made the rounds. He returned to the rear of the house. His face was grave. He called Jody to him. Flag had trampled back and forth across the tobacco seed-bed. The young plants were almost ready to set out. He had destroyed nearly half of them. There would be enough for the usual patch for Penny's own use. There would be no money crop, as he had planned, for storekeeper Boyles at Volusia.

"I don't figger Flag done it malicious," he said. "He were jest racin' back and forth and it were somethin' to jump on, was all. Now you go set up stakes all through the bed amongst the plants and all around the bed, to keep him offen the rest of 'em. I should of done it before, I reckon, but I never studied on him rompin' in that pertickler place."

Penny's reasonableness and kindness depressed Jody as his mother's rage had not done. He turned away disconsolately to do the job.

Penny said, "Now it jest being' accidental-like, we'll not say nothin' to your Ma. Hit'd be a pore time for her to know it."

As Jody worked, he tried to think of a way to keep Flag out of mischief. Most of his tricks he considered only clever, but the destruction of the seed-bed was serious. He was sure that such a thing would never happen again.

**Marjorie Kinnan Rawlings** (see entries 232-235) will forever be associated with Cross Creek, the tiny, remote town in Florida's mossy north-central region where she lived for many years and wrote her most famous books, including a collection of autobiographical pieces appropriately titled *Cross Creek*, which ends with these haunting words: "It seems to me that the earth may be borrowed but not bought. It may be used but not owned . . . . Cross Creek belongs to the wind and the rain, to the sun and the seasons, to the cosmic secrecy of seed, and beyond all, to time."

236. Rivera, Beatriz. **Playing with Light**. Houston, TX: Arte Público, 2000. 240p.

Using a technique known as crosscutting, Beatriz Rivera juxtaposes two stories: The first about a small group of privileged Cuban-American women living in present-day Miami who come together to discuss a novel set in a dressmaking factory in 19th-century Havana; and the second is about a *lectore* (reader) in 1870 who reads aloud to poor women working in a Havana dressmaking factory from a futuristic novel set in Miami in the 20th century. "The expertly handled twist is that the historical characters are reading the story of the Miami characters and vice versa. Eventually, the two worlds collide, leaving the reader dazzled by the implications" (*PW*, Sept. 4, 2000, p. 85). Anyone interested in contemplating the intertwining of Cuban and American history will find this innovative novel rewarding.

237. Robinson, Kevin. **Mall Rats: A Stick Foster Mystery**. New York: Walker, 1992. 197p.

At wheelchair-bound *Orlando Sentinel* reporter Stick Foster's wedding a nice old lady, Martha Galliger, is murdered, her punch containing enough crack, PCP, and amphetamines, in the words of the crime lab, "to kill a circus elephant." Stick—star of two other Kevin Robinson mysteries set in Orlando, Florida, *Split Seconds* (1991) and *A Matter of Perspective* (1993)—gets right on the case and quickly identifies a group of marginalized teens known as the mall rats as his number one suspect. "Robinson offers a detailed look at the reality of wheelchair living, and he exposes a distinctly unphotogenic aspect of the Florida landscape: mall mania" (*BL*, May 1, 2001, pp. 1602-03).

238. Robinson, Spider. **Callahan's Con**. New York: Tor, 2003. 304p.

Whimsy and science fiction meet head-on in Spider Robinson's various Callahan novels, known for their unpredictable plots, screwball characters, outlandish wordplay, wacky wisdom, and the strangest saloons this side of Uranus. In *Callahan's Key* (2000), barkeep Jake Stonebender, his wife Zoey, and assorted eccentrics move from Long Island, New York, to Key West, Florida, where they mobilize to save the universe from impending annihilation. In **Callahan's Con**, a burly Key West Mafioso called Little Tony Donuts puts the arm on Jake for protection money, whereupon Jake's super brainy daughter, Erin Stonebender Berkowitz, devises an elaborate scheme to scam Mr. Donuts that involves time travel and Florida's Fountain of Youth. Robinson's far-out tales have many fans, but be warned—his sf is an acquired taste.

239. Rorby, Ginny. **Dolphin Sky**. New York: Putnam, 1996. 240p.

Called stupid because she has difficulty reading, 12-year-old Buddy, who lives in a village in Florida's Everglades, becomes preoccupied by the plight of captive dolphins forced to perform stunts at a tacky local attraction. She naturally empathizes with these intelligent sea mammals, especially after her insensitive father declares they are "too dumb" to care about being imprisoned and exploited. Eventually Buddy's life changes when she's diagnosed with dyslexia, a reading disability. By working hard to overcome the handicap, she gains a measure of poise and self-confidence and in the end is able to help her beloved dolphins. Though mainly for young people (ages 10+), the novel will appeal to many adults as well. "Believable characters, convincingly portrayed relationships, a deeply moving plot and a wealth of intimate details of Everglades life combine to make this debut a real winner" (*PW*, Mar. 25, 1996, p. 85).

240. Rudloe, Jack. **Potluck**. Williamston, MI: Out Your Backdoor Pr., 2003. 282p.

In his acknowledgments, Jack Rudloe notes that this novel started out as "a non-fiction book about the shrimping industry, called 'Shrimper's Log.' It would've been the first overview of this way of life. However, it didn't take long for a very different story to emerge, which I called 'Potluck.' I want to thank the many people who helped me with the work. Some are in prison, others are dead, and some will remain anonymous." A highly respected North Florida environmentalist and author of half a dozen nonfiction titles on marine conservation, Rudloe knows the state's shrimp business inside out. In **Potluck** he conveys how difficult it is for small, independent entrepreneurs to make a living today—and how great the temptation is to use their boats to earn big money hauling illegal freight, including drugs, guns, and human cargo. The novel's protagonist, Preston Barfield, is basically an honest captain of a shrimper working in the Gulf of Mexico off the Florida coast who out of economic necessity becomes involved in some very nasty business. "The pressure, the competition with foreign shrimpers and the drugs that corrupted a small coastal shrimping town are all told in this gripping novel" (*FM*, Sept. 2003, p. 7). Note: Because Rudloe's novel was published as an original paperback by a small press in Michigan, it received little attention from reviewers and as a result few libraries, including those in Florida, acquired it. Interested readers can normally borrow the book through their public library via interlibrary loan, or it can be purchased directly from the publisher or from an online bookseller.

From **Potluck**:

Preston grabbed another handful of cable, "Can't do it, Charlie. Those shrimp might show any time. Hell, they may show tonight. The water's still cold, but I've seen it happen before. The first boat on the scene is the one that makes the money. And I need to make some money bad. Mary's gonna have that baby in a couple of months, and the doctor said there's complications. What little insurance we got won't cover the half of it."

His deckhand nodded glumly. He knew Preston was three payments behind on his truck with the finance company, and two payments behind on his own boat, all due to doctor bills. But he also knew that he'd be lucky if he shared a hundred dollars this trip after deducting expenses, and that was a week's work.

Charlie offered testily, his teeth starting to chatter from the biting north wind, "Those boys packing out that freighter don't have them kinda problems. They're rolling in money. I think we ought to make a dope run down to Colombia and get in on some of this easy money. At least we wouldn't be freezing to death down there, that warm tropical weather, and those good-looking women. I know one boy who made the run, said he about screwed himself to death down there."

Preston gave him a hard look, so he dropped the subject.

241. Russ, Wilma. **Quivering Earth: A Novel of the Everglades.** New York: McKay, 1952. 252p.

While not well-known and not a writer of first rank, Wilma Russ did produce one memorable novel, **Quivering Earth**. Set in Florida's Everglades in the early years of the 20th century, the story begins when Pop Gundyhill, a curmudgeonly Cracker who hates "civvyzation" and lives secluded deep in the Glades with his dog Whimpie, finds and cares for a half-wild white girl of six or seven who somehow survived an Indian raid that killed her family. Pop and the orphan girl, whom he calls Keeta (short for M'skeeter, a corruption of mosquito), develop a close father-daughter relationship in the first section of the novel, the old geezer teaching the child about the joys and dangers of living in the Everglades, one of the largest and most labyrinthine swamps in the world. In the second section, Pop and Keeta, now an adolescent, join up with a construction gang working on an Everglades reclamation project. Among the people they meet are Hitty Bell Lacey, who cooks for the crew; Domingo, a sinister half-breed who attempts to rape Keeta; and Mark Wingate, a cultivated young man from the North who must return home but tells Keeta before he leaves, "When I get ready to build my world down here, you're the kind of girl I am going to need to help me." In the final third of the book, Hitty convinces Pop that he needs to take Keeta, who's now grown into an attractive teen on the cusp of womanhood, "out of this God-forsook swamp." They make their way to a town near Lake Okeechobee, where Keeta works in a respectable boardinghouse owned by Pop's estranged wife, Vera, and is pursued by Fayte Delane, a dashing man from Tampa who loves to dance the rigadoon. But, predictably, Mark returns to claim Keeta, Pop reconciles with Vera, and the saga ends happily. "Miss Russ has provided a love story that is pretty contrived but not too obtrusive. It shouldn't distract you from some very nice nature descriptions, a lusty gang of secondary characters, and a general atmosphere of earthy wholesomeness which is pleasantly refreshing" (*Saturday Review of Literature*, Apr. 5, 1952, p. 34).

242. Rust, Ann O'Connell. **Pahokee**. Orange Park, FL: Amaro Books, 1992. 284p.

Between 1988 and 1992 Ann O'Connell Rust wrote and published The Floridians, a five-volume series of historical novels beginning with *Punta Rassa* (1988), followed by *Palatka* (1989), *Kissimmee* (1990), *Monticello* (1991), and finally **Pahokee**—the titles all names of Florida frontier towns. Filled with many characters and much interesting history and local color, the novels focus on the lives of pioneer women in different parts of the state during the period 1877 to 1928. **Pahokee**, for instance, covers the years 1899-1928, the story concluding with the disastrous Lake Okeechobee hurricane that killed approximately 2,500 Floridians. At the beginning of each novel author Rust, a Florida native born in Canal Point, a small town on Lake Okeechobee, notes, "The history is as accurate as is needed for the story line, and all the characters are fictional."

243. Salvatore, Diane. **Paxton Court**. Tallahassee, FL: Naiad, 1995. 256p.

Four recently retired gay and lesbian couples from New York City who have been friends for years buy adjacent homes on Paxton Court in Lakeside Leisure, a fictional Florida retirement community. Eager to unwind from stressful careers, the eight newcomers simply want to enjoy their golden years quietly relaxing in the sun. But when they flaunt their sexual orientation by painting their houses purple, Bunny Seagrit, a local straight arrow, leads a petition campaign to ban the provocative color and, by insinuation, the "Paxton perverts" themselves. When the community clubhouse adds insult to injury by denying one of the couples a family discount, a lawsuit further inflames the situation. These civil problems, plus incidents of infidelity and reversion to old workaholic habits, prompt the homosexual retirees to reassess their goals and commitments. One reviewer found the novel "fresh and funny," adding "thankfully, the author doesn't grandstand on gay issues but instead concentrates on the dynamics of senior-citizen love, proving herself wise in the ways of the heart, the mind and the libido" (*PW*, Oct. 16, 1995, p. 44).

244. Sanchez, Thomas. **Mile Zero**. New York: Knopf, 1989. 349p.

To date Thomas Sanchez has written five serious, richly textured novels that critics tend to either swoon over or dislike intensely: *Rabbit Boss* (1973), *Zoot-Suit Murders* (1978), **Mile Zero** (1989), *Day of the Bees* (2000), and *King Bongo* (2003). Of these, **Mile Zero** is the best known and the only one with a Florida locale. The story, which takes place in Key West, the state's small, exotic city located at the end of the Overseas Highway at mile marker zero (symbolically the end of the world), makes the point that this little piece of paradise has been repeatedly and shamefully defiled by avaricious and insensitive outsiders ranging from developers to drug dealers to tourists to boatloads of illegal refugees. An eccentric cast of characters populates the novel, including St. Cloud, once an idealistic Vietnam War protester and now an alcoholic burnout; MK, a ruthless Vietnam vet and South American drug runner; Lila, a young Southern woman trying to escape the clutches of MK who shot her husband, Roger; Zobop, an avenging killer and enigmatic deliverer of haranguing monologues in which he crowns himself "the Great Corrector" and advocates destruction as an act of cleansing; and Justo, a black Cuban-American policeman intent on apprehending Zobop. **Mile Zero** received mixed reviews, as these two samples indicate: "Its brilliantly contrived plot uncoils with the suspense of a thriller. Nothing is gratuitous: characters and actions are linked in a hidden web, sometimes with devastating irony. And it is funny, a comic masterpiece crackling with backhanded wit and laugh-out-loud humor" (*NYTBR*, Oct. 1, 1989, p. 7); "It is not a good sign that [the author's] hollow radical blarney is being mistaken for literature" (*New Republic*, Apr. 1, 1990, p. 31).

From **Mile Zero**:

It is wrong to try to cheat death [says Zobop in one of his monologues]. Do you remember 1906, when the army of laborers building Flagler's Overseas Railroad relied on crude barometers, which were nothing more than water-filled glass jars with weeds on the bottom? No, you remember nothing. When the weeds in those jars began to float toward the top it signaled air pressure was dropping and a vengeful wind from Africa was on the rise. On an October night of 1906 the weeds floated right to the top of the jars, but it was already too late, winds were storming over a hundred miles per hour, snapping steel cables anchoring the houseboat barracks of Flagler's army. The Eye of the Hurricane was bearing down without pity, sharks were rising in the twenty foot tidal surge. Many of the screaming men swilled vials of laudanum from first-aid kits, minds going adrift as waves smashed into houseboats. A Gray Ghost appeared from the Eye of the Hurricane, it flung boats, machines and men southward into the churning Gulf of Mexico. In a puff the Gray Ghost reduced Flagler's grandiose army to fish bait. Why do I tell you this, you ask? Is it because of my distaste for Flagler, a corrupt old Capitalist in a straw bowler hat who sacrificed the lives of hundreds of work-a-day blokes in the construction of his get-rich-at-any-price scheme, to make of the Florida Keys nothing more than a concrete and iron railroad spur to South America, an elaborate dock of dreams where a cardinal Capitalist could pile ever higher his plunder from the planet, his crude barrels of crude oil, his sagging sacks of gold? No, that is not why I tell you this. That is history you should know, the simplicity of greed itself. I tell you this because my brain is waterlogged and the weeds are rising fast. Do not be so blind as to think there is a prescription for exemption you can swill like laudanum before the howling wind of retribution arrives. Do not think there is a route of escape across land or water. Do not try to cheat death. Do not forget, four hundred years before

Flagler began construction of his pornographic greed scheme, the Spaniards named many of these martyred Keys *matar hombre*, kill man. *Matar hombre*, that is what I aim to do.

245. Sayles, John. **Los Gusanos**. New York: HarperCollins, 1991. 475p.

Marta de la Peña—a beautiful, guileless Cuban exile working as a nurse in Miami in the early 1980s—has an obsessive desire to avenge the death of her brother, Ambrosio, a poet who died before his prime during the Bay of Pigs fiasco two decades earlier. The plot centers on Marta's efforts to organize a guerrilla force that will slip into Fidel Castro's Cuba and commit a terrorist act in memory of her brother. Author John Sayles, who's both an acclaimed film director (e.g., *Return of the Seacacus 7*) and a skillful writer, not only knows how to create spellbinding action scenes but has a knack for weaving relevant history into the story and developing memorable characters, a task easily accomplished in this instance due to the many shady operatives involved in the U.S.-Cuba conflict. "Focusing on the vicissitudes of Marta's extended family in both Havana and Miami, he [Sayles] reviews 50 years of Cuban-American relations. An exciting, instructive, and highly readable novel" (*LJ*, Apr. 15, 1991, p. 128). Note: The book contains some untranslated Cuban-Spanish street slang, but the meaning of *gusanos* in the title is clear. It's Castro's name for Cuban exiles: worms.

246. Schrecengost, Maity. **Panther Girl**. Gainesville, FL: Maupin House, 1999. 130p.

Intended mainly for young readers (ages 8-12), this edifying historical novel takes place in the Florida territory in 1843, a year after the end of the brutal Second Seminole War and two years before Florida became a U.S. state. Hugh MacKenzie, a Scottish immigrant, and his wife, Sarah, and their precocious six-year-old daughter, Mariah (through whose eyes the story unfolds), move from Georgia to the Tampa Bay area, then very much a wilderness. In fact, the city of Tampa, which was not chartered until 1855, was then a rude military installation called Fort Brooke. The family's pioneering adventures, hardships, and relations with the Native American population, especially as experienced by the bright, inquisitive Mariah, comprise the bulk of the book, though also included are a famous Seminole Indian legend (retold by Mariah), a glossary of frequently used Seminole terms (such as *chickee*, *katca*, and *sofkee*), and helpful black-and-white illustrations by Sal Salazar. Note: **Panther Girl** won the 1999 Patrick D. Smith Award for Florida Historical Fiction. Note also: Maity Schrecengost, an experienced elementary school teacher, is also the author of *Tasso of Tarpon Springs* (1997), an adventure story for young people about a Greek boy who comes to Tarpon Springs, Florida, in 1905 to work as a sponge diver.

From **Panther Girl**:

Mariah moved her blanket and snuggled down between her parents. Daddie told a wonderfully scary story of Indians and tomahawks. Of Indian raids, burned villages, and children taken captive. When he got to the part about scalps dripping with blood, Mariah gasped. Daddie smiled in the darkness.

"Hugh! For pity's sake," Sarah chided, "that's enough."

"Daddie, is that story true?" Mariah demanded.

"Of course not. I just made it up to take your mind off the chiggers."

"But could the story be true?"

Daddie hesitated. "Well, parts of it could be true. You know about the trouble there's been with the Indians."

"But would the Indians do anything bad to us? We haven't done anything mean to them."

"I'm sorry to say, lass, it doesn't work that way. White men took the Indian's land and did some bad things to them. They've broken treaties and lied to the Indians. We're white people. And to the Indians white people are the enemy.

"We're not so different," Daddie went on. "If a bunch of Indians came runnin' out of the bushes there, we'd figure they were out to scalp us, wouldn't we? We wouldna guess they came to make a friendly call."

"Hugh!"

"All right, all right," Daddie chuckled. "Best get to sleep, lass, before we give your mother a hissy fit."

247. Schumacher, Aileen. **Rosewood's Ashes**. Philadelphia: Intrigue Pr., 2001. 356p.

Rosewood, a black community of about 150 people near Cedar Key on Florida's Gulf Coast that white vigilantes burned to the ground in 1923 after killing half a dozen residents and terrorizing the rest, was a real place. The town ceased to exist after the survivors fled and never returned, their land later expropriated by whites and the event conveniently hushed up for decades. Late in the 20th century, however, this atrocious hate crime began to be talked about openly and soon it attracted front-page attention in Florida and around the country when victims or their descendants sought monetary compensation. The Rosewood tragedy provides the backdrop for Aileen Schumacher's skillfully constructed debut thriller featuring David Alvarez, a police detective, and his lady love, Tory Travers, a woman who knows Rosewood's ugly past well. The fictional story begins with an ambitious undertaking to write a revisionist history of Florida that emphasizes both the accomplishments and tribulations of the state's African Americans and other minorities. When Amy Cooper, an academic working on the project, is killed by an explosion at the Gainesville airport while on an information-gathering trip concerning Rosewood, Alvarez and Travers become embroiled in what turns out to be a highly suspenseful mystery. Note: In an afterword, Schumacher details what is historically true in the novel and what is pure fiction.

248. Sellers, Heather. **Georgia Under Water**. Louisville, KY: Sarabande Books, 2001. 220p.

Georgia Jackson, an intelligent but ambivalent Florida teenager, narrates most of the action in this collection of nine linked stories that range from explosive scenes provoked by dysfunctional parents (alcoholic father; mentally disturbed mother) to a realistic depiction of truck-stop sex outside the little town of Christmas, Florida. The book obviously has natural appeal for young adults and is indeed recommended for readers in this age group; but make no mistake: **Georgia Under Water** is very much a grown-up rendering of the problems and frustrations faced by a pubescent girl struggling to come to grips with adulthood. "Unlike other coming-of-age fiction, this collection flaunts its messy contradictions and offers no safe place from which to view the family's destruction. **Georgia Under Water** is as disturbing, and frequently as absorbing, as adolescence itself" (*NYTBR*, Jun. 17, 2001, p. 22).

249. Shames, Laurence. **Florida Straits**. New York: Simon & Schuster, 1992. 256p.

The author of a series of well-crafted, high-energy, saucy-funny mysteries set in Key West, Laurence Shames is sometimes compared with such masters of contemporary Florida crime fiction as Elmore Leonard and Carl Hiaasen—good company by anyone's standards. Thus far he has produced eight novels beginning in 1992 with **Florida Straits**, followed by *Scavenger Reef* (1994), *Sunburn* (1995), **Tropical Depression** (see entry 250), *Virgin Heat* (1997), *Mangrove Squeeze* (1998), *Welcome to Paradise* (1999), and *The Naked Detective* (2000). Shames's plots often involve New York (pronounced New Yawk) area characters who relocate to the sunny climes of Key West. In **Florida Straits**, for instance, young Joey Goldman, the illegitimate son of a Mafia don and a Jewish manicurist, leaves the Big Apple for America's southernmost city because he's tired of being treated like an errand boy, a gofer, a zero. He's quite certain he'll have no difficulty establishing his own criminal enterprise in the Keys—after all, a street-smart New Yawker like Joey Goldman shouldn't have any trouble handling some Florida Crackers, right? But the local mob has much more muscle than Joey imagined, and when retired mafioso Bert the Shirt advises him to get lost, Joey's reduced to selling condo time-shares. In the end Shames's abject but somehow likable antihero learns to love Key West and ultimately chooses respectability over the rackets. Along the way there are some fine lines describing the Florida city and its unique ambience.

250. Shames, Laurence. **Tropical Depression**. New York: Hyperion, 1996. 293p.

In Laurence Shames's fourth breezy Key West crime novel, Murray Zemelman, who's known as "the Bra King" (he owns Beauty-Breast, Inc., a New Jersey brassiere manufacturing firm), has become suicidal despite gobbling large quantities of Prozac. In a "final squirt of panic," Murray decides not to kill himself; instead he drives nonstop from Jersey to Key West to start a new life, leaving everything behind—the lingerie business, the palatial house, the trophy wife (a former model aptly named Taffy). Once in Key West, he rents a condo from Joey Goldman (first encountered in **Florida Straits**; see entry 249) and then meets up with an acerbic Native American, Tommy Tarpon, who claims to be the last surviving member of the Matalatchee, an obscure Florida Indian tribe (and creation of Shames's rich imagination). Together Murray and Tommy scheme to have the tribe declared a "sovereign nation" by the U.S. Government so they can open a legal gambling casino on the only remaining Matalatchee land, a squalid little island off the South Florida coast. Complications occur when a crooked state senator and a Miami mobster want in on the action. "Shames doesn't quite match the inspired whackiness of Carl Hiaasen or the artful characterizations and plotting of Elmore Leonard, but he knows how to put his tongue in his cheek—and he keeps it firmly, entertainingly, in place throughout" (*PW*, Jan. 1, 1996, pp. 56; 58).

From **Tropical Depression**:

He sprang up from the sofa, took a spin out to the balcony. When he got there the sun was just emerging from behind a small and fluffy cloud. The ocean twinkled, clean heat returned to the world, and absurdly, the Bra King took this as an omen. He scratched his head with gusto, was on top of things once more. He went back to the striped sofa, which was already taking on the potent feel of headquarters.

He called his office in the garment district of Manhattan, got his friend and number-two man, Leslie Kantor, on the line.

"Murray," Kantor said, "you okay? Taffy called last night. You didn't go home, you didn't come in—"

"I started to come in," the Bra King interrupted. "But the day got off to a really shitty start, so I said fuck it and retired."

"Excuse me?"

In the distance, very soft, the sound of swatted tennis balls.

"Retired, Les. Resigned. Quit. I'm in Key West. Palm trees. Coconuts."

The line went silent save for the faint scream of tearing paper. Murray had known Les Kantor for a lot a years, knew him like a book. He knew Les had retrieved his pack of Tums from his left-hand trousers pocket and was trimming down the wrapper with a perfect thumbnail. "Coconuts," he murmured at last.

"Coconuts, Les. And I'm divorcing Taffy."

251. Sher, Ira. **Gentlemen of Space**. New York: Free Pr., 2003. 304p.

It's 1976 and Florida junior high school science teacher Jerry Finch wins a trip to the Moon on the (fictitious) Apollo 19 mission, leaving behind wife Barbara and nine-year-old son Georgie—and, shockingly, an unborn child conceived with Georgie's teenage babysitter. Media coverage, heavy from blastoff, becomes frenzied when Jerry's infidelity leaks to the press and reaches fever pitch when he disappears in space and his fellow astronauts come home without him. Though Jerry never returns, Georgie, who recollects the story some years later, receives celestial phone calls—real or imagined?—from his father in which Jerry ponders a mystical connection between humans and the heavens. "This is a beautiful, eloquent first novel that dares one to use clever phrases like 'rising star' and 'out of this world'" (*BL*, Mar. 15, 2003, p. 1276).

252. Shropshire, Mike. **The Pro**. New York: St. Martin's/Thomas Dunne, 2001. 269p.

After professional golfer Franklin Delano "Del" Bonnet, the teller of this waggish tale, is banished from the PGA tour for allegedly engaging in oral copulation with a lady while driving under the influence, he winds up in the boonies as the club pro at Caloosahatchee Pines, a fictional downmarket golf community for senior citizens on the outskirts of Punta Gorda on Florida's Gulf Coast. After nine years at Caloosahatchee Pines, Del's pushing 50 and the world of big-time golf is a distance memory. But fate intervenes: A sales rep working out of his station wagon introduces Del to a new, handmade driver with a huge "kryptonite" club head that improves his game so much he joins the Senior Tour, where he's backed by newly acquired patron and lover Dottie Ridge, a 70-year-old former Rockette who's got plenty of green plus a "perfectly contoured ass." Mike Shropshire's irreverent slice of the golfing life has been lauded as a "brilliantly comic diversion .... The locker room patois, much of it scatological, fits the scenario and may limit the audience, but a more hilarious look at the trappings and rituals of a country club sport would be hard to find" (*PW*, June 18, 2001, p. 60). Note: Shropshire is best known for his book *Seasons in Hell* (1996), a nonfiction account of one of the worst baseball teams in history, the 1973-75 Texas Rangers.

From **The Pro**:

The good people at Caloosahatchee Pines largely agreed that I was a pretty good teacher when it came to the basics of setting up a golf swing ....

But in the modern world, the simple ability to communicate no longer remains sufficient. That lesson came with the unexpected arrival of Tyler LaGrange. Tyler was elected president of the board at Caloosahatchee Pines six months before, and he thought the golf pro needed to provide monthly projection charts for all of the golfing members. Like if Arlene Portwood, age eighty-eight, was shooting 130, Tyler wanted me to get her down to 127 whether Arlene wanted to or not and, if she didn't, then Tyler LaGrange wanted me to appear before the board and explain why. LaGrange was a young guy, not a day over sixty, and still active as the regional marketing director for some brewery, and that partially explained his fetish with sales projections.

LaGrange disagreed with my marketing strategy, that consisted of a sign in the pro shop that read, THERE'S NOTHING SPECIAL ABOUT OUR GOLF BAGS, BUT YOU CAN'T LICK OUR BALLS. He wanted to get rid of the sign. In fact, Tyler LaGrange wanted to get rid of me. How come? Because he thought I had a "thing" for his wife, Jerri, that's why. Or even worse, LaGrange thought that Jerri might have had a "thing" for me. The club president pictured me as somebody who appeared in his wife's masturbation fantasies. The fact was that Jerri, while gifted with a cheerful personality and fine soprano voice, had the torso and legs of Sam Huff [a legendary pro football player].

253. Skurzynski, Gloria & Alaine Ferguson. **Deadly Waters**. Washington, DC: National Geographic, 1999. 160p.

Written by a mother-daughther team and aimed primarily at juvenile readers (ages 10+) but relevant for anyone interested in Florida's fragile environment and particularly its endangered species, **Deadly Waters** concerns a rash of mysterious manatee deaths in the Everglades. While their scientist parents are busy investigating the problem, Jack Landon (age 12), his sister Ashley (10), and foster brother Bridger (14) get involved by chance and in due course uncover key clues to what's killing the gentle creatures. "An engaging read, the story features likable protagonists and plenty of action and suspense. Children also get information about the Everglades ecosystem, the dangers of pollution, and the need for environmental awareness and responsibility" (*BL*, Oct. 15, 1999, p. 446). Note: This is the fourth novel in the authors' National Parks Mystery series, all of which star the intrepid Landon kids.

254. Slate, Sam J. **Satan's Back Yard**. New York: Doubleday, 1974. 262p.

Before Florida could become part of the United States (eventually the 27th state in 1845), the territory had to be acquired from Spain, the dominant power in the region from 1513 (when the Spaniard Ponce de León claimed it for his country) to the early 19th century. Sam Slate's "tale of historical intrigue" (*PW*, May 6, 1974, p. 61) deals not only with the American desire to obtain Florida and Spain's reluctance to part with it, but efforts in 1817 by a renegade "patriot" army led by Gregor MacGregor to seize the territory and establish an independent nation—a bloody venture that at the time earned Florida the dubious sobriquet, "Satan's backyard." While Slate's novel adheres to the broad contours of historical fact and includes appearances by major political figures of the day (Thomas Jefferson, Andrew Jackson, James Madison, James Monroe, etc.), the plot is driven by the derring-do of a fictional protagonist, Jonathan Ames, a former U.S. Army officer who infiltrates and spies on MacGregor's forces at the behest of James Madison. MacGregor of course failed to achieve his goal, and in the novel Ames is amply rewarded for his contribution toward bringing about that end. "Slate has a gift for characterization, and a sense of the big scene. His battles, duels, and hair-breath escapes are exciting" (*LJ*, Aug. 1974, p. 1987).

**From Satan's Back Yard:**

Madison said he was pleased to see Ames so well and fully recovered from his injuries. "Mr. Crawford sent me copies of your Florida dispatches. They were excellent. Only an hour ago the President [James Monroe] told me your timely report on Aury gave him the information he needed to justify the seizure of Amelia Island."

An embarrassed Jonathan stammered his thanks. Once again, under Madison's shrewd examination, he described the success and the failure of the patriot army.

"Was it really a failure?" mused Madison. "I wonder. It's tragic that MacGregor didn't liberate Florida when, with one decisive move, he could have captured St. Augustine. But we now control Amelia and St. Augustine. This gives us a wonderful opportunity to force Spain to cede Florida and to accept a satisfactory boundary for the Louisiana Territory. Don't you think so, Bill?"

"Yes, Jemmy. I believe Madrid is at last convinced it's better to sell Florida before we just take it. Both MacGregor and [Andrew] Jackson proved how easy that is."

"Then, Mr. President," asked Ames, "you think this time we'll really get Florida?"

"Indeed I do, Jonathan. Spain is now a second-rate power. Despite her imperious bad manners, she can't hide this fact from the rest of the world."

255. Slaughter, Frank G. **Fort Everglades**. New York: Doubleday, 1951. 340p.

Frank Slaughter (1908-2001), a surgeon turned writer who lived in Jacksonville for most of his life, produced a number of popular historical novels set in Florida, including *The Golden Isle* (1947), *Storm Haven* (1953), *Apalachee Gold* (1954), *Flight from Natchez* (1955), **The Warrior** (see entry 256), and **Fort Everglades**. The latter takes place during the Second Seminole War (1835-42) in what today is Miami (then called Fort Dallas, on which the author's fictional Fort Everglades is based); and the plot, as is often the case in Slaughter's tales, centers on a doctor in extremis. "The author has lost none of his gift for dramatizing surgery—whether he's operating on a moonlit island or in the Seminole chieftain's own palm-thatch house, with the whole tribe watching" (*NYTBR*, Mar. 4, 1951, p. 20).

From **Fort Everglades**:

He [Dr. Royal "Roy" Coe] turned to his patient at last in response to Dr. Barker's low-voiced summons. Instruments were ready at the bedside, such as they were; there were even enough sutures to close his incision if he kept it small. He took the girl's pulse, making an occasion of that simple routine, holding the massed glare of a hundred eyeballs with his outward calm unshaken. As he had expected, the beat was thready but sustained enough to give him hope. The girl's forehead was cool, and she was still sleeping deeply under the narcotic. He had only to turn back an eyelid and check the constriction of the pupil to guess the nature of the potion. Almost certainly it was the seeds of the coontie plant, the cyclamen whose roots furnished a gruel called *sofkee* and whose seeds were a powerful narcotic.

"Can we risk an internal examination?"

Dr. Barker shook his head. "Even an Indian midwife wouldn't dare. We'd be shot down where we stand."

Roy nodded grimly and drew in his breath as he flicked aside the white doeskin blanket that covered the patient's body, exposing the naked flesh beneath. The watchers sighed in unison, and he heard a musket being cocked behind the crazy dance of the fire. The expected shot did not come as he let his fingers outline the operative area and the probable cause of the swelling that had distended the abdomen like a monstrous drum.

256. Slaughter, Frank G. **The Warrior: A Novel of Osceola and the Seminole War of 1835**. New York: Doubleday, 1956. 255p.

The Second Seminole War, which began in 1835 and lasted seven years, occurred after the United States had acquired the Florida territory from Spain in 1821 but before Florida achieved statehood in 1845. It was a cruel, vicious struggle between the Seminole people living, hiding, and fighting in remote areas of the territory and white settlers aided by the U.S. military, which was charged with relocating the Native American population to land west of the Mississippi River as per the Indian Removal Act passed by the U.S. Congress in 1830. Frank Slaughter's **The Warrior** is a lucid fictional account of the activities of the great Seminole leader, Osceola, during the first year of that conflict. Told in the words of Osceola's white "blood brother," Charles Paige, a character imagined by Slaughter, the story offers readers a fair and historically valid rendering of the period and of why Osceola, though a bitter enemy of the American government, has long been regarded a true American hero. Note: **The Warrior** served as the basis for the feature film *Naked Under the Sun* (1957), a dramatization of Osceola's life and ultimate imprisonment at Fort Moultrie in South Carolina, where he died in 1838.

257. Smith, Ed Ray. **Blue Star Highway: A Tale of Redemption from North Florida**. Atlanta: Mile Marker 12 Pr., 1998. 286p.

Set in a fictitious North Florida town called Oceanside in 1962, this comforting yarn about a good-hearted 14-year-old boy, Marty Crane, who's in trouble with the law, has the potential to appeal to both adult and YA readers. As part of his punishment while serving a two-month sentence in the Ocean County Juvenile Detention Center, Marty must write a detailed explanation of how he got into his current predicament. "The result is a rambling, rollicking account of Marty's first crush, description of a horrendous Florida hurricane, musings on religion, and lessons about racial bigotry" (*BL*, Feb. 15, 1999, p. 1060).

Born in 1927, Mississippi native **Patrick D. Smith** (see entries 258-260) came to Florida in 1966 to work as director of college relations at Brevard Community College in Cocoa, a job he held for 22 years until retiring in 1988. But it is as a writer of historical novels set in Florida that has earned Smith so many accolades, including being named "The Greatest Living Floridian" in 2002.

258. Smith, Patrick D. **Angel City**. St. Petersburg, FL: Valkyrie Pr., 1978. 190p.

**Angel City**, a proletarian novel reminiscent of John Steinbeck's *Grapes of Wrath* (1939), exposes the harsh, ineffably sad conditions and injustices migrant workers faced in Florida in the 1970s (and to some extent continue to experience today). By way of preparation for writing the book, Patrick Smith, one of Florida's premier storytellers and author of the much admired **A Land Remembered** (see entry 260), observed the plight of the migrants firsthand, working for a time incognito in the fields around Homestead, Florida. Note: In 1989 Pineapple Press reprinted **Angel City** as part of its second *Patrick Smith Reader*, which also includes Smith's first novel, *The River is Home*, and an introduction by Kevin M. McCarthy that provides valuable background information about both the novels and author Smith. (For the record, *The River is Home* was originally published by Little, Brown in 1953 and takes place not in Florida but the Mississippi Delta, where Smith was born and grew up.) Note also: In 1980 CBS aired a made-for-TV movie adaptation of **Angel City** starring Ralph Waite.

259. Smith, Patrick D. **Forever Island**. New York: Norton, 1973. 192p.

Patrick Smith's **Forever Island** is a powerful story told from the point of view of Charlie Jumper, an aging Seminole Indian who has lived in the Big Cypress area of the Everglades for 60 years but now confronts the trauma of being driven out by a housing development built by and for "the white man." There's a foreboding sense throughout that no matter how hard Charlie tries to save his home and way of life, he can't win: He's up against an implacable force that has no use or sympathy for the Charlie Jumpers of the world. For instance, when he tries to negotiate buying the land he always thought he owned with his particular currency (animal hides and the like), Mr. Riles, the white man's agent, explains, "Mr. Jumper, the new owner of that land is not a man; it's a corporation.

I can't speak to a corporation about fish and pelts and snake skins. They'd think I've lost my mind." Note: In 1987 Pineapple Press reprinted **Forever Island** along with another of Smith's Florida novels, *Allapattah*, in its first *Patrick Smith Reader*, which also contains an informative introduction by Edgar W. Hirshberg, a Florida English professor. Originally published by Manor Books in 1979, *Allapattah* (a Seminole word for crocodile) takes place in the Everglades and concerns the difficulties young Seminoles confront in modern Florida.

260. Smith, Patrick D. **A Land Remembered**. Sarasota, FL: Pineapple Pr., 1984. 403p.

Winner of the Florida Historical Society's 1986 Tebeau Prize for the year's "Most Outstanding Florida Historical Novel" and more recently voted "Best Florida Book" by readers of the popular magazine *Florida Monthly* (Sept. 2005, p. 23), Patrick Smith's **A Land Remembered** follows the fortunes of three generations of the MacIvey family, a hardy lot who went from impoverished North Florida backwoods Crackers in the late 1850s to Miami movers and shakers worth millions a century later. Teeming with high-spirited action and robust characters, the saga is dominated by a succession of strong MacIvey patriarchs from Tobias to Zechariah to Solomon—men who personify the panoramic sweep of Florida history from the pioneering days after statehood to the boom period following World War II. The novel ends questioning the deep-rooted assumption among today's Florida business and political elites that rapid growth and development are absolutely necessary for the state's continued well-being. Note: Pineapple Press reports that **A Land Remembered**, now in its 14th hardcover printing, "is truly a book that has succeeded by word of mouth. Readers recommend it to others and its following grows and grows." It is also available in a paperback edition, and in 2001 the publisher issued a two-volume Student Edition. Accompanied by a 64-page Teacher's Manual, the Student Edition is an abridged version of the novel, reformatted and rewritten for young readers ages 9+.

From **A Land Remembered**:
After the war [World War II] it started again, another boom, not as frenzied as the madness of the 1920's but boom nevertheless. MacIvey Development surged forward, dredging and filling, building tract houses with their St. Augustine lawns and transplanted cabbage palms, blocking off the ocean beaches with towering condominiums and gigantic apartment complexes, moving westward into the Everglades from Hollywood and Fort Lauderdale and Pompano and Boca Raton and Lake Worth. Sol was no longer an active part of it, turning the management of the company over to eager young executives he hired; but before he realized what was happening he had created a juggernaut that would not stop until the last swamp was drained, the last tree felled, and the last raccoon left to scrounge scraps from garbage cans or starve.

261. Standiford, Les. **Bone Key**. New York: Putnam, 2002. 329p.
Add the name Les Standiford to South Florida's current crop of first-class crime novelists, a lengthy list headed by Carl Hiaasen, Elmore Leonard, James W. Hall, Edna Buchanan, James Grippando, Laurence Shames, Barbara Parker, Paul Levine, Nancy Pickard, Jonathon King, and Julliane Hoffman. Standiford, director of the creative writing program at Florida International University in Miami, is best known for his mysteries starring building contractor John Deal, a decent fellow who seems incapable of avoiding trouble wherever he goes. The Deal series began in 1993 with *Done Deal* and now includes *Raw Deal* (1994), *Deal to Die For* (1995), *Deal on Ice* (1997), **Presidential Deal** (see entry 262), *Deal with the Dead* (2001), **Bone Key** (2002), and *Havana Run* (2003). **Bone Key** finds Deal, accompanied by his tough-talking crew chief, ex-con Russell Straight, in Key West exploring the possibility of his company, DealCo Construction, getting the contract for a major new development project. Deal isn't in town long when he intervenes in an incident involving police brutality and a young black hustler, Dequarius Noyes, who later winds up dead in Deal's hotel room clutching the label of a very expensive

bottle of vintage wine. Deal investigates, but no one is talking; even an old flame, Annie Dodds, whom he runs into out of the blue, is strangely ambivalent. Resolution of the case turns on Deal's figuring out how Noyes's death is related to the hijacking of a shipment of wine that occurred some 70 years earlier during Prohibition days. "Taut suspense and great atmosphere add up to the real deal" (*BL*, May 1, 2002, pp. 1483-84).

From **Bone Key**:

"I never figured you for a wine drinker," Russell persisted. It was easier to talk, now that the steel band on the open-air porch had packed it in. Their raucous syncopation had been replaced by piped-in piano Muzak. "Anybody'd look at you, they'd say there's a beer drinker and a half."

Deal paused, his glass halfway to his mouth. In truth, he'd been at the checkout counter of Sunset Corners up in Miami, a case of light beer in his cart, when he'd started down this other path. Iron Mike, one of the owners of the package store, caught a glance at what Deal purported to buy and insisted there was a less painful way to drop a few pounds. Mike talked, Deal listened, and the light beer had gone back on the shelf, replaced by a case of Merlot and a pamphlet-sized book on how to shed a few pounds without losing your mind.

The rest had been history, Deal mused, staring down at his glass. A more expensive history. He tasted the wine, then tried another sip. Maybe he *should* have asked for the cork, he thought. "I like beer," he said to Russell. "But then I went on this diet."

262. Standiford, Les. **Presidential Deal**. New York: HarperCollins, 1998. 304p.

In Les Standiford's fifth Deal thriller, South Florida building contractor John Deal is about to receive a presidential medal for saving a boatload of Cuban refugees from drowning in Biscayne Bay when all of a sudden terrorists in police uniforms attack the awards ceremony, killing and wounding some and kidnapping the fetching First Lady and, as fate would have it, Deal himself.

Whisked away and locked up on a remote island in the Bahamas, the two hostages survive a horrendous hurricane and other indignities before being liberated, thanks in large part to the efforts of Vernon Driscoll, a former Miami homicide investigator and Deal's best bud. Once free, Deal tackles the big questions: Who was behind this brazen assault? And what was its real purpose? "There are few mega-surprises here, but the author handles deftly the scenes in which Deal and the First Lady are alone together, offered with a tenderness uncharacteristic of the genre" (*LJ*, May 15, 1998, p. 117). Note: Standiford also writes Florida nonfiction, most notably *Last Train to Paradise: Henry Flagler and the Spectacular Rise and Fall of the Railroad that Crossed an Ocean*, a splendid history of Flagler's misbegotten venture published in 2002 by Crown.

263. Stark, Richard. **Flashfire**. New York: Mysterious Pr., 2000. 288p.

Most readers won't recognize the name Richard Stark, but when they learn it's a pseudonym for talented writer Donald Westlake, interest should immediately zoom. **Flashfire**, a mystery that takes place among the tall condominiums that line South Palm Beach along Florida's Intracoastal Waterway, features the exploits of Parker, an agreeable and seasoned criminal who's appeared in more than 20 Stark novels, most published two or more decades ago. In **Flashfire**, an aggrieved Parker travels to the Sunshine State to retrieve his fair share of the proceeds from a bank robbery, money denied him by dishonorable cohorts. "This is great, dirty fun" (*PW*, Sept. 18, 2000, p. 90).

264. Stevens, Blaine. **The Outlanders**. New York: Jove, 1979. 476p.

Blaine Stevens is a pen name used by Florida-born Harry Whittington (1915-89), a prolific writer of steamy historical novels that draw on actual events and include real public figures. **The Outlanders**, one of Whittington's best efforts, portrays the manly doings of Ward Hamilton, a fictional railroad tycoon operating in post-Civil War Florida. In addition to being tough as old saddle straps, Hamilton possesses a shrewd head for business. For instance, when Governor Marcellus Lovejoy Stearns (who held the office from 1874 to 1877) signed controversial legislation authorizing the leasing of state convicts for use by private companies, Hamilton was among the first to take advantage of this source of ultra-cheap and virtually unregulated labor. The story also contains a fair amount of soft-core passion ("He caught her head in his hands, just above his towering column, her hot, wet breath enflaming his whole body. 'Let me suck it,' she pleaded") as well as the obligatory destructive Florida hurricane that confounds the main characters' best laid plans.

From **The Outlanders**:

In late January, the first freight car departed Tallahassee with a company of prisoners bound to Lake City, to begin work repairing the gradings, creek bridges, roadbeds and railjoints of the New East Florida & Gulf Central Railroad. The editor of the *Ocala Banner* wrote: "This man Hamilton is risking the peace, tranquility, and constitutional rights to security and freedom of all the rest of us in order to harvest the fruits of cheap prison labor. Like so many 'outlanders'—those quick-buck adventurers who invade our lovely homeland seeking fortunes, without that vital obligation to our soil felt by us natives—Hamilton is recklessly thinking only of one thing: profit. The day they set the convicts free in North Florida, at the whim of this Yankee plunderer, may well be the blackest day of infamy in Florida's history."

People stood in sullen silence along the station platforms and trackbeds, watching the first convict train roll slowly east. Each prisoner was wrist-shackled, his chain run through large metal eyebolts embedded in two-by-fours set around the walls. The inmates could sit down on the flooring or stand up, but they had little space to move around, crowded in the cars like cattle.

265. Strasser, Todd. **Against the Odds: Gator Prey**. New York: Pocket Books/Minstrel, 1999. 136p.

A small plane carrying four people—13-year-old Justin; his mother; her boyfriend; and his teenage daughter, Rachel—crashes in the Everglades. The passengers survive but must cope with medical problems, vile weather, and wild beasts, including lurking, beady-eyed alligators. And the teenagers, who had just met and instantly disliked each other, have the added burden of learning tolerance and how to make the best of a horrendous situation. "The fast-paced suspense and Justin and Rachel's developing friendship combine for an engrossing story of survival and getting along with others in times of crisis" (*BL*, Mar. 1, 1999, p. 1214). Readers ages 10+ will find this short novel a rewarding experience.

266. Stuckey-French, Elizabeth. **Mermaids on the Moon**. New York: Doubleday, 2002. 256p.

The central character in this sensitive story of self-discovery is a 38-year-old woman named France who up until the disappearance of her mother, Grendy, had been leading a satisfying life in Indiana working in a by-women-for-women art gallery. But when Grendy, who performs in an underwater mermaid attraction comprised of older women (the "merhags") at fictional Mermaid Springs in Florida, abruptly leaves her job, minister husband (a compulsive womanizer), and autistic grandson (the son of France's deceased sister, Beauvais) with no explanation other than an ambiguous note saying she taking off to "find herself," France drops everything and hurries to Florida to find her mother—and in the process finds herself. "As refreshing, crisp, and tangy as a summer drink, this is a beguiling read" (*LJ*, June 15, 2002, pp. 96-97). Note: **Mermaids on the Moon** is author Elizabeth Stuckey-French's first novel. She teaches creative writing at Florida State University in Tallahassee.

267. Swain, James. **Sucker Bet**. New York: Ballantine, 2003. 304p.

James Swain not only writes action-packed mysteries about the nerve-racking world of big-time gambling, he's an accomplished card handler who knows most if not all the tricks and scams used by "crossroaders" (gambling cheats). His protagonist, Tony Valentine, a former Atlantic City (New Jersey) cop who's relocated to Florida and now works as a consultant specializing in identifying and catching casino con artists, first appeared in *Grift Sense* (2001), followed by encore performances in *Funny Money* (2002), **Sucker Bet** (2003), *Mr. Lucky* (2005), and *Deadman's Poker* (2006). Tony's home base is Florida, but his work takes him to major gambling venues all over the country, such as Atlantic City and Las Vegas. In **Sucker Bet**, arguably the best of the series to date, a fictional Micanopy Indian reservation casino located in the Everglades just west of Miami hires him to track down a crooked blackjack dealer who dealt a player 84 consecutive winning hands before disappearing. Odds are readers will find the pages turning faster than a well-oiled roulette wheel as the plot heats up. "The gambling details are a treat, the banter is worthy of a place at Elmore Leonard's table, and the Floridian sense of absurdity draws on [Carl] Hiaasen without seeming derivative" (*BL*, Mar. 15, 2003, p. 1281).

268. Swarthout, Glendon. **Where the Boys Are**. New York: Random House, 1960. 239p.

**Where the Boys Are** is historically an important Florida novel, not because it's great literature but because it was instrumental in establishing Florida's image—still strong today—as a prime location for American college and high school students to celebrate the rites of spring. In other words, the novel helped create a tourism bonanza that has never stopped giving. Narrated by Merrit, a sweet Midwestern coed who talks directly and candidly to the reader, and set in Fort Lauderdale, the state's first and probably still best known spring break destination, Glendon Swarthout's story contains all the key elements—sun, fun, beaches, tans, alcohol, all-night parties, sex, and freedom, freedom, freedom—that spring break offers young people seeking hedonistic getaways every March and April. Today, the novel remains a fascinating and readable, if campy, artifact of the 1950s. Note: A highly popular film adaptation starring Connie Francis and also titled *Where the Boys Are* came out soon after publication of the book.

From **Where the Boys Are**:
Biologically, they come to Florida to check the talent. By that I mean to inspect and select. When a *Time* reporter asked one girl why she migrated she said because "this is where the boys are." You've seen those movie travelogues of the beaches on the Pribilof Islands up by Alaska where the seals tool in once a year from the Bay of Fundy or someplace to pair off and reproduce. The beach at Lauderdale has a similar function. Not that reproduction occurs, of course, but when you attract thousands of kids to one place there is apt to be a smattering of sexual activity. And the terrific thing is that many of the boys are from the Ivy League: Harvard, Princeton, Yale, etc. A lot of them go to Bermuda and Nassau to snob around with girls from Eastern schools but the intelligent ones, having heard about Midwestern girls, tear down here to see if it's true. So if you are a girl and want to meet the authentic Ivy League article; and who doesn't; Lauderdale is where to go.

269. Sweeney, Joyce. **Free Fall**. New York: Delacorte, 1996. 228p.

Four adventuresome teenage boys become lost in an underground cave in the Ocala National Forest in Central Florida. As their ordeal drags on and desperation mounts, festering conflicts among the youngsters surface, adding a tense interpersonal dynamic to the story. "Sweeney mixes excitement with finely crafted characters and credible psychological underpinnings to deliver a powerful punch" (*BL*, July 1996, p. 1819). **Free Fall** is aimed mainly at young readers (ages 12+), but adults interested in a good story will also find the book satisfying. Note: Joyce Sweeney's first book, *Center Line*, published in 1984 and partially set in Florida, won the Delacorte Press Prize for the year's outstanding first YA novel.

270. Thompson, Maurice. **A Tallahassee Girl**. Boston: Houghton Mifflin, 1881. 355p.

In its day **A Tallahassee Girl**, a novel that takes place in and around Florida's capital city during the post-Civil War

Reconstruction period, was both a commercial success, selling well throughout the country, and a source of pride among residents of Florida, then a largely undeveloped state with a small population of 325,000. The book's narrative focuses on Miss Lucie La Rue, daughter of a prominent judge who lived "like a lord" before the war but suffered financial hardship after the defeat of the Confederacy and the end of slavery. Lucie—described as "the handsomest, loveliest, most noteworthy girl in Florida"—is of course the Tallahassee girl, "a charmer [who] sings like a mocking-bird in May" and whose hand is eagerly sought by suitors. The author, Maurice Thompson (1844-1901), a prominent 19th-century writer, lawyer, and politician, based the story on a visit to Tallahassee, which included social calls on fellow writer Ellen Call Long, then in the process of completing her polemical novel, **Florida Breezes** (see entry 166). Long's beautiful daughter, "Nonie," is thought to have been Thompson's inspiration for Lucie; another prominent character in the book, Lawrence Cauthorne, a writer, appears to be a version of Thompson himself. **The Tallahassee Girl** also contains numerous firsthand descriptions and observations that furnish valuable insights into Florida's cultural, political, and economic circumstances during Reconstruction. Note: Thompson's novel has long been out-of-print and only a limited number of copies are available via interlibrary loan or the secondhand book trade. The hope is the book will eventually be reprinted by the University Press of Florida, Florida Classics Library, or similar publisher with a strong interest in Florida history and literature.

From **The Tallahassee Girl**:

The city of Tallahassee is not very old. Its site was chosen by the territorial commissioners in 1823. The Capitol, a stuccoed brick building fronting both east and west with a heavy-columned portico, was built some time after. In obedience to a social law in force in the South, a number of very wealthy and highly educated families drew together around this prospective urban centre; and at the time of the breaking-out of the war of Rebellion, the little city had spread itself over the crown and down the embowered slopes of Capitol Hill, overlooking a region at once the most fertile, the most picturesque, and the most salubrious to be found south of the North Carolina mountains.

271. Tracy, Donald. **The Hated One**. New York: Simon & Schuster/Trident Pr., 1963. 189p.

In 1952 the town of Live Oak, then a rigidly segregated community in North Florida, was the scene of a sensational real-life murder case in which an affluent "Negress," Ruby McCollum, shot and killed her lover, a prominent Caucasian doctor and local politician. McCollum's trial—a travesty of justice in Jim Crow Florida—received national attention, including reportage by Florida's foremost African-American writer of the day, Zora Neale Hurston (see entries 121-123). Inspired by the McCollum saga, Don Tracy's novel concerns a disgraced alcoholic white lawyer, Frank Coombs, who returns to his hometown in fictional Tangerine County in North Florida to defend a "no-count nigra girl," Coralee Preston, accused of an interracial murder in the 1950s. The case seems open and shut against Coralee, and Coombs, the story's narrator, is vilified by the town's bigoted white citizenry, but in the end a kind of raw justice prevails. Filled with unrelenting tension, bolstered by a flawed but persevering hero, and written in the convincing style of someone who's been there, this noir thriller has all the hallmarks of a modern crime classic. Note: Originally published in 1963, **The Hated One** has recently been reprinted in its entirety in **Orange Pulp: Stories of Mayhem, Murder, and Mystery** (see entry 209). Note also: William Bradford Huie wrote a nonfiction account of the McCollum case, *Ruby McCollum: Woman in the Suwannee Jail* (Dutton, 1956), that was heavily censored at the time in Florida; in 1964 New American Library reissued the book in a paperback edition.

From **The Hated One**:

I certainly hadn't forgotten that Tangerine County, North Florida, could be hot in September. But until I hit the palmetto and scrub pine stretch that flattened out beyond the Suwannee I didn't remember just how blazing, dizzying, sweat-soaking hot it really was.

I'd been away in the north for eight years and perhaps my blood really had thickened in spite of the doctors' pooh-poohs about such things. Or maybe it was the hangover that made the heat close in on me, smother me, even though I kept the old Ford at sixty-five over the straight, flat country road.

The drinks I'd had that morning had long since faded away. There was the need for another and I called myself a damned fool for not getting a pint at one of the liquor stores clustered close to the Georgia-Florida line, just over the St. Mary's River. After all, what difference did it make whether or not Frank Coombs came back to his old home town half in the bag?

272. Tremayne, Peter. **Swamp**. London, England: Sphere Books, 1985. 185p.

The titular "swamp" in Peter Tremayne's horror tale turns out to be the Everglades National Park, Florida's massive 1.5 million-acre wetland. Deep in this watery wilderness lurks Tremayne's main character, a giant reptile capable of knocking down small buildings with a flick of its tail and incapable of being stopped by mere bullets; as one character observes, "Even a bazooka might not harm that thing." Some traumatic event—which the reader learns about only at the end of the story—has caused this normally reclusive creature to leave its lair and seek out and kill humans with terrifying savagery. Park ranger Pete Pirelli and Native American tracker Miccosukee Mike lead the hunt for the rampaging beast, and eventually there's a man-versus-monster showdown in a far-off Glades ghost town, a confrontation complicated by a devastating hurricane that just happens to be roaring across the area at the time. Note: British author Tremayne, probably best known for his Sister Fidelma mystery series set in the 7th century, has written a number of tantalizing potboilers about scary creatures, from zombies and vampires to the swamp thing in this book. Note also: In 1993 **Swamp** was reprinted and distributed in the U.S. by Severn House, a publisher in Sutton, England.

From **Swamp**:

Summoning courage, Pirelli moved forward into the gloom.

The smell was vile; unutterable. He felt he wanted to retch but fought down the impulse. He moved forward a few more steps into the gloom and then, taking his courage in both hands, he switched on the torch [flashlight], sweeping it quickly around. The passing of his beam did not reveal any menacing creature inside.

Calming the swift beat of his heart, Pirelli now gave a more leisurely sweep around. The cavern must have been thirty feet high and perhaps the same in length and width, giving the impression of a square cave. There were certainly signs of recent habitation. Bones and decaying vegetation strewn across the floor.

"It's all right, Mike," called the ranger softly. "There's nothing in here."

Miccosukee Mike followed him in and peered around in the gloom.

"Shine your torch across there," he instructed quietly.

Pirelli did so.

The stabbing beam revealed five curious egg shapes. The two men, hands over their noses to act as filters to the loathsome odours, walked across. The shapes were almost three feet in length, were cracked and broken. A mucus-like liquid spilled from them.

273. Trocheck, Kathy Hogan. **Crash Course**. New York: Harper Collins, 1997. 256p.

Truman Kicklighter, a retired reporter who first appeared in the author's *Lickety-Split* (1996), finds life at the Fountain of Youth Residential Hotel in St. Petersburg, Florida, dull, so he's never happier than when there's a mystery he can poke his curious nose into. In this instance the case involves Jackie, a black waitress at the hotel who buys a secondhand Corvette that turns out to be a lemon and, when she complains, the car is stolen and her unctuous car salesman turns up dead—in the vehicle. Naturally Kicklighter snoops around and, with help from Jackie and a newsstand dwarf named Ollie, uncovers criminal activity galore. "Although the book is set in Florida heat and Highway 19 congestion, Trocheck . . .

keeps readers cool with lively wit, memorable characters, and cutting prose. A great read" (*LJ*, Mar. 1, 1997, p. 106).

274. Troop, Alan F. **The Dragon DelaSangre**. New York: NAL/ Roc, 2002. 304p.

Fantasy fiction doesn't get much more fanciful than Alan Troop's unusual yarn, a monster novel that will appeal to both adult and young adult devotees of the genre. Peter DelaSangre and his father—a pair of dragons living on an island off the coast of Florida—are able to assume human form and together they operate a thriving business on the mainland. In addition, they eat people, though discreetly, not wanting to call attention to themselves or their lifestyle. After his father dies, Peter sniffs out, courts, and marries Elizabeth, a lovely lady dragon, but human enemies constantly threaten the couple's well-being. "An exciting, inventive, unique novel with, in Peter, a surprisingly sympathetic protagonist" (*BL*, Mar. 1, 2002, p. 1099). Note: Sequels to **The Dragon DelaSangre** include *Dragon Moon* (2003) and *The Seadragon's Daughter* (2004).

275. Truluck, Bob. **Street Level**. New York: St. Martin's/Thomas Dunne, 2000. 217p.

Winner of the Best First Private Eye Novel of 1999 (an award sponsored by Private Eye Writers of America and St. Martin's Press), Bob Truluck's **Street Level** is a hard-boiled tale of extortion and murder that mostly takes place in less desirable neighborhoods of Orlando, Florida. It begins when Isaac Pike, a wealthy homosexual, decides life simply won't be complete unless he becomes a father. Toward that end he deposits a dollop of his semen at a fertility clinic, so it's readily available when he finds the right woman to bear his heir via artificial insemination. The plan goes awry, however, when Pike's semen is stolen and the thief and some of his cohorts claim to have used it to impregnate a teenage topless dancer, Crystal Johnson, who shakes her boobies in a downscale Orlando bar. The bad guys contact Pike, threatening to abort the fetus—his child!—unless he comes across with a bundle of cash. Pike responds by hiring Duncan Sloan, a flippant, foulmouthed, not terribly competent gumshoe to locate and rescue Crystal. At first Sloan turns down the job as too difficult: All that's known about the young lady is that she's Caucasian, is probably in the Orlando area, might be pregnant, and has a tattoo of an eyeball on her backside—or, as Sloan puts it, "just another white girl with ink on her ass." But soon he relents and accepts the case, which heats up when Crystal's parents are murdered. "Uncharacteristic descriptions, dry humor, and Orlando setting add more spice to the mix. Exciting and adventurous" (*LJ*, Aug. 2000, p. 165). Note: Truluck's second Duncan Sloan thriller, *Saw Red* (2003), is also recommended for Florida crime fiction aficionados.

276. Updike, John. **Rabbit at Rest**. New York: Knopf, 1990. 544p.

Over a period of 30 years, from 1960 to 1990, John Updike, one of the truly great writers of our time, produced a remarkable quartet of linked novels—*Rabbit Run* (1960), *Rabbit Redux* (1971), *Rabbit is Rich* (1981), and **Rabbit at Rest** (1990)—that beam an intense light on the life of one Harry "Rabbit" Angstrom, a much flawed but always stimulating 20th-century middle-class American hero. **Rabbit at Rest**, which opens during the winter of 1989, finds Rabbit on Florida's southern Gulf Coast where he and wife Janice have recently acquired a condo and become "snowbirds"—northerners who flock to the Sunshine State for five or six months every year to escape the cold, snow, and ice. He's now 55, semi-retired, conspicuously overweight, an angina sufferer, and has death on his mind: "Standing amid the tan, excited post-Christmas crowd at the Southwest Florida Regional Airport, Rabbit Angstrom has a funny feeling that what he has come to meet, what's floating in unseen about to land, is not his son Nelson and daughter-in-law Pru and their two children but something more ominous and intimately his: his own death, shaped vaguely like an airplane. The sensation chills him, above and beyond the terminal air-conditioning." For the most part Rabbit views Florida as a "mass-produced paradise," a distasteful, superficial place "full of big white soupy power-steered American cars being driven by old people so shrunken they can hardly see over the hood." Only about a third of **Rabbit at Rest** takes place in Florida, but in those roughly 200 pages Updike provides a brilliant portrait of the state as seen through the jaded eyes of Rabbit Angstrom. **Rabbit at Rest** won the 1991 Pulitzer Prize for fiction and has been correctly called "the saddest and deepest of the 'Rabbit' novels" (*LJ*, Oct. 1, 1990, p. 118). Note: It's not absolutely necessary to have read the earlier books to appreciate **Rabbit at Rest**. On the other hand, anyone will be the poorer for not having read them all.

277. Van Wert, William. **What's It All About?: A Novel of Life, Love, & Key Lime Pie**. New York: Simon & Schuster, 1996. 247p.

This humorous and often wise book lacks much of a plot. Rather, it's mostly a compilation of entertaining pronouncements and observations uttered by 79-year-old raconteur Hiram Walker, a randy widower who's president of a mobile home park association in Bonita Springs, just north of Naples on Florida's Gulf coast. Old Hiram thinks he knows it all and loves to pontificate about everything, from religion to food to the reading habits of Americans to how to be successful in business in his adopted state: "It don't take a lot of brains to make a good living in Florida. Florida has her fair share of fools. It just takes a certain amount of cussedness, keeping the wheels greased here and there, and sometimes putting the quietus on a busybody or two." As might be expected, Hiram runs his park, populated entirely by seniors, with an iron hand, though his rules and methods are constantly being challenged by Cyrus Applebee, a retired lawyer. And sometimes the park's contrary widow ladies Hiram courts give him fits. "This is an uproarious book about aging and living" (*LJ*, Apr. 1, 1997, p. 156).

278. Veciana-Suarez, Ana. **The Chin Kiss King**. New York: Farrar, Straus & Giroux, 1997. 311p.

Based on an experience close to the author, this emotionally rich novel relates how three generations of Cuban-American women living in a cramped Miami duplex—Cuca (the matriarch), Adela (Cuca's daughter), and Maribel (Adela's daughter)—come together to minister to the first member of the family's fourth generation, Maribel's infant son, Victor Eduardo, born with severe birth defects. All the men involved have either died or absconded; only the women are there for the dying child. A talented writer, Ana Veciana-Suarez has been praised in a review of **The Chin Kiss King,** her first novel, for having "an ear for the intonations of bilingual speech and an eye for bicultural nuance" (*PW*, June 2, 1997, p. 49). More recently Veciana-Suarez wrote *Flight to Freedom* (2002), a fictionalized story for young adults about a girl like herself leaving Cuba for a new life in Miami.

279. Watson, Sterling. **Deadly Sweet.** New York: Pocket Books, 1994. 373p.

The backstory that informs this tense ecological thriller is the accusation that for years South Florida's very big and very profitable sugar industry has been polluting the area's lakes and wetlands, including the Everglades. Set partly in a prominent sugar town closely resembling Clewiston (located in Hendry County on the southern edge of Lake Okeechobee), the plot centers on bringing to justice the person or persons who killed Corey Darrow, a young, idealistic environmentalist and thorn in the side of powerful sugarcane grower Lofton Coltis. Corey's sister, Sawnie, asks Eddie Priest, an ex-attorney and ex-drunk who now sells boats in the Gulf Coast city of St. Petersburg, to get involved in the investigation: Not only did Eddie once practice environmental law, he had romantic feelings for Corey; and, as fate would have it, she was murdered just after leaving his place. A likely suspect—Harry W. Feather, a malevolent Native American who works for Lofton Coltis—is quickly identified, but proving his guilt and motivation is another matter. "Finely crafted characters, places, and events all bring a present-day Florida to life—with an added hint or two of Southern decadence" (*LJ*, Sept. 1, 1994, p. 219). Note: Author Sterling Watson, who's taught literature and creative writing at Eckerd College (in St. Petersburg) for a number of years, currently has five novels to his credit, all with Florida locales but quite different issues and themes. In addition to **Deadly Sweet,** they are **Weep No More My Brother** (see entry 280), *The Calling* (1986), *Blind Tongues* (1989), and *Sweet Dream Baby* (2002).

280. Watson, Sterling. **Weep No More My Brother.** New York: Morrow, 1978. 300p.

No sooner had Farel "Fare" Odum received his Ph.D. in English literature from the University of Florida than he learns that the man who murdered his beloved brother, Charles Ed, was about to be incarcerated in Union Correctional Institution, the old Florida State Prison at Raiford in North Florida. Fare immediately applies for and gets a job teaching convicts at the prison, the idea being to place himself in a position to avenge his brother's death. Of course the best laid plans don't always yield the desired results and in Fare's case they go horrendously awry, sparking unanticipated chaos, violence, and personal anguish. A powerful writer, Sterling Watson offers a sensitive, gut-wrenching depiction of the men and conditions at the Raiford prison. "Watson's novel is taut, hard, [and] imaginative as it provides a portrait of prison and of a man who willfully becomes enmeshed in its life and its psychology" (*PW*, Apr. 10, 1978, p. 67).

From **Weep No More My Brother:**

It was cold outside. The bonfires, four of them, beckoned. Fare remembered that there had been the madness, then the merriment. Now, as he surveyed the yard, strewn with broken chairs, clothing, plastic crockery, gutted mattresses, flattened basketballs, piles of books from the library, it looked as though madness had given way to despair. As he stood on the ramp before descending to the yard, he glanced to his left and right, up and down the sides of the building. Not far away, in the shadows to his left, a man squatted, shitting. Beyond him, within the stink of him, three men pushed another to the wall. The victim was a young man, whose head lolled. A crude bandage covered an enormous lump at his temple. One of them held a knife to his throat. The man with the knife poked it upward once, twice, and Fare could see in the darkness that the young man tried by clawing with his hands at the wall to raise himself upward from the knife. The other two men stood on either side. The squatting man said, "Let him down a little." The blade lowered slightly, and the boy whimpered, catching his breath. They began to remove his clothing. The man who had been relieving himself stood, glanced at Fare, turning his head half-around without moving his shoulders, buckled his trousers and walked over to join the others.

Fare walked toward the fires. He looked back once. They were over the boy, one of them giving up the knife to another. He saw the white flash of pumping buttocks in the darkness.

281. Weaver, Beth Nixon. **Rooster**. Delray Beach, FL: Winslow, 2001. 308p.

An outstanding first novel written mainly for YA readers (ages 12+) but also of interest to adults seeking an engrossing story, **Rooster** takes place in rural Central Florida during the turbulent 1960s when sexual freedom, rock music, and recreational drugs became hallmarks of America's youth culture. The narrator, Kady Palmer, 15, yearns to have wealth, celebrity, popularity, and a splendid mansion to live in. Instead, her family is dirt-poor and can only afford a small, cramped house—Kady calls it a "hovel"—in a citrus grove where her father is trying to grow orange trees. Kady's dream of moving up socially suddenly seems possible when she meets Jon, an affluent teen from across the lake who quickly becomes her best beau, enticing her with expensive gifts and marijuana parties with his hip friends. All goes swimmingly until one evening a brain-damaged youngster nicknamed Rooster who lives next door to Kady and idolizes her surreptitiously follows her to one of Jon's parties, where he eats a brownie laced with pot, climbs a tree, and tries to fly—a misadventure that has serious consequences for both Rooster and Kady. Note: The book was reprinted in a paperback edition in 2005.

282. Wetlaufer, Suzy. **Judgment Call**. New York: Morrow, 1992. 431p.

Eager for her "big break," beautiful young Miami newspaper reporter Sherry Estabrook finds herself the leading lady in a heart-stopping serial murder case in this fine first novel. "Poor judgment is the leitmotif of the book. Sherry's is evident in everything she does, from choosing boyfriends to harassing her nasty neighbors, but her worst offense is to trust a 16-year-old assassin" (*BL*, Apr. 15, 1992, p. 1484). Suzy Wetlaufer, a former *Miami Herald* reporter, covers much the same criminal territory as Edna Buchanan (see entries 24-26) and John Katzenbach (see entries 136-137), both of whom also once worked for the *Herald*.

From **Judgment Call**:

"Hey, wait a minute!" Sherry cut him off. She was taking one last look at the corpse, and suddenly she noticed something she hadn't seen during her initial once-over. There were four slender lines—cuts, actually, as if they'd been made with a paring knife or an ice pick—carved into the dead man's forehead. "Hey, wait a minute," she repeated. "Hey, Teddy, you see those marks in the victim's forehead? You see what I'm talking about?" She stooped down and gestured with her pen.

Wasynczuk took a quick look around to make sure none of his superiors had made it to the scene to catch him fraternizing with the enemy. None had—this hit was small time—and then he knelt down to check out Sherry Estabrook's odd observation. And in fact, she was right. The guy's forehead was sliced up, not too badly, but enough that it was obvious the killer was trying to leave his mark.

"Looks like we got a regular Zorro at work," he moaned. "I'm telling you, Sherry, they get more ballsy every day."

283. White, Randy Wayne. **Everglades**. New York: Putnam, 2003. 340p.

In **Everglades**, Marion "Doc" Ford, an introspective marine biologist and former U.S. intelligence operative living in a stilt house in a snug marina on Sanibel Island on Florida's southern Gulf Coast, makes his tenth appearance as Randy Wayne White's durable series hero. As the story opens Doc, a big man who's been drinking heavily (to quiet his demons), is woefully out of shape but nevertheless responds with dispatch to a request for help from an ex-lover, Sally Minster, whose wealthy developer husband has come a cropper in the Everglades while working for a religious cult headed by a charismatic albeit treacherous guru named Bhagwan Shiva: It seems the Bhagwan has an elaborate scheme cooking to con a small Indian tribe out of its land. As usual, Doc's hippy sidekick, Tomlinson, tags along, adding a mystical touch of Zen to the proceedings. Not only is the novel a ripping good mystery, it convincingly captures the Glade's steamy atmosphere and offers a trove of fascinating lore about that exotic area of Florida. In addition, readers will appreciate how deftly White manages to convey Doc Ford's complex persona, which includes both a savage psyche and a tender soul.

284. White, Randy Wayne. **The Man Who Invented Florida**. New York: St. Martin's/Thomas Dunne, 1993. 304p.

This third Marion "Doc" Ford novel—*Sanibel Flats* (1990) and *The Heat Islands* (1992) introduced Randy Wayne White's series character—focuses on Doc's uncle, Tucker Gatrell, a boastful old coot who swears he's discovered Florida's true Fountain of Youth. The state has had several, all bogus, but Uncle Tuck insists his fountain, a sulfur spring gurgling up from a pre-Columbian Indian mound on the edge of the Everglades, is the real thing. Why is he so certain? Because its restorative waters, he says, have caused his gelded horse to grow brand-new testicles! Doc reluctantly gets involved when two government agents and a TV fishing personality disappear in the mangrove swamps of Southwest Florida, but it's Tuck and his Indian pal, Joseph Egret, who dominate the story, which turns on the issue of ownership of the land where the reputed miraculous fountain is located. "White offers an eclectic vision of Florida with his laid-back prose but pays close attention to various 'characters,' especially Marion's braggart uncle. Upbeat, literate, fascinating, and clever: manna for deeper readers" (*LJ*, Nov. 1, 1993, p. 151).

285. White, Randy Wayne. **Ten Thousand Islands**. New York: Putnam, 2000. 336p.

Recently some critics have suggested Randy Wayne White belongs in the same company as John D. MacDonald, the undisputed grand master of Florida mystery writers (see entries 171-174). It's too soon of course to know where White will eventually end up in Florida's literary pantheon, but there's no question he's already made a powerful impression with his succession of intellectually rewarding Doc Ford thrillers, which got off to a rousing start in 1990 with *Sanibel Flats*. Subsequent titles include *The Heat Islands* (1992), **The Man Who Invented Florida** (see entry 284), *Captiva* (1996), *North of Havana* (1997), *The Mangrove Coast* (1998), **Ten Thousand Islands** (2000), *Shark River* (2001), *Twelve Mile Limit* (2002), **Everglades** (see entry 283), *Tampa Burn* (2004), *Dead of Night* (2005), and *Dark Light* (2006). A case can be made that the best of these is **Ten Thousand Islands**, a terrific story that seamlessly interweaves early Florida Native-American history with the all-too-frequent contemporary crime of desecrating and looting ancient archaeological sites. The tale, which takes place mostly on Marco Island and environs in the Ten Thousand Islands region of Southwest Florida, has plenty of action; for instance, at one point Doc punishes an evildoer by nearly ripping off one of his ears: "People don't realize how tenuously the human ear is attached to the head. I gave Derrick a painful demonstration." But White's main concern here, as in all the Doc Ford novels, is the Sisyphean search for human motivations and morality. "Former CIA agent Ford is a reluctant warrior who, once engaged, goes after the bad guys with a lethal mix of tradecraft and righteous indignation. Both are cranked into overdrive in this satisfying straight-ahead thriller, nicely overlaid with the reverberations of prehistory" (*BL*, May 1, 2000, pp. 1625-26).

From **Ten Thousand Islands:**

Marco Island is a community of block-and-stucco, landscaped lots, fairways and beach condos, everything laid out as symmetrically as a Midwestern community college. It illustrates the tidy Toledo-by-the-Sea approach to development that has become the template of modern Florida. The effect is all the more striking because Marco lies several miles deep into the confluence of a great saw grass and mangrove wilderness.

Until the mid-sixties, Marco was a fishing and clamming village. Enter three brothers, the Mackles [see entry 176], who decided to work a classic Florida finesse, but on a grand scale: presell lots to snow-weary northerners and use the cash to finance the infrastructure of an entire city; a city that had yet to be built.

For months, the Mackles ran ads in major newspapers touting a new golf and retirement resort in the Ten Thousand Islands. It was billed as a world-class facility even though no facilities existed. What did exist were artists' renderings and little diorama cities that real estate agents flogged at high-pressure sales "parties" that promised free trips to Florida.

The gambit worked. It's easy to push sunshine in The Great Gray North. They sold millions in raw property and used the profit to build precisely what they had promised, including a mazework of canals to create more "waterfront" lots.

The result? Marco was an environmentalist's nightmare, but a triumph of business ingenuity.

286. White, Robb. **The Lion's Paw.** New York: Doubleday, 1946. 251p.

A juvenile classic that many adults remember reading and loving when they were in grade school, **The Lion's Paw** relates the adventures of three spunky runaway children who traverse Central Florida in a small sailboat called the *Lion's Paw*. Traveling from east to west through rivers, canals, and lakes with the final destination Captiva Island off Florida's Gulf Coast, the youngsters—Ben, 15, who's searching for his father; and Penny, 13, and her brother Nick,

9, escapees from an orphanage—must deal with situations "that might daunt many grown-ups" (*LJ*, Jan. 1, 1947, p. 85). Author Robb White (1904-93), a graduate of the U.S. Naval Academy at Annapolis, wrote a number of other novels featuring courageous characters and daring exploits but none has achieved the lasting popularity of **The Lion's Paw**. Note: Ralph Ray's full-page illustrations nicely enhance the printed text. Note also: Mickler House Publishers (in Chuluota, Florida) reprinted the novel in 1983; however, the book is no longer in print, nor is it widely available in libraries in either the original or reprint edition, and copies on the secondhand book market tend to be quite expensive. A new, reasonably priced reprint edition would be most welcome and should do well in the marketplace.

From **The Lion's Paw**:

The alligator appeared suddenly right astern. It came whooshing up through the muddy water, and as it broke the surface it opened its jaws and came for the dinghy.

To Nick it seemed that everything stopped moving except the rushing jaws of the 'gator. The creek, the woods, the sky were silent, and the sunlight made everything crystal-clear. He saw muddy water in the bottom of the dinghy. He saw his little alligator lying motionless but still grunting on the yellow, varnished blade of one of the oars. He saw a turtle, its shell glossy, sitting on a log.

He saw the teeth of the alligator's upper jaw and saw a silver drop of water fall from one of them. The inside of the thing's mouth was soft-looking and dead white and wet and it hung in smooth folds from the top jaw, sagged in the bottom of the mouth. Back where the throat was the white, folding flesh looked as though it were puckered up a little, closing the throat. Muddy water swirled slowly around the lower front teeth.

The gaping jaws seemed to grow bigger and bigger as they swam straight toward him. To Nick the white, tooth-ringed mouth seemed to be huge, engulfing everything.

For long seconds Nick squatted perfectly still in the bilges of the dinghy as the jaws slid swiftly toward him. He couldn't breathe; he couldn't move a muscle as he stared at the jaws.

Then everything broke apart like an explosion.

287. Wilder, Robert. **Flamingo Road**. New York: Putnam, 1942. 342p.

An epic soap opera of a novel that's as compulsively enjoyable today as it was when first published more than 60 years ago, **Flamingo Road** is the haunting story of pre-World War II love, lust, greed, and corruption in the mythical Florida city of Truro, reputedly modeled on DeLand, seat of Volusia County located northeast of Orlando. Readers quickly get to know the main players: Handsome but morally irresolute Field Carlisle; lovely Lane Ballou, a saintly prostitute who craves respectability and in particular a residence on upscale Flamingo Road; unscrupulous, nasty, "elephantine" Sheriff Titus Semple, the local political Svengali; bosomy Lute-Mae Sanders, whose hospitable brothel does a booming business servicing some of Florida's finest gentlemen; and Dan Curtis, Lane's sugar daddy. Robert Wilder's easy style is distinguished by realistic dialogue and pitch-perfect figures of speech, as in "If Lute-Mae Sanders ever opened her mouth, honey, this county and most of the state would split open like a dropped watermelon." Note: A film version of **Flamingo Road** starring Joan Crawford appeared in 1949, and later the novel inspired a successful TV series with Morgan Fairchild in the lead role.

From **Flamingo Road**:

"You're acting like a child." Even as she spoke Lane was thinking Dan ought to know that Titus's plans were changed. For one reason or another the Sheriff had decided Field wasn't strong enough to carry a campaign. "Truro's your home, people like you. Titus isn't everything."

"He is when you're in my shoes."

"Well, then, you've been wearing them too long." She was incensed at the whining note in his voice. Remembering how he once had been, confident, unafraid, she almost shuddered. "What's happened to you, Field? Where have you gone?"

She realized immediately this was a mistake. He wanted to be sorry for himself, openly with abused explanation. His body sagged helplessly.

"He kicked me out like I was a stray dog. After all I've done."
Lane couldn't control her feelings. "You haven't done anything.
For years Titus Semple has been carrying you around. You've let
him make you soft, fat, and frightened. Tell him to go to hell, find
something to do if you don't want to stay in politics. This is your
town as much as his. Fight him for a piece of it."

There was an indefinite sneer around his lips. "Sure, it's easy
enough for you to say." He glanced around the room. "You've done
all right, haven't you? From Lute-Mae's to Flamingo Road on your
behind." He laughed slobberingly.

288. Wilder, Robert. **God Has a Long Face**. New York: Putnam,
1940. 461p.

Robert Wilder (1901-74), a bestselling novelist from the 1940s
through the 1960s, is regrettably no longer in favor with the reading
public, though much of his fiction remains as fresh and cogent as
that produced by some of today's most popular storytellers. Wilder
grew up in Daytona Beach and a number of his novels take place
in Florida, including **Flamingo Road** (see entry 287) and several
historical novels that trace the state's progress from the pioneering
days of the 19th century to its emergence as a tourist and retirement
mecca in the 20th century. **God Has a Long Face,** chronologically
the second book in this trilogy, recounts the exploits of the Burgoyne
family, led by "General" Basil Wallis Burgoyne, a tall, vigorous,
unlettered but enormously shrewd native of Cincinnati, Ohio, who
after the Civil War determined that he and his progeny would play
a key role in the development of Florida, then a sparsely populated
state rich in land and natural resources. "The reader who began by
marveling at the General, and only half believing in him, will be
surprised to find before the story is done that he has developed an
honest regard for the tough, blustering, kind-hearted, disappointed
old rascal" (*NYTBR*, Nov. 17, 1940, p. 6). Other titles in Wilder's
historical trilogy are *Bright Feather* (1948), an honest depiction
of the vicious conflict between Florida's white settlers and Native
Americans during the Second Seminole War (1835-42), and **The
Sea and the Stars** (see entry 289).

289. Wilder, Robert. **The Sea and the Stars**. New York: Putnam, 1967. 382p.

This novel completes Robert Wilder's trilogy dealing with Florida's history from pre-statehood to modern times (see entry 288 for descriptions of the other two titles, **God Has a Long Face** and *Bright Feather*). **The Sea and the Stars** chronicles the life and loves of business tycoon Stoddard "Tod" Lathrop, whose grandfather originally brought the Lathrops to Florida from Rochester, New York, at the beginning of the 20th century. Using a combination of fact and fiction, Wilder vividly describes the state's boom-and-bust economy during the turbulent 1920s, 1930s, and 1940s, and how during that time Tod Lathrop got rich as a real estate entrepreneur with a visionary eye for commercial development on a grand scale. "The story is partly autobiographical (Mr. Wilder, like Lathrop, came to Florida as a boy), partly historical, and partly fictional, and despite its lack of a formal plot, holds the reader's interest to the end" (*LJ*, Apr. 1, 1967, p. 1513).

290. Willeford, Charles. **Miami Blues**. New York: St. Martin's, 1984. 192p.

Though now acknowledged as "one of America's best noir mystery novelists" (*PW*, Jan. 1, 1996, p. 36), Arkansas-born Charles Willeford (1919-88) spent a large chunk of his writing career toiling in the literary lower depths, churning out book reviews and cheap paperback potboilers, some—for example, *Whip Hand* (1961)—happily published under a pseudonym. Willeford grew up in California, joined the army at 16 where he spent the next 20 years, and after leaving the service moved to Florida, settling in South Miami. Not until **Miami Blues** appeared in 1984 did he begin to be recognized as a master of the hard-boiled crime story. That novel—a compelling thriller about a psychopathic South Florida thief and murderer (Junior Frenger), a gullible hooker (Susie Waggoner), and a vulnerable but determined Miami homicide cop (Hoke Moseley) whose paths intersect with grievous consequences—was quickly followed by three others featuring the gritty Hoke Moseley character: *New Hope for the Dead* (1985), *Sideswipe* (1987), and **The**

**Way We Die Now** (see entry 292). Note: **Miami Blues** has been reprinted a number of times, most recently in 2004. Note also: A highly successful film adaptation of the novel was released in 1990 with Alec Baldwin, Jennifer Jason Leigh, and Fred Ward in the principal roles.

291. Willeford, Charles. **The Shark-Infested Custard**. Lancaster, PA: Underwood-Miller, 1993. 272p.

Four bachelors living banal lives in a Miami singles-only apartment complex become good buddies, but the strength of their casual friendship is sorely tested one night when one of the men, on a bet, brings home a 14-year-old street girl along with her drug dealer. All's cool—until the girl suddenly dies of an overdose and in the ensuing chaos the dealer is killed. Morally vacuous, the panic-stricken guys dump both bodies in the victims' car and leave it in a nearby parking lot, after which they return to their building to concoct a cover-up story about where they were that night. "Some readers are sure to be offended by the socially unredeemable nature of this story, but others will admire Willeford's refusal to compromise. Up close, emptiness is always offensive" (*BL*, Apr. 15, 1993, p. 1499). Note: Though published after Willeford's death in 1988, **The Shark-Infested Custard** was written in the 1970s and is an amalgam of two works: A short story called "Strange" that originally appeared in *Everybody's Metamorphosis* (1988), a limited edition collection of stories privately published by Dennis McMillan; and a novel entitled *Kiss Your Ass Goodbye* (1987), also published by McMillan in an edition limited to 442 hardbound copies. Note also: **The Shark-Infested Custard** has recently been reprinted in paperback by Dell.

292. Willeford, Charles. **The Way We Die Now**. New York: Random House, 1988. 245p.

**The Way We Die Now**—Charles Willeford's fourth and final Hoke Moseley novel (see entry 290 for information about the series)—ironically appeared just before the author's own death. It finds Hoke, Willeford's memorable Miami homicide detective, undercover in Immokalee, a rough, rural town in Southwest Florida widely known as a major agricultural center, especially for tomatoes and watermelons. Immokalee naturally has a large, constantly shifting population of poor migrant farmworkers, and in **The Way We Die Now** a brutish grower is suspected of using illegal immigrants from Haiti and keeping them in virtual slavery until, when too old or sick to work, they are killed and discarded like any other worn-out farm animal. Posing as a down-and-out drifter (made easier due to the loss of his dentures), Hoke sets out to gather evidence and eventually bring a callous murderer to justice. "A snake-mean slice of South Florida lowlife" (*Time*, Aug. 8, 1988, p. 74). Note: A new paperback edition of the novel was published in 2005 by Vintage Crime.

From **The Way We Die Now**:

It had been at least eight years since Hoke had been in Immokalee, driving through without stopping on a trip to Fort Myers, but he didn't think the little town had changed much. There was a fresh coat of oil on the main drag, and he didn't remember the stoplight's being there at the dogleg into Bonita Springs. But the buildings were just as ancient, and there was a fine layer of dust over everything. Hoke walked to the nearest gas station and asked the attendant, a teenager wearing a white "Mr. Goodwrench" shirt, for the key to the men's room.

"Hell, you know better'n that," the kid said. "You're s'posed to use the place down by the pepper tree. Get outa here! My john's for customers."

The rejection astonished Hoke at first, and for a moment he considered taking the key off the doorjamb, where it was hanging, wired to a railroad spike, and using the toilet anyway. But the moment passed. His cover was working; he looked like a tramp, and he was being treated like one.

293. Williams, Carol Lynch. **The True Colors of Caitlynne Jackson**. New York: Delacorte, 1997. 172p.

A grim but compelling tale for readers of all ages but especially young people, Carol Lynch Williams' novel is about two resourceful half sisters, 12-year-old Caitlynne (known as "Caity" and the story's narrator) and 11-year-old Cara, who are forced to survive on their own after being abruptly abandoned by their abusive, mentally unstable mother (their fathers are long gone). After Mom's stormy exit, Caity and Cara travel on bicycles from their home in Central Florida to their grandmother's in New Smyrna Beach on the Atlantic Coast, a long and dangerous trip that tests their stamina, tenacity, and courage. "Scenes showing the girls' attempts to soothe each other's physical and emotional wounds add a strong undercurrent of tenderness to this often harrowing drama" (*PW*, Dec. 16, 1996, p. 60). Williams has also written other first-rate YA novels with a Florida locale, including *Kelly and Me* (1993), *Adeline Street* (1995), and *Christmas in Heaven* (2000).

From **The True Colors of Caitlynne Jackson**:

The edge of Sanford [a Florida city northeast of Orlando] is where the fields begin. The smell of cabbage and dirt was thick in the air. We passed a dead skunk and one squished cat. We passed a sign that said Osteen 16 Miles. Sixteen more miles. I knew this was the beginning before a very long end, but I didn't know if I could make it.

Cara looked as tired as I felt.

"We're almost there," I said to her over my shoulder. "We only have a few more miles."

Cara didn't say anything.

It took us forever to get to the tiny town of Osteen. Mostly what we saw there was dogs. And lots of dead animals, some mashed so badly I couldn't even tell what they had started out as.

We stopped to rest. Up ahead I could make out the road that would eventually get us to New Smyrna. If we didn't wind up like the armadillos and skunks we were passing. Squished flat.

294. Williams, Joy. **Breaking & Entering**. New York: Vintage, 1981. 279p.

A gifted writer, Joy Williams is author of *The Florida Keys: A History & Guide* (8th ed., 1997), a Baedeker extraordinaire, plus many short stories and two novels set in Florida, *The Changeling* (1978) and **Breaking & Entering**. The latter vividly describes the nihilistic existence of Willie and Liberty, young married drifters who break into Florida vacation beach homes whose owners are not in residence, and for brief periods the couple lives the life of the owners, wearing their clothes, drinking their booze, swimming in their pools, sleeping in their beds, etc. An "utterly original novel . . . . It's a profoundly sad story in which the search for self has become a drift toward death. Williams' characters walk through life squinting, disoriented, like Mersault in Camus's *The Stranger*" (*American Libraries*, June 1994, p. 608).

From **Breaking & Entering**:

At daybreak, it was still raining. Rosy-fingered dawn bloomed elsewhere, in higher, purer altitudes perhaps, where the heart beats more slowly. Liberty was dreaming the things she dreamed in stolen houses—churches and flowers and suitcases, bowls and water and caves. She stirred, and felt that Willie was standing over her, staring at her. And that was part of the dream, she thought, for Willie to be studying her so solemnly, as though he were choosing something. She was a woman in a house, sleeping. She looked at Willie, safe in her sleep-looking. She looked at him and saw herself, the form he would have her assume, a woman in a house, sleeping.

Later, she opened her eyes and saw Clem's [the dog] muzzle aimed at her, several inches away, his tail wagging slowly. She knew Willie had gone. When he hadn't returned in an hour, she and Clem left too.

The Florida sky, the color of tin, squeezed out rain. It fell on stone and seed alike. Across the street from the Umbertons, a neighbor's lawn consisted of large white stones dumped on black vinyl. The rain fell on that. It fell on a sheriff's car that drove slowly past. The deputy was opening a Twinkie wrapper with his teeth. He grinned at Liberty as though she shared with him the criminal goodness of Twinkies. The car went around a corner and the street was empty. Heat rose like smoke from the damp pavement.

295. Wilson, Jon. **Bridger's Run**. Sarasota, FL: Pineapple Pr., 1999. 256p.

Eponymous hero Tom Bridger is a brash, good-looking, adventurous, and wealthy young man from New York who comes to Florida in 1885 in search of mysterious treasure and a disappeared uncle, Mike McGinnis. The novel, which takes Bridger from Jacksonville to Tampa and pits him against several nasty villains, is part of the publisher's Cracker Western series. Florida frontier tales reminiscent of Zane Grey and Louis L'Amour, the series currently contains seven titles, most by Lee Gramling, including his exciting **Ghosts of the Green Swamp** (see entry 85).

296. Wimberley, Darryl. **Strawman's Hammock**. New York: St. Martin's/ Thomas Dunne, 2001. 288p.

Practically all of Florida's numerous fictional crime fighters, public and private, are white. It's refreshing therefore to encounter Darryl Wimberley's series of mysteries starring an African-American detective, Barrett "Bear" Raines, who plies his trade in and around sparsely populated Lafayette County in the Big Bend region of North Florida. Thus far Raines has been center stage in three well-received thrillers: *A Rock and a Hard Place* (1999), *Dead Man's Bay* (2000), and **Strawman's Hammock** (2001). Each offers a suspenseful plot, plausible characters, and a clean, economical style. In **Strawman's Hammock**, arguably the best of the three, Raines is working for the Florida Department of Law Enforcement as a special agent when he's encouraged by a prominent local businessman to run for county sheriff. The situation gets sticky when Raines' inquiry into a horrible murder—a young female migrant farm worker is shackled and left to be eaten alive by a rabid dog in a wooded area called Strawman's Hammock—fingers his backer's son as the likely perpetrator. "Highly recommended for all lovers of mainstream hard-boiled mysteries" (*BL*, Oct. 1, 2001, p. 302). Note: Florida native Wimberley has also written a non-Raines novel, *A Tinker's Damn* (2000); set in North Central Florida during the Depression years of the 1930s and early 1940s, it concerns a turbulent relationship between father and son and appears to be heavily autobiographical.

297. Woods, Stuart. **Orchid Beach**. New York: HarperCollins, 1998. 320p.

A bestselling crime novelist with nearly 30 titles to his credit, Stuart Woods specializes in contemporary mysteries featuring tight plots, short chapters, smart dialogue, lively characters, and dollops of titillating sex. In 1998 he introduced series heroine Holly Barker in **Orchid Beach**. When Holly, a 37-year-old U.S. Army sergeant, lost a sexual harassment case against her superior, a colonel, she quit the military and applied for and got the position of deputy police chief at Orchid Beach, a small, fictional community in Florida. But the night before she arrives in town the chief of police and his best friend are murdered. Shaken but resilient, Holly takes over the chief's job and aided by two new acquaintances—Jackson Oxenhandler, a local attorney (and soon to be Holly's lover), and Daisy, a wonderfully intuitive Doberman—she launches an investigation into the killings that eventually leads to a nasty nest of wealthy right-wing fanatics. *Orchid Blues* (2001) and *Blood Orchid* (2002) also feature Holly as Orchid Beach's top cop, but in *Iron Orchid* (2005) she leaves Florida to join the CIA, which prompted one reviewer to observe "Holly loses much of her sparkle away from the Florida sun" (*BL*, Sept. 1, 2005, p. 8). Note: Other novels by Woods with a Florida locale include *Choke* (1995), set in Key West, and *Cold Paradise* (2001), which features New York policeman-turned-lawyer Stone Barrington, another Woods series character, on a case that brings him south to Palm Beach. Note also: In *Reckless Abandon* (2004) and *Dark Harbor* (2006), Woods brings Stone Barrington and Holly Barker together in action-packed thrillers that take place in New York City and Maine respectively.

298. Woolson, Constance Fenimore. **East Angels**. New York: Harper, 1886. 591p.

Constance Fenimore Woolson (1840-94), a great-niece of popular 19th-century American writer James Fenimore Cooper, was a leading female novelist of her day. Born in New Hampshire, she later lived in Ohio and traveled widely in the U.S. and Europe. After her father's death in 1869 Woolson spent considerable time in St. Augustine, Florida, a city she held in great esteem and used as the locale for a collection of short stories, *Rodman the Keeper* (1880), and two novels, *Horace Chase* (1894) and **East Angels**, her deepest and most successful book. Set during the post-Civil War period, **East Angels** is a lengthy, leisurely paced social novel dominated by the romantic sensibilities of two complex and quite different women: self-centered Edgarda "Garda" Thorne and self-sacrificing Margaret Harold. There's a large supporting cast, including two well-drawn male characters, Evert Winthrop and Lanse Harold; and the title character—East Angels itself, a St. Augustine plantation mansion—radiates a protean sense of place from beginning to end. Regrettably, this excellent novel, written more than a century ago, is now largely forgotten, but those fortunate enough to have read it (or who will read it) are among the elect, literarily speaking. It is not far-fetched to suggest that **East Angels** belongs in the same company as George Eliot's *Middlemarch* (1871-72), her long, woman-centered epic novel published in the latter 19th century that continues to be read, studied, enjoyed, and admired today. Note: In 1999 Reprint Services Corporation published a reprint edition of **East Angels** in library binding as part of its Notable American Authors series; also, in 1986, Classic Textbooks published the novel in a paperback edition; and in the 1970s Research Publications added a microfilm edition to its Wright American Fiction series (reel W-54, number 6102).

From **East Angels**:

Evert Winthrop had spent his childhood and youth in New England, he had visited all parts of the great West, in later years he had travelled extensively in the Old World; but this was his first visit to that lovely southern shore [Florida] of his own country which has a winter climate more enchanting than any that Europe can offer; to match it, one must seek the Madeira Islands or Algiers. In addition to climate, Winthrop was beginning to discover that there were other things as well—old Spanish houses like the one through which he was now passing [East Angels], a flavor of tradition and legend, tradition and legend, too, which had nothing to do with Miles Standish and his companions, or even with that less important personage, Hendrik Hudson. There was—he could not deny it—a certain comparative antiquity about this southern peninsula which had in it more richness of color and a deeper perspective than that possessed by any of the rather blank, near, little backgrounds of American history farther north. This was a surprise to him. Like most New-Englanders, he had unconsciously cherished the belief that all there was of historical importance, of historical picturesqueness even, in the beginnings of the republic, was associated with the Puritans from whom he was on his father's side descended.

299. Wyatt, Wyatt. **Catching Fire**. New York: Random House, 1977. 272p.

The critics did not exactly go wild over Wyatt Wyatt's comic novel when it appeared nearly three decades ago: "Wyatt's comedy love story, possibly intended as a fable, is engaging, funny in spots and for a first novel distinctly promising. It does not, however, make a power of sense" (*PW*, Feb. 7, 1977, p. 90); A.J. Anderson (in *LJ*, Feb. 15, 1977, p. 516) liked the book even less, calling the plot "as shapeless as a punctured balloon" and the dialogue "only once removed from gibberish." Still, **Catching Fire**, much of which takes place in Florida at the fictional Hotel Paradise (based on the real Langford Hotel on East New England Avenue) in the real city of Winter Park, was then and remains today an amusing novel in a kooky sort of way. After being burned (literally and figuratively) by an aggrieved husband, Norman Foreman receives extensive skin grafts, the epidermis courtesy of a pig, which earns him the inevitable nickname "pigman." As a result, Norman takes a temporary vow of chastity, a promise made extra difficult due to being aggressively pursued by a deaf femme fatale named Spider who wears only a string bikini. Other wacky characters populate

Norman's world, including Captain Smokes, a 91-year-old midget; Offernel Farrington, a retired carnival showman and scam artist; a noseless guy called, for obvious reasons, no-nose Floyd; and a one-eyed Frenchman who's really from Montana. Yes, it's true: Wyatt's comedy requires a special—some might say twisted—sense of humor.

300. Wylie, Philip. **The Best of Crunch and Des**. New York: Rinehart, 1954. 404p.

Best known for *Generation of Vipers* (1942), a savage nonfiction critique of American institutions, Philip Wylie (1902-71) also wrote a goodly amount of fiction, including 59 entertaining short stories published over many years in the *Saturday Evening Post* featuring Crunch Adams and Desperate "Des" Smith, old Florida salts who operate a charter fishing boat, the *Poseidon*, out of Miami. Among the 21 stories in **The Best of Crunch and Des** (all of which originally appeared in the *Post* between 1939 and 1948) are such timeless yarns as "Widow Voyage," "Crunch Catches One," "Crazy Over Horse Mackerel," "Fish Bites Man," "Bait for McGillicudy," and "Eve and the Sea Serpent." Note: *Crunch and Des: Classic Stories of Saltwater Fishing*, published by Lyons & Burford in 1990 and edited by Wylie's daughter, Karen Wylie Pryor, is another collection of selected Crunch and Des fish tales; it contains 22 stories, including 12 not in **The Best of Crunch and Des**, plus a preface by Pryor entitled "My Father, Phil Wylie." Note also: **Florida Stories** (see entry 184) includes "Widow Voyage," accompanied by an informative two-page introduction by editor Kevin McCarthy.

301. Yancey, Richard. **A Burning in Homeland**. New York: Simon & Schuster, 2003. 352p.

This ambitious first novel takes place in fictional Homeland, a small Central Florida town. There's nothing small, however, about the issues involved: passion, betrayal, vengeance, death. In 1960 a suspicious fire destroys the home of Homeland's Baptist minister,

Ned Jeffries, who suffers terrible burns in the blaze. Jeffries' wife, Mavis, and their ten-year-old daughter, Sharon Rose, are not hurt and go to live with a local family, the Parkers, whose young son, Shiny, relates the story. The fire revives memories of a notorious murder committed two decades earlier by Halley Martin, then a young, uneducated orange grove worker in love with his employer's beautiful daughter, Mavis Howell, who after Halley went to prison became Mrs. Ned Jeffries, the preacher's wife. Now 20 years later, Halley, his hands brutally maimed by a fellow inmate, has just been released from prison and is back in Homeland, an angry man—angry at Ned Jeffries, a man of God who befriended and helped him in prison but then turned around and stole the woman he loved. "Told in flashback, Mavis and Halley's stories finally converge, with tragic consequences for all .... Dripping with atmosphere and drama, it's a pleasure as guilty as a third helping of pecan pie" (*BL*, Jan. 2003, p. 854).

302. Yglesias, Helen. **The Girls**. Harrison, NY: Delphinium Books, 1999. 224p.

A poignant account of four Jewish sisters—Eva, age 95; Naomi, 90; Flora, 85; and Jenny, 80—confronting the humiliations of old age, this ironically titled short novel typifies Helen Yglesias's best fiction, which focuses on family relationships, both loving and bitter. The characters are well delineated, as is the Florida setting: Yglesias "presents a social and cultural travelogue of Miami Beach's various districts and neighborhoods—sweeping from the gaudy vulgarity of opulent hotels to down-at-the-heels elderly residences and nursing homes" (*PW*, Aug. 23, 1999, p. 48). Note: The author is the ex-wife of Jose Yglesias (see entries 303-304).

303. Yglesias, Jose. **The Truth About Them**. New York: World Publishing, 1971. 215p.

The author of 14 books including ten novels, Cuban-American writer Jose Yglesias (1919-95) is most closely identified with Ybor City, a multicultural enclave in Tampa, Florida, where he grew up an ardent champion of the rights of working people. Two of his most powerful novels, **A Wake in Ybor City** (see entry 304) and **The Truth About Them**, draw on his early memories and stories told by his parents, grandparents, and numerous aunts, uncles, and cousins. In **The Truth About Them**, for instance, "them" refers specifically to Yglesias's large, motley Hispanic family that began its American odyssey when his grandmother, the matriarch, arrived in Ybor City from Cuba as a young girl in 1890 and went to work in one of the many local cigar factories. The novel's main character and narrator, a left-wing journalist who's obviously a close copy of Yglesias himself, recounts the saga of his immigrant tribe's journey over several generations, emphasizing its strengths and successes rather than its failures and discontents. "Blood is thicker than dogma in this book. It glows with a respect for human dignity. It delights in the brio of a close-knit clan who are broke but not poor. It celebrates those ethnic distinctions that add salt to civilization" (*NYTBR*, Jan. 9, 1972, p. 32). Note: In 1999 Arte Público issued a paperback reprint of **The Truth About Them** as part of its Pioneers of Modern U.S. Hispanic Literature series.

304. Yglesias, Jose. **A Wake in Ybor City**. New York: Holt, Rinehart & Winston, 1963. 284p.

Pulsating with hot-tempered characters and emotional political declarations, Jose Yglesias's first novel brings together a fractious group of Cuban-American kinfolk in Ybor City (a heavily ethnic section of Tampa, Florida) ostensibly to grieve the death of a family member. But it's 1958, the eve of the Fidel Castro-led revolution against the military regime of Fulgencio Batista in Cuba, and the great issue before the assembled mourners is: Which side are you on? Some, including Elena Villaneuva and her husband Jaime (Batista's press secretary), ardently support the "legitimate" government of Cuba whereas others, such as Elena's brother Robert and his friend Esteban, sympathize with Castro, who's waiting in the Sierra

Maestra mountains to launch his bid for power. A passionate tale of deeply divided cultural and ideological loyalties, this novel remains as fresh and, yes, as relevant today as when it was first published more than 40 years ago. Note: Along with Yglesias's **The Truth About Them** (see entry 303), **A Wake in Ybor City** is currently available in a paperback reprint by Arte Público.

From **A Wake in Ybor City**:

"You are wrong, Elena," he [Robert] said. "Those young rebels may be fools, but they are in the right, like the cigar makers were fools to go on strikes that they never won. Believe me, when I first left Tampa I hated it as much as you do, but there was something to hate where I went, too. The thing is I've learned not to hate myself the way the Americans here want us to hate ourselves."

"Psychology! Psychology!" Elena said. "If that's the best you can come up with, they're right to despise you."

"All right, all right," Robert said. "All I mean is, if you're going to live in Cuba you ought to hate what those foolish rebels hate."

"They hate the foreigners who have taken their lands and the politicians who have taken their liberties!" Esteban held out an arm and pointed a finger at Elena, as if he were addressing a gathering. "They will throw *you* out. You, who hate your home town, are a foreigner there and a good friend of their politicians. You're an imperialist. You have no country."

"You cheap orator," Elena said. "Money buys any country. It can buy even you."

Esteban paused only a second. "Money only buys whores!"

Elena raised a hand then clenched it to keep herself from slapping him. "You whoring son of a whore!"

Jaime moved quickly and stood between Elena and Esteban. "Take it back," he said, and held his hand up, the palm stiffly open.

"Blood suckers," Esteban said. "We will kill you all!"

Jaime brought his hand down swiftly and slapped Esteban across the face. "Take it back," he said, and raised his hand again.

305. Ziegler, Irene. **Rules of the Lake: Stories**. Dallas, TX: Southern Methodist Univ. Pr., 1999. 193p.

A collection of 12 interrelated stories plus a brief prologue and lengthy epilogue, **Rules of the Lake** concerns the coming of age of Annie Bartlett in rural, pre-Disney Central Florida between the years 1965 and 1972. Young Annie, who dreams of becoming a mermaid like those at the famous Weekie Wachee Springs attraction near her home, loves to swim, especially in local Widow Lake, which holds momentous significance for her and her family. It's where her mother drowned: "My mother swam every morning before breakfast, which was against the rules. My father was strict about the rules of the lake, and one was No Swimming Alone, but I guess she figured she could get away with it as long as she snuck it in before he woke up." Author Irene Ziegler deftly uses the lake as a symbolic expression of the wider world, where things often appear placid or pleasant on the surface but underneath untold dangers lie in wait. "Ziegler ably inscribes the natural beauty of Florida as backdrop to a tumultuous domestic narrative about upsetting the balance of things and facing the hope as well as the fear that comes with change" (*PW*, Nov. 1, 1999, p. 76).

# BIBLIOGRAPHY

Barlow, Margaret. "Illuminating Manuscripts: Florida's Literary Scene," *Florida History & the Arts*, Summer 2001, pp. 14-17.
   Described by the author as "a small sampling of the wealth of literary resources" currently available in Florida, Barlow's article identifies major awards, grants, festivals, workshops, and publishers of interest to the state's writers and readers.

Born, Judy. "'Florida: Land of Mystery' Revisited," *Florida Libraries*, Nov.-Dec. 1997, p. 135.
   A follow-up to Nancy Pike's "Florida: Land of Mystery" (see below), this single-page article includes information about John D. MacDonald's Travis McGee novels and a couple of Florida bookstores specializing in mysteries, plus a list of recent thrillers set in the state.

Gardner, Jeanette C. *An Annotated Bibliography of Florida Fiction, 1801-1980*. St. Petersburg, FL: Little Bayou Pr., 1983. 220p.
   Gardner's invaluable bibliography annotates 1,100 works of fiction set in Florida published in the 19th century and first eight decades of the 20th century. "The term 'Florida fiction' as used in this bibliography refers to books and stories with a setting in some part of the state. The work of a Florida author is not included unless a Florida setting is used. The Florida location may occupy the entire time of the story, or appear only briefly. Both adult and juvenile titles are used" (Introduction, p. ix). Gardner strives for "coverage as comprehensive as possible" for the dates covered.

Glassman, Steve & Maurice J. O'Sullivan, editors. *Crime Fiction & Film in the Sunshine State: Florida Noir.* Bowling Green, OH: Bowling Green State Univ. Popular Pr., 1997. 192p.

The 11 scholarly but quite readable essays that make up this unique collection deal with various aspects of Florida crime fiction in both print and movie mode. For instance, "Noir: Keys Style," written by a University of New Hampshire professor who retired to the Florida Keys, examines why the Keys and especially Key West hold such fascination for some mystery writers and filmmakers.

McCarthy, Kevin M., editor. *The Book Lover's Guide to Florida.* Sarasota, FL: Pineapple Pr., 1992. 512p.

Summed up by one authority as an "extensive literary travel guide," this indispensable tome furnishes basic information about more than 1,700 writers and 2,200 books associated with Florida and the state's "book culture." The guide, which emphasizes books published since 1950, is divided into 10 chapters, each an extended essay offering an overview of the literary output and landmarks of a specific region (e.g., DeLand to Lake Okeechobee; Greater Miami; Siesta Key to Tampa). There are also a number of substantial essays throughout the book on various subjects such as science fiction, mysteries, and literary magazines in Florida.

McCarthy, Kevin M. *Twentieth-Century Florida Authors.* Lewiston, NY: Edwin Mellen Pr., 1996. 252p.

This book contains biographical profiles of 14 contemporary Florida fiction and nonfiction writers: E. W. Carswell, Harry Crews, Marjory Stoneman Douglas, Hampton Dunn, David Kaufelt, Stetson Kennedy, Eugene Lyon, Richard Powell, Jack Rudloe, Marjory Bartlett Sanger, Jerrell Shofner, Frank Slaughter, Patrick Smith, and Charlton Tebeau. The profiles average 16 pages in length and are based on McCarthy's interviews with the writers as well as his study of their works.

O'Sullivan, Maurice. "Florida Literature," *FHC FORUM: The Magazine of the Florida Humanities Council*, Fall 2003, pp. 22-25.

This informative article takes a critical look Florida's literary history. Among the issues explored is this interesting question: "Aside from Zora Neale Hurston and Ernest Hemingway, Marjorie Kinnan Rawlings and John D. MacDonald, how many Florida writers can most people name? With the oldest literary tradition in North America, why are we so little known?"

O'Sullivan, Maurice & Steve Glassman. "From the City of Angels to the Magic Kingdom," Introduction to **Orange Pulp: Stories of Mayhem, Murder, and Mystery** (Gainesville, FL: Univ. Press of Florida, 2002), pp. 1-20.

O'Sullivan and Glassman provide an excellent concise history of crime fiction in Florida in the introduction to their anthology, **Orange Pulp** (see entry 209). Major and minor authors are identified and briefly discussed, and all works cited are listed A-Z by author on pages 17-20.

Ott, Bill & Brad Hooper. "A Hard-Boiled Gazetteer to Florida," *Booklist*, May 1, 2001, pp. 1600-03.

Mysteries set in Florida that feature a series character—for example, Carl Hiaasen's Skink, James W. Hall's Thorn, Les Standiford's John Deal, Randy Wayne White's Doc Ford—are briefly noted in this useful geographically arranged roundup. It updates an earlier article, "Art Deco Armageddon: Crime Fiction in Florida" in *Booklist* (June 1 & 15, 1994, pp. 1778-79).

Pike, Nancy. "Florida: Land of Mystery," *Florida Libraries*, Aug.-Sept. 1994, p. 342.

Pike points out that in the early 1990s Miami became "our nation's new whodunit crime capital thanks to its glitz, glamour, and Art Deco hotels along with corpses, cocaine, and killers." She then cites a number of recent thrillers that back up the claim.

Rowe, Anne E. *The Idea of Florida in the American Literary Imagination.* Baton Rouge: Louisiana State Univ. Pr., 1986. 174p. Without doubt, this small, well-written book is the best analysis of Florida literature currently available. Rowe, a longtime professor of English at Florida State University, closely examines the effect of Florida on the work of such influential writers as William Bartram, Ralph Waldo Emerson, Harriet Beecher Stowe, Constance Fenimore Woolson, Stephen Crane, Henry James, Ring Lardner, James Branch Cabell, Marjorie Kinnan Rawlings, Ernest Hemingway, and Wallace Stevens. "Neither a study of Florida authors nor a history of the state in literature, the work offers, with historical and biographical contexts, a perceptive interpretation" (*Choice*, Nov. 1986, p. 480). Note: In 1992 Rowe's book was reprinted in a paperback edition by the University Press of Florida.

# Author-Title-
# Subject-Locale Index

Books reviewed in *Florida on the Boil* are printed in **bold** type. All other books and monographs are printed in *italic*.

Numbers following authors, titles, subjects, and locales refer to ENTRY numbers in the guide, *not* page numbers. The only exceptions are references to the guide's caricatures and material in the Preface, Introduction, and Bibliography. For example, Janette C. Gardner's *An Annotated Bibliography of Florida Fiction, 1801-1980* is referred to in the Introduction and also listed in the Bibliography; the index entry reads as follows:

> *An Annotated Bibliography of*
> *Florida Fiction, 1801-1980*
> (Gardner), *see* Introduction,
> page 20; *see also* Bibliography,
> page 277.

Titles that begin with a number are entered as though the number is spelled out. For example, the short story collection **100% Pure Florida Fiction** is indexed as if it were spelled **One Hundred Percent Florida Fiction.**

Surnames beginning with Mac are listed before those beginning with Mc. For example, MacDonald precedes McBain. If in doubt about the spelling of a Mac/Mc author, check both possibilities. The abbreviation St. (as in St. Augustine) is spelled out and filed under Saint.

Ocala, 34, 46, 63, 232
Ocala National Forest, 235, 269
Ocean Ridge, 156
Ocklawaha River & environs, 191, 234
*Octopus Alibi* (Corcoran), 39
O'Dell, Scott, 208
*Off the Chart* (Hall, J.), 93
oil & oil drilling off Florida's coast, 48
Okaloacoochee River, 129
Okeechobee, Battle of, 63
Okefenokee Swamp, 126
old age, *see* senior citizens
*One Hot Summer* (Garcia-Aguilera), 78
**100% Pure Florida Fiction** (Hubbard & Wilson), 119
"The Open Boat" (short story by Crane), *see* Introduction, page 20
Orange Bowl, 10, 15
**Orange Crush** (Dorsey), 58; *see also* 57
Orange Pulp: Stories of Mayhem, Murder, and Mystery (O'Sullivan & Glassman), 209; *see also* 81, 86, 271; *see also* Bibliography, page 279
**Orange Winter: A Story of Florida in 1880** (Medary), 191

oranges, orange juice, & orange groves, 23, 42, 82, 185, 186, 191, 281, 301
**Orchid Beach** (Woods), 297
*Orchid Blues* (Woods), 297
Orlando, 40, 42, 44, 67, 123, 168, 169, 237, 275; *see also* Hurston caricature, page 121
*Orlando Sentinel*, 237
Osceola, 30, 34, 46, 96, 126, 138, 219, 256
Osteen, 293
O'Sullivan, Maurice J., 209; *see also* 81; *see also* Bibliography, pages 278 & 279
Ott, Bill, *see* Bibliography, page 279
**The Outlanders** (Stevens), 264
Overseas Highway, 244
Overseas Railroad, *see* Florida East Coast Railway
Owens, Janis, 210; *see also* Introduction, page 24
owls, 108
**Ox and the Prime-Time Kid** (Ney), 205
*Ox Goes North* (Ney), 205
*Ox, The Story of a Kid at the Top* (Ney), 205
*Ox Under Pressure* (Ney), 205

**Pahokee** (Rust), 242
*Palatka* (Rust), 242

Printed in the United States
111226LV00001B/5/A

9 781425 717254